CONTEMPORARY ISSUES IN HIGHER EDUCATION

CONTEMPORARY ISSUES IN HIGHER EDUCATION

Self-Regulation and the Ethical Roles of the Academy

Edited by

John B. Bennett
and
J. W. Peltason

AMERICAN COUNCIL ON • MACMILLAN PUBLISHING
EDUCATION COMPANY
NEW YORK

Collier Macmillan Publishers
LONDON

Copyright © 1985 by Macmillan Publishing Company and American Council on Education

All rights reserved. No part of this book may be reproduced or transmitted in any form or by any means, electronic or mechanical, including photocopying, recording, or by any information storage and retrieval system, without permission in writing from the Publisher.

Macmillan Publishing Company
866 Third Avenue, New York, NY 10022

Collier Macmillan Canada, Inc.

Library of Congress Catalog Card Number: 84-26172

Printed in the United States of America

printing number
1 2 3 4 5 6 7 8 9 10

Library of Congress Cataloging in Publication Data
Main entry under title:

Contemporary issues in higher education.

   1. University autonomy—United States—Addresses, essays, lectures.   2. Universities and colleges—United States—Finance—Addresses, essays, lectures.
3. Industry and education—United States—Addresses, essays, lectures.   I. Bennett, John B. (John Beecher), 1940-   .   II. Peltason, J. W. (Jack Walter), 1923-   .
LB2331.4.C65   1985   378.73   84-26172
ISBN 0-02-902660-1

Contents

Contributors	vii
Preface	ix
Introduction. John B. Bennett and J. W. Peltason	xi

Part One   Self-Regulation: The Concept   1

Self-Regulation Within Postsecondary Education. JOHN B. BENNETT, ELAINE H. EL-KHAWAS, AND ROBERT M. O'NEIL   3

Part Two   Self-Regulation and Institutional Relations   27

"Thy Firmness Makes My Circle Just": Professional Schools in the University. TIMOTHY S. HEALY, S.J.   29

Institutional Advancement and Funding. FRANK H. T. RHODES   49

Equity and Quality in College Education: An Essential American Priority. ROBERT H. MCCABE   71

The Politics of Accreditation and the Role of COPA in Self-Regulation. C. GRIER DAVIS, JR. AND ROBERT H. STROTZ   103

Part Three   Self-Regulation and Academic Inquiry   121

Intercollegiate Athletics. DEREK BOK   123

The Nature and Integrity of the Undergraduate Degree. JERRY W. MILLER   147

Potential Conflict of Interest Issues in Relationships Between Academia and Industry. ELISABETH A. ZINSER   169

"Self-Regulation of the Use of Human and Animal Subjects in Academic Inquiry. KARL J. HITTELMAN AND ERICA J. HEATH   215

Part Four   The Future   **245**

   The Role of the Academy in a Nuclear Age. THEODORE
   M. HESBURGH, C.S.C.   247

Contributors

John B. Bennett
Director, Academic Affairs and Director, Office on
  Self-Regulation Initiatives
American Council on Education
Washington, District of Columbia

Derek C. Bok
President
Harvard University
Cambridge, Massachusetts

C. Grier Davis, Jr.
Director, Institutional Relations
Northwestern University
Evanston, Illinois

Elaine H. El-Khawas
Vice President, Policy Analysis and Research
American Council on Education
Washington, District of Columbia

The Reverend Timothy S. Healy, S.J.
President
Georgetown University
Washington, District of Columbia

Erica J. Heath
Administrative Analyst
Human and Environmental Protection Committee
University of California-San Francisco
San Francisco, California

The Reverend Theodore M. Hesburgh, C.S.C.
President
University of Notre Dame
Notre Dame, Indiana

Karl J. Hittelman
Associate Vice Chancellor for Academic Affairs
University of California-San Francisco
San Francisco, California

Robert H. McCabe
President
Miami Dade Community College
Miami, Florida

Jerry W. Miller
President
Association of Independent Colleges and Schools and
 Immediate Past Vice President for Academic Affairs
 and Institutional Relations, American Council on
 Education
Washington, District of Columbia

Robert M. O'Neil
President
University of Wisconsin System
Madison, Wisconsin
President-Designate, University of Virginia
 (September 1985)

J. W. Peltason
Chancellor
University of California-Irvine and Immediate Past
 President, American Council on Education
Irvine, California

Frank H. T. Rhodes
President
Cornell University
Ithaca, New York

Robert H. Strotz
President
Northwestern University
Evanston, Illinois

Elisabeth Zinser
Vice Chancellor for Academic Affairs
University of North Carolina-Greensboro
Greensboro, North Carolina

Preface

SELF-REGULATION WITHIN HIGHER EDUCATION, though perhaps a new term, is not a new idea. Colleges and universities have always taken pride in their traditions of collegial governance and their defense of academic freedom—and both are essential elements of self-regulation in higher education. Likewise, institutions have always stubbornly sought ways to defend their independence against powerful donors and legislators; such independence is both a condition and an expression of self-regulation.

Because it is a fairly new term, though, self-regulation has a certain elasticity, and so one must decide just how broadly to cast its net. In general terms, we can say that self-regulation is nongovernmental, self-imposed, self-policing, coordinated activity. It involves enlightened institutional self-interest and presupposes appropriate institutional self-regard. "The basic idea is that academic institutions, either individually or collectively, voluntarily deal with problems without waiting for regulations to be imposed by external bodies."[1]

Always an important concept, self-regulation is increasingly so in these days of heightened social and institutional complexity. The alternatives to self-regulation include judicial, legislative, or bureaucratic regulation, as well as decisions left solely to market forces. In the first three alternatives, important decisions usually wind up being made by those outside higher education and unfamiliar with its idiosyncracies as well as its genius. Then the result for everyone involved is usually marked inefficiency or ineffectiveness. Likewise, although "letting the market decide" works well in many cases, the market itself contains no safeguards against undesirable and compromising practices. So there seems to be no desirable alternative to self-regulation.

Self-regulation is not always easy, however. No institution wants to put itself at a competitive disadvantage in attracting students, faculty, or other resources. As a result, there can be underlying tension among individual institutions as well as between them and the common self-regulation structures chosen to represent them or to whom they have delegated authority. Another tug is between the integrity of the educational enterprise and the demands from outside for public accountability. This conflict shows itself in many ways, but almost always there is some tension between efforts to develop knowledge and to serve society. Under such stress, good will can evaporate. Even when abundantly present, it needs the structure that principles of good practice can provide.

The Office on Self-Regulation Initiatives of the American Council on Education (ACE) was created in June 1978 in order to promote the concept within the higher education community. This book extends the work of the office, in part by reflecting upon it but mostly by advancing the cause for which it was established.

Although this book has been jointly edited and both editors take full responsibility, the lion's share of the work has been done by the senior editor. He, therefore, deserves most of the credit for whatever editorial contributions have been made to the outstanding work of the authors as well as most of the editorial blame, if indeed any is deserved.

JOHN B. BENNETT
Washington, D. C.

J. W. PELTASON
Irvine, California

Note

1. Elaine El-Khawas, "Self-Regulation and Collegiate Athletics," *Educational Record*, Vol. 60, No. 4, pp. 511f.

Introduction

THE CHAPTERS THAT FOLLOW WERE WRITTEN SPECIFICALLY for this collection. They are presented in two main groups, though all deal with interconnected issues. One focuses in various ways on institutional relations—internal as well as external—as they bear upon self-regulation issues. The other treats issues of self-regulation touching more directly upon academic inquiry and integrity.

The chapter by John B. Bennett, Elaine H. El-Khawas, and Robert M. O'Neil sets the context by elaborating upon the concept of self-regulation in higher education—its history and its character in a time of social and political transition—and by tracing the work of the ACE Office on Self-Regulation Initiatives. Two levels of self-regulation activity are identified: the institutional level, at which ultimately everything must be done, and the associational or agency level, at which assistance can be provided.

Closest to home in self-regulation is the way in which each institution chooses to organize itself. Within every university there are potentially profound values at stake in the relationships of one school or college to another and to the whole. In reminding us of the core mission of higher education, Timothy S. Healy, S.J., identifies several of these values and illustrates the importance of judiciousness in the establishment and review of these relationships. The potential for mischief is great, particularly when values alien to the university are introduced through the professional schools. Relationships among institutions are no less important for self-regulation in higher education. The diversity of American postsecondary institutions is a key source of their strength, but excessive competition can become corrosive. Frank H. T. Rhodes reviews the history and strength of our dual system, delineates the tensions presently existing between the public and the independent sectors of postsecondary education, and argues the importance of specific forms of cooperation. Displaying insufficient cooperation, the postsecondary community will inevitably generate a backlash within important public constituencies. Cooperative efforts are not easy to foster, though, given the growth of competitive forces and influences.

Public expectations can set important challenges for self-regulation. Robert H. McCabe addresses affirmatively the question whether access and quality can go together and argues forcefully that both community colleges and four-year institutions have responsibilities to regulate themselves accordingly. Open-door institutions can produce high-achieving students and even selective-admissions institutions should provide additional resources for full human development. Ultimately the national interest is at stake when large numbers of disadvantaged students face restricted access to postsecondary opportunities. McCabe concludes with a variety of recommendations, including program redirection, on how better to meet both goals of access and quality.

A key instrument of community self-regulation outside the individual institution is accreditation. Accreditation issues figure prominently in several of the chapters and the activity itself is addressed at length in the chapter by C. Grier Davis, Jr., and Robert H. Strotz. The authors review some of the history and examine both the increasing role of the government in accreditation activity and problems connected with specialized accreditation.

Other chapters address self-regulation issues relating more specifically to academic inquiry and integrity. Discussing a particularly inflamed area, Derek Bok speaks to some of the vexing and highly publicized issues surrounding intercollegiate athletics and the abuse of academic integrity and student potential. He provides a helpful review of recent efforts to attack these problems, efforts conducted both under ACE and NCAA auspices. This review includes a variety of thoughtful suggestions, addressed to presidents both as individuals and collectively, as members of athletic conferences, and of NCAA. Jerry W. Miller broadens the scope of concern by addressing the topic of undergraduate degrees—their meaning and components as well as the problems inherent in assuring their integrity. He pays particular attention to the problems of basic academic skills and of specialized accrediting agencies and concludes with a list of concrete suggestions.

Elisabeth A. Zinser then directs our attention to the variety of cooperative relationships being established between campuses and industry. She provides a helpful classification of these relationships and indicates the range of conflicts of interest that can occur. These relationships offer significant promise for both academe and society, but care is required in structuring and monitoring them.

Self-regulation issues touching directly on academic integrity are involved also in the use of human and natural subjects in the conduct of academic inquiry. Karl J. Hittelman and Erica J. Heath provide a helpful introduction to the topic, indicating how we got where we are and suggesting a wide range of considerations for institutions at which such inquiry is conducted. They remind us of the need to clarify the goals informing any institutional self-regulation program and to adjust questions of authority and of the extensiveness of the program accordingly.

The concluding chapter, by Theodore M. Hesburgh, C.S.C., reminds us again of the essential moral character of the university and presents the case for attending to the radical challenges to civilization which the age of nuclear weapons demands. He argues forcefully that these challenges are like no other the academy has seen and, as a result, require unprecedented responses. The self-regulatory character of the academy everywhere underlies and undergirds his argument.

Other issues could doubtless have been included under the theme of self-regulation. Certainly the need for close attention to self-regulation will not diminish, and its importance to the academy will ever remain. For apart from its organizational importance, its moral claims are not long to be denied.

CONTEMPORARY ISSUES IN HIGHER EDUCATION

PART ONE

Self-Regulation:

The Concept

Self-Regulation Within Postsecondary Education

JOHN B. BENNETT
ELAINE H. EL-KHAWAS
ROBERT M. O'NEIL

The Ongoing Need for Self-Regulation

Several rather different issues now before American higher education make quite clear the need for renewed institutional attention to self-regulation. Three examples provide illustration. The most comprehensive and serious example is the growing public perception that the quality of higher education is slipping. Both standards and performance are in question and statements such as Chester Finn's are becoming more common: "Searching national scrutiny of the quality of higher education is in order."[1] His concerns range across the board and include low admissions and graduation standards, inadequate faculty performance, poor internal institutional governance, and excessive smugness, even self-righteousness, in the self-regard of higher education. To Finn's concerns could be added others: the seemingly endless scandals in collegiate athletics, the apparent unwillingness of adminstrations or faculty organizations to do anything about incompetent faculty, and the continuation of diploma mills. These and other unedifying dimensions of higher education do nothing to secure or preserve public respect.

One indication of this slipping public respect is that congressional attention to the notion of adequate student academic progress has recurred, this time with the suggestion that the federal government should mandate a minimum grade requirement for those receiving federal financial aid. This proposal would directly involve federal agencies and officials in what has traditionally been the responsibility and prerogative of institutional faculties and academic administrators. On the other hand, some argue that as the source of financial aid the government has the right—indeed, perhaps the obligation—to determine that this aid is used in appropriate ways, thereby indicating lack of confidence in the integrity of current institutional practices.

The second example of the need for self-regulation is the emerging problem of conflict of interest of both faculty and institutions engaged in research that could lead to the development of commercially valuable products. An illustration would be the researcher who has a financial interest, or even a management position, in a company that is contributing support through the university to his or her research. Actually, the conflict can be between faculty member and university, faculty member and sponsoring entity, university and sponsoring entity, or among all three. Such conflict of interest would be a serious threat to the integrity and freedom of academic research and instruction.

Several ethical issues seem to be involved here. One is the tension, if not conflict, between traditional faculty obligations to teaching, research, and service, and the opportunity for individual fame and fortune. Pursuit of the latter inevitably has some impact upon the former—as the availability of the faculty member and his or her interest in students and departmental affairs diminish. Likewise, curriculum or course objectives can become tilted toward special, externally funded research projects, and students can be enlisted in efforts out of proportion to their educational good. Certainly, traditional faculty objectivity may slip (or appear to) when financial stakes are involved, and the question of excessive secrecy must be faced. One must wonder, too, about the conditions under which institutions should expect externally funded research as a condition for faculty advancement: preferential treatment for those generating extrainstitutional revenue can become a problem.

An associated issue is the integrity with which the research is actually conducted. Recent disclosures at major institutions of falsification of data as well as of plagiarism of material have drawn public attention to the potential for scandal at the very heart of the academic enterprise. Everyone must be concerned about the breech of a trust that is absolutely indispensable to scholarship. Equally clearly, the only effective solution rests in various forms of self-regulation within the research community itself.[2] The problem becomes more complex when the research in question is collaborative in character; in such cases the primary investigator may want periodically to inquire as to the authenticity of the work and should make appropriate public announcement when fraud is discovered.

A third area calling for increased institutional self-regulation is one in which academe has yet fully to distinguish itself: equity for women and minorities. Far from taking a bold leadership position, higher education seems for the most part to have done no better than other sectors of society in demonstrating its commitment to broader gender and racial participation and representation. A special opportunity seems present now that the government is widely perceived to have relaxed its enforcement concerns. For now academe can deal with the issue in a positive and uncoerced manner.

A host of other self-regulation issues could be mentioned, and indeed many are explored in subsequent portions of this book. All reflect in one way or another current pressing concerns about responsibility and accountability in American higher education. These concerns are developing at the same time that the currency and fashionableness of references to "self-regulation" have increased. In this new mood people speak with caution about depending on the government to protect the public good. Instead, the emphasis now is more toward individuals and institutions alike regulating themselves and the government getting off their backs. The Reagan administration has underscored this attitude in a variety of ways, all of which deemphasize—if not always minimize—federal regulation.

There are good reasons for regarding this deemphasis as a timely development, at least in higher education. The past two decades have witnessed a veritable surge in federal requirements. Taken individually, none of the numerous governmental demands on higher education may be objectionable, but as the recent Carnegie Foundation report on governance suggested, the most serious problem has been the *cumulative* impact of these federal interventions. "In one year the University of California reported filing 229 'unique' reports with 32 separate federal agencies. The president of another university recently complained that within a three-week period his institution had been subjected to compliance reviews by no fewer than four different federal agencies. Recipients of federal grants are now subject to 59 legislative and regulatory requirements regarding administration and social policy."[3] Time spent in this sort of paperwork and duplicative response is time taken away from academic planning. The problem has not been simply federal, as state agencies, boards, and legislatures have added their share of directives and requirements to those of the federal government.

Understandably, then, representatives of higher education have recently emphasized self-regulation as a much more efficient form of governance than government mandates. It is also often more appropriate. Government mandates, coming as they do from individuals and agencies external to higher education and often unfamiliar with its traditions and circumstances, are usually clumsy. They secure some objectives at the expense of other social or academic values. Governmental regulation can also be unreasonable—selecting only one or two acceptable ways to address reforms or to accomplish objectives and requiring complicated, often uncoordinated, record-keeping and reporting, sometimes presented as though all institutions were already both guilty and unrepentant. The results have too often been meager, and the energies and good will of the parties involved are quickly exhausted by compliance with the reporting requirements.

Accordingly, the stress should now be on self-regulation, as an essential expression and means of institutional integrity rather than simply as a reaction to external mandate. Within higher education, self-regulation should mean voluntary and coordinated regulation by the community broadly understood—both as parts and as a whole. Certainly it is appropriate that higher education institutions be faithful to this concept of self-regulation. It is in these institutions especially that collective wisdom on the human race, its nature, and its forms of organization is analyzed, argued, and transmitted. Of all places it is right here that reason should be in full sway, reinforcing the importance of self-regulation as community self-initiative and self-direction.

In fact, these institutions have engaged in such forms of self-regulation from their beginnings. There is a rich heritage to be renewed and expanded. Issues of academic direction and of instructional balance have always preoccupied institutions, and traditions of self-governance regarding research, curriculum, and peer evaluation are especially strong. The Carnegie report refers to the functions relating to teaching and research as the "essential core of academic life" and understands them as including "the selection of faculty, the content of courses, the processes of instruction, the establishment of academic standards, and the assessment of performance [as well as] the conduct of campus-based research and the dissemination of results."[4] On individual campuses there has always been some viable form of collegiality or self-governance on these issues. To be sure, new forms such as collective bargaining have sometimes developed in response to changing pressures. Typically, though, faculty and administration together have been determined to control internal affairs. External forces have rarely been welcome unless, as with unions, they are supporting issues determined by at least some of the participants to be appropriate.

Similarly, there has been much self-regulation in the past among campuses. Individual institutions of higher education have voluntarily come together to establish agreements and to make common cause on any number of issues. Notable examples come readily in mind. The establishment of the College Entrance Examination Board in 1900 vastly facilitated common understandings on college entrance requirements. The American Association of University Professors was established in 1915, and in 1940, together with the Association of American Colleges, it distributed the now widely influential "Statement of Principles on Academic Freedom and Tenure." The National Collegiate Athletic Association was established to promote cooperative arrangements in athletics. Of course, the most widely known examples of voluntary self-regulation in higher education are the accrediting associations.

So self-regulation is hardly new in higher education. But the need for doing it well is ever with us and certainly the present times display no diminished requirements. Bigness and rapid social-technological change have joined with an increased public cynicism about the honesty of institutions generally.[5] Certainly the competition among campuses for students is now well known. The result is the uneven and rather precarious degree of public trust and respect with which many higher education institutions are currently regarded. And matters could get worse, for the critical attention presently paid to secondary education is bound to shift in part to higher education soon. Scrutiny will not be confined to departments and colleges of teacher education, for concern about the integrity of undergraduate instruction more broadly can be anticipated. Too many students are graduating without adequate levels of competency in basic academic skills.[6] Institutions simply must pay more attention to self-regulation. Otherwise, public favor and support will diminish and a renewed emphasis upon further external mandates and controls can be anticipated.[7]

These are important concerns, but the most fundamental reason for paying renewed and sustained attention to self-regulation is simply its particular appropriateness to higher education. Effective self-regulation is the mark of a vigorous and responsible institution and of a healthy and creative profession and community, especially one dedicated to discovering and transmitting knowledge.

The Areas of Self-Regulation

Each higher education institution has self-regulatory responsibilities to at least three different publics: its internal public, including students, faculty, and staff; other institutions of higher education; and the larger environing society. Specific situations will vary widely, but some general comments can be made.

INTERNAL PUBLIC

With regard to their students, institutions regulate themselves in a variety of ways. The traditional area of course and degree requirements comes immediately to mind. But matters usually regarded only as academic can also become consumer-related and indeed societal issues. Thus, the very adequacy of instruction itself can become problematic, as the characteristics, interests, and needs of the student body shift in a time of rapid social and technological change. Not only broad curricular requirements but also ethnic and gender balance in instructional materials can attract attention. Likewise, such matters as when classes are scheduled and the frequency with which courses are offered are matters in which students often take a keen interest. Students have always had an interest in grading practices, but now they are much more prone to exploring appeal procedures. And there is growing interest by many parties in the proprieties governing institutional advertising and student recruiting, and in the policies for both the award and transfer of credit.

Underlying these matters is the fact that at the very core of education is a special trust—one easily misused or abused. Not unlike the relationship between physician and patient, the teacher is to promote the true interests, the fundamental good, of the students. Physician and teacher are both midwives to natural processes—to assist, not impede, the drive toward health and knowledge. Like the patient in relation to the doctor, the "traditional" student is especially dependent upon his or her faculty members and vulnerable to the abuse of their station. For their part, faculty members can find it all too easy to interpret the attentions of students as relating personally to them rather than through them to the inquiry or the material at hand. As a result, teaching with both enthusiasm and integrity can sometimes be quite a challenge. The difficult instructional task is to be transparent to the inquiry and the material presented while at the same time utilizing the strengths of one's personality.

Associations can help to promote a climate in which appropriate faculty professional norms can flourish. The American Association of University Professors (AAUP) in particular has been instrumental in clarifying many of these professional norms and in gaining wider national acceptance of them. Nonetheless, there is much more it could do. Individual faculty members as well as institutions can violate academic freedom and merit censure. As a professional organization, the AAUP would strengthen its standing within higher education were it to promote standards of individual behavior more aggressively.[8]

Still, it remains to each institution to establish and to nurture structures of governance that effectively promote appropriate behavior in its special situation. Each institution must devise ways of making clear its commitment to the special conditions and trusts of learning. It must be made known that unprofessional behaviors such as racial stereotyping or sexual harassment by faculty and staff simply will not be tolerated. Institutions must also address the harassment of intellect through redundant or obsolete courses and programs or by those faculty who have ceased to be interested or interesting. There is no reason that simple dullness should be perpetuated, much less enshrined. Methods for encouraging program review and professional renewal and growth must be in place and must be effective. Specific expectations regarding the conduct and publication of research as well as appropriate community service are but two other examples of faculty matters on which each institution must provide clarity.

Another area calling for institutional attention is viable and fair procedures for systematic evaluation of tenured faculty and administrators.[9] Additionally, the current need of most institutions to reduce increases in expenses calls for the construction of fair and workable salary policies. Likewise, program redirection and reduction demand equitable processes and outcomes—ones that do not automatically reverse recent gains in equal opportunity and affirmative action. And the relationship between faculty and nonfaculty is on most campuses an issue calling for regular and ongoing sensitive attention. Effective self-regulation in these areas may require the revamping of institutional reward systems.

All of these internal publics or constituencies offer both opportunities and requirements for effective self-regulation. Vigorous institutions will be paying attention.

OTHER INSTITUTIONS

The nation has a rich variety of institutions of higher education. These provide a second public to each other, for there are vast differences among institutions with respect to governance, tradition, and mission, as well as in reputation and price. To date, the community of higher education has done fairly well in establishing common understandings on such matters as definitions of credit, admission notification and policies, and recruiting practices.

Still, further cooperation between and among these institutions must be fostered and acceptable practices supported—particularly as competition for precious resources tightens. Workable understandings between the public and private sectors of higher education regarding acceptable and unacceptable fundraising behaviors and approaches must be developed. Another continuing challenge to the whole community of higher education is to distinguish those institutions whose departure from traditional delivery systems is a function of bold experimentation from those institutions that are simply careless in observing standards or are oblivious to them altogether.

Institutions with obvious common denominators such as location or size have often found it advantageous to come together in consortia to promote student or faculty exchange, fundraising, cost savings through joint purchasing, or other collective activities. Most of these involvements are fairly stabilized and enjoy collective acceptance, but other joint activities—such as intercollegiate athletics—cry out for far more disciplined self-regulation.

THE ENVIRONING SOCIETY

In addition to viable self-regulatory understandings within and among the various institutions, there must be effective relationships between each campus and its larger, environing society. Societies ought to have a large interest in the basic integrity of their educational institutions, for no healthy society can long tolerate the attitude that truth is unimportant. Of course there may be a variety of stratagems used to disguise this fact and/or the truth in question. But these illusions must ultimately be set aside.

Precisely because of this necessity, academic institutions are often prone to demanding a degree of freedom society may find irritating or even threatening. Frequent critics as well as observers of social practice, institutions need to be shielded from reactions to unpopular or unfashionable comments or activities. This shielding is a vital function of the governing board. In fact, it is the lay board that makes possible the fact of significant institutional self-regulation.

Self-regulation presupposes a certain amount of freedom from societal control, and only if each institution is protected from excessive intrusions from without will it have energies to spend on effective and responsible self-direction. Trustees and regents must be prepared to draw the line in defense of their institutions and to allow these energies to be spent. This function requires that governing boards interpret the institution to the public as well as defend it from unwarranted attack.

At the same time, it is the board that as representative of the public calls the institution to recognize the obligations that follow from presence within, and partial sponsorship by, society. That is, governing boards must encourage self-regulation, a step beyond simply permitting it to happen. The board must focus some attention of the institution upon the needs of the environing society and encourage appropriate self-direction. Thus, the governing board is at once buffer and transmitter. Each function heightens both the possibility and the need for institutions to be truly self-regulatory.

Each institution will need to identify areas in which it can contribute appropriately and even creatively to wider community need or growth. For many, this is an especially exciting area of self-regulation—as individual institutions work to serve and support wider community projects and values. In the process, self-regulation becomes especially important in such matters as institutional development and fundraising, in the selection of and arrangements governing sponsored research, and in special contractual arrangements with communities and businesses to provide educational programs.

In all of these areas, narrow institutional self-interest will eventually destroy public respect. The relations of an institution with its external publics parallel those with its internal constituencies. That is, within a college or a school, excessive competition or narrowness of vision among constituent departments detracts from the underlying unity. Beyond some point, that unity is broken or stretched so thin that internal efficiency and external identity are lost. So too, within a region—and by extension nationally—failure of individual institutions to display appropriate conduct contributes to a diminished public regard of all. The actions of a few can jeopardize and depreciate the value of all.

The Locus of Self-Regulation

Central to effective self-regulation in all of these broad areas are deliberate and systematic review and assessment by campus groups and officials, and then by external peers, of institutional objectives, practices, and accomplishments. Accordingly, we can speak of two levels of self-regulation within higher education. The first, and primary, level is at the individual institution and refers to those practices and activities within each institution whereby it develops, implements, and monitors its use of principles of good practice, both administratively and academically. It is only at the institutional level that principles designed to promote integrity can actually be made to work. Even externally mandated regulatory measures must be implemented at the campus level. Accordingly, this primary level is ultimately also the final level.

On some issues, it is the decisions and behavior of individual faculty that will promote self-regulation. On other issues, faculty senate committees (such as curriculum, personnel, or long-range planning committees, or review boards on human subject research) function to promote effective self-regulation. In still others, the effective decisions rest with various administrative offices. Almost always, though, it is the institution as a whole working through its parts that is effective in self-regulation.

Although the individual institution is the locus of ultimate self-regulatory efficacy, activity at the secondary level can facilitate matters. Playing a key role at this secondary level of self-regulation are the various accrediting agencies. Products of the institutions, the accrediting agencies and associations are nongovernmental, voluntary agencies organized, supported, and governed by the postsecondary community as a whole. Accreditation is an early example, as well as a key mechanism in, the self-regulation of higher education. In fact, what are now known as the regional accrediting associations were an obvious historical product of efforts to regulate from within the community.[10] The key objective in accreditation activities is to determine and to support the adequacy of institutional policies and practices—and so to attest "that an institution or program has clearly defined and educationally appropriate objectives, that it maintains conditions under which it is reasonable to expect that they will be achieved, that it appears to be accomplishing them, and that it can be expected to continue to do so."[11]

In this context, self-study is as essential for institutions as it is for individuals. In fact, the self-study and self-assessment activities that are part of standard accreditation processes play an important role in self-regulation. As an operational principle, self-study follows necessarily from taking seriously the principle of diversity within higher education. It thereby shows the inappropriateness of holding each institution to some detailed, rigid a priori set of external expectations.

Self-evaluation is indeed at the heart of self-regulation, for a disposition to be seriously engaged in self-evaluation is really a prior condition for peer comment to be effective. And, of course, peer comment is itself indispensable. It is peers to whom one turns for corroboration of one's own judgment and for enlargement of perspective. For peers, by definition, are those judged to have both sufficient experience and access to relevant standards.

It is peers in this sense, not bureaucrats or regulatory strangers, who run accrediting agencies. Collectively established and implemented, agencies are structured either institutionally (as in the national and regional associations) or programmatically (as with the specialized agencies). Typically, both types of accrediting agencies have twin objectives. On the one hand, they provide a measure of assurance to the public that adequate academic programs are in fact presented within the accredited institution. On the other, they encourage and promote institutional efforts to improve quality.

Thus accrediting agencies are to be both evaluative and supportive. Some individuals see these two objectives as in conflict, if not outright incompatible. There can certainly be tension, but efforts toward both objectives must be supported and enhanced. The public needs the assurances of quality, which are best provided by those who have relevant expertise and who have nothing to gain from misrepresentation. At the same time, these experts have every professional reason to want to suggest and to encourage appropriate improvements.

Unfortunately, there is evidence that regional and specialized mechanisms alike can stand improvement. Both the Carnegie report on governance and the report of the ACE Commission on Quality suggest that regional accreditation needs to be taken much more seriously—particularly by those professionals who are presently "too busy" to serve.[12] The Carnegie report describes such service as a matter of responsible citizenship, much like jury duty. And the ACE report urges that more administrators and faculty members from highly regarded institutions participate. Regional accrediting agencies can hardly be taken seriously by the public in the absence of respect by educators themselves.

Specialized accrediting agencies can present a special problem. Because their focus and membership are relatively narrow, they are surrounded by opportunities to advance the needs and interests of their own practitioners ahead of those of the public, thereby becoming guilds. When this happens, it is the conditions of employment for their members, rather than such genuine issues of accreditation as the quality of graduates, that seem to be advanced. Indeed, the Carnegie report suggests that precisely such self-enrichment is occurring and that this area of accreditation "actually threatens the integrity of the campus."[13] Obviously, effective self-regulation is endangered when special interests are being served behind the cloak of respectability.

The solution to this problem appears to rest in much closer involvement of the whole higher education community in self-regulatory organizations such as the Council on Postsecondary Accreditation (COPA). In fact, COPA functions as a back-up level of self-regulation to assure that other members at the secondary level are functioning appropriately. Institutions should refuse dealings with agencies not recognized by COPA and should press COPA itself for strong collective action on agency abuse. Wide circulation of proposals and comments on them can obviate some of the self-serving problems. In fact, such breadth of involvement of the higher education community seems to be the only way in which narrow self-interest can be overcome.

The concept of accreditation—and the attendant associations and procedures—is clearly a key part of the machinery available for effective self-regulation within higher education. It is important and it needs to be strengthened in the ways indicated. But there are also other resources, and among them is the ACE Office on Self-Regulation Initiatives.

The ACE Office on Self-Regulation Initiatives

With the support of co-sponsoring associations, this office was established in 1978 by the American Council on Education in order to focus national attention on the need to strengthen higher education's activities in self-regulation. In fact, one of the charges was to promote "self-regulation as a viable alternative to governmental regulation." Another objective was to reinforce institutional mechanisms for dealing with ongoing self-regulation issues as well as with new developments on which the public looks to higher education for special leadership. More broadly phrased, its goals are "1) to foster wider awareness of and commitment to self-regulatory procedures; 2) to stimulate action on issues where self-regulation is appropriate; 3) to provide coordination and assistance to existing activities with self-regulatory aspects; and 4) to serve as a continuing national focus for issues relating to self-regulation."[14]

An Advisory Committee was appointed early on to assist the office in developing program directions and objectives. The Committee has been keenly aware of the diversity of higher education institutions. Indeed, members have been selected to be broadly representative of this diversity and have worked to support institutional variety and to repudiate arbitrary standards, or those skewed in favor of one institutional sector or region. Committee discussions have also been consistent in showing it to have no intention of being yet another external influence on institutions, but rather to aim at broad expressions of what in essence seems appropriate in higher education administration.

There are three main components in the approach of this office and its Advisory Committee. The first is the development, in concert with others, and the distribution nationally, of guidelines for recommended institutional good practice. The second is the collaboration with other associations in alerting campus administrators to the need for prompt implementation of the national policy recommendations. And the third is the requesting of relevant associations to assume leadership in appropriate follow-up activities such as the conduct of workshops, the provision of technical assistance, and the development of advisory publications.

To date, the practice of the office has been collaborative in character. Those associations, offices, and individuals possessing the relevant expertise have been pressed into taking the leadership role on individual issues. Review of proposed guidelines has deliberately been widespread. Certainly the development of policies by those who are to be affected by them is a time-honored and effective management tool. Of course, one must be careful that the process of review is wide enough to identify special interests and deflect them. But with this approach, the prospect for desirable outcomes is much brighter than when measures are simply presented.

Terminology is also important. For instance, the distinction between guidelines and standards can be variously drawn. The ACE position is that guidelines are to be understood as constructed on the basis of logically prior standards, and guidelines are to be aids to the application of these standards. In this sense, guidelines are created at certain points, whereas standards are rooted in fundamental community perceptions and so are less bound to specific times and places. The difference is somewhat relative, to be sure, but it functions importantly in self-regulation.

The difference is important because appeal is made to standards in the application, interpretation, and revision of guidelines. They, not guidelines, are primary. As a result, guidelines can be counterproductive when presented too strongly, as though they were themselves standards. Individuals and institutions must be permitted to sense for themselves the "fit" between the guidelines and the underlying and warranting standards. Judging that there is indeed such a fit seems to be a prior condition for the full acceptance and effective implementation of the guidelines. Of course, any effective implementation will usually require further adjustments to reflect individual circumstances.

The trick, then, is to develop guidelines of substance that also recognize the huge variety of institutional type, practice, and tradition in this country. They must be neither too prescriptive nor too vague. In this respect, the agenda is at the same time limited and ambitious. Both the diversity of institutions and the history of individual campus autonomy pose a great challenge to the effort. The expectation is that each institution will give thoughtful attention in its review so that already existing as well as resulting policies are consistent with both the guidelines and institutional purpose and values. To date, nine guidelines have been issued by the office, on topics ranging from tuition refunds, admissions practices, and credit transfer policies to satisfactory progress for students receiving financial aid. Each of these guidelines has evolved and developed in different ways, with each reflecting the specific issues that prompted efforts to prepare guidelines as well as the consensus that emerged on the elements of good institutional practice regarding those issues.

The office's experience in developing the guidelines on tuition refund policy offers an illustration of the developmental process. Agreement among representatives of several education associations to try to develop guidelines on the subject emerged from a recognition that federal officials were raising legitimate questions about the extent to which colleges maintained fair and equitable tuition refund policies. What was just as clear, however, was the sense that no single formulation could adequately capture the range of circumstances affecting refund policies that would need to be taken into account by the thousands of collegiate institutions in the United States. Refund policies judged fair for a small residential college, for instance, might be very inappropriate for a commuter institution whose clientele are primarily part-time students.

The challenge was to develop a statement that would encompass the broad principles that should guide tuition refund policies while also offering prototypical language that campuses might adopt or adapt as they reviewed their own statements. Guided by the advice of the Advisory Committee, members and staff of the National Association of College and University Business Officers (NACUBO) embarked on a time-consuming and detailed canvass of existing tuition refund policies and of administrator's opinions on the components of good administrative practice regarding tuition refund. Gradually a pattern emerged, and a consensus was established that certain components might be considered basic building blocks of good policy. Also, the policies of particular institutions were identified by many as exemplary in certain ways.

Once a draft statement was prepared that reflected such components of good practice, it received wide circulation and request for comment. Association staff and college and university personnel alike were asked to offer comments. NACUBO itself published a draft version of the statement in its monthly newsletter with a call for comments. This process produced a number of refinements in the draft, such as the addition of a phrase or a change in wording that would make the statement more applicable to different institutional circumstances.

The resulting statement, approved by NACUBO's advisory board and by ACE's Advisory Committee in 1979, was very successful. Within a year of its distribution, the associations had received varying types of evidence that many institutions had adopted its terms and that many other colleges and systems of colleges and universities had used the statement as the basis for their own review and development of new tuition refund policies. To a surprising extent, individual colleges adopted in their own policy entire sections of the guidelines. Equally gratifying was the acceptance of the guideline by the U.S. Department of Education.

Other efforts to promote self-regulation on higher education issues have taken different directions, although still attempting to offer substantive advice that respects the diversity of institutional types and practices. For example, it seemed inappropriate to expect any single set of guidelines to encompass the variety of concerns that were being voiced several years ago about whether campus administrators were giving adequate management attention to their administrative arrangements for student financial aid. The form in which substantive advice was assembled therefore did not result in guidelines. Rather, a short monograph was developed that organized numerous principles of good administration and that cited examples of institutional practice that knowledgeable administrators considered valuable.[15]

The drafting process resembled that conducted for the guidelines on tuition refunds. A review and assessment of existing practices, along with a careful analysis of federal program expectations and requirements, helped to set the outline for what was needed. A draft statement was prepared and circulated among a wide variety of campus administrators for comment. Here, too, the review comments not only added to the clarity of the document but also helped to suggest more generic language. The resulting paper made clear that its intent was to provide materials for thoughtful reviews of campus policies by individual administrators. Its fundamental aim was to be a resource in assisting campus leaders to discharge their own responsibilities for proper oversight of financial aid programs. It pointed to good procedures and essential principles, but was not prescriptive. It imposed a heavy obligation upon institutional leaders, expecting that they would find a method for regularly assessing their financial aid administration and policies.

A third way in which the office has promoted the concept of self-regulation is illustrated through its quite recent sponsorship and conduct of several activities related to the concept of periodic evaluation of tenured faculty performance. Rather than issuing guidelines or writing a manual, the office planned, organized, and conducted—together with the American Association of University Professors—a Wingspread conference at which the nature and character of such evaluation was explored. Subsequently, the office made presentations at the annual meetings of several associations and conducted special workshops at which participants discussed how to initiate or refine systems of periodic evaluation of the performance of tenured faculty members.

In these three different ways, the office has pursued its general mandate to assist colleges and universities to become more self-governing and more self-conscious about the adequacy of their institutional policies. There is an underlying recognition that an important part of the self-regulatory process rests on the willingness of campus administrators to reexamine policies and procedures in the light of new and changing concerns. The effective role of the education associations is to alert campus leaders to emerging issues and to provide advisory materials of sufficient substance to express the essential components of good policy while allowing flexibility of institutional response.

Even during the office's initial months of activity, it was evident that an important task was to be a source of expertise and guidance for other associations that wished to respond to accountability pressures. Each year, representatives of various associations have sought out ACE's advice on how they might handle certain public concerns affecting their constituents. On other occasions, the office has responded to requests for examples of policy guidelines and statements or has offered advice on ways that such statements might be crafted so that they espouse necessary principles without becoming overly prescriptive. At various times, this role had meant that advice is given to another association to the effect that they should not develop guidelines on a subject, that the ones they are considering would be onerous to institutions, or that the guidelines they have produced are exemplary.

The need for self-regulation will not end and the work of the office will continue in these and other ways. New initiatives will be developed as new circumstances permit and dictate. For instance, the office is currently developing a second series of self-regulation statements to supplement the Guidelines series. This second series will include resource materials on issues of keen interest to many, perhaps most, institutions—though not all, as is the case with the Guidelines series. Candidates for this second series, to be called Resource Documents, include suggestions of self-regulatory issues involved in campus/business linkages and in campus security.

The Effectiveness of Self-Regulation

Regardless of the specific issue, in the last analysis institutions must have the courage to take the difficult steps in self-governance. In this sense, self-regulation is simply the moral dimension of management. Self-regulation is regulation in connection with certain normative concepts of how members of the higher education community *ought* to behave. For instance, many institutions appear to the public to lack either the capacity or the courage to deal with incompetent faculty members. Part of this problem doubtless resides in the public's disposition to believe the worst. This may be a form of anti-intellectualism. But not all—or probably even much —of the problem can be dismissed so easily. Who, after all, can assert with confidence that his or her institution has clean hands, that it is presenting the students with the *best* possible instructors and that its resources are being deployed in the most efficient manner?

Certainly it is never easy to arrange, promote, or sustain cooperation and a community of true self-regulation. And a time of reduced and constricted financial resources tends to accelerate competition rather than cooperation. Inevitably, some community-generated policies or recommendations will work against one part of the community or unduly favor another.

An additional problem is associated with difficulties of monitoring acceptable conformance with community standards. Who has time to do this for 3,000 institutions? Even if there were viable means of monitoring, there is almost a complete lack of workable sanctions, other than moral. And even these are not easily administered, there being no central authority. As a result, those members of the community that violate common standards are rarely publicly rebuked by the community as a whole. Even more rarely are they excommunicated, expelled, or in other ways publicly excluded. Renewed attention must be paid to the need to assure the public that violations of standards do not go unheeded. Ultimately, though, one must rely "on voluntarism as a free market principle—if the guidelines make sense, then people will use them."[16]

As we noted earlier, one strong reason to give serious attention to self-regulation activities is to avoid onerous federal and state involvment in areas that are the rightful responsibility of the higher education community. After all, the most valuable asset and endowment of higher education is public confidence. The public expects its educators to govern themselves and to display in their individual and collective behavior traces of the wisdom they are charged to transmit. More than simply an asset, public confidence is indispensable to higher eduction. The evidence and fruits of self-regulation provide assurances to the public that appropriate standards are in fact observed and that the occasional abuses are just that—occasional.

Equally important is the sense that the higher education community itself should work directly and diligently to address those problems subject to public concern. Certainly the primary responsibility for institutional integrity and academic quality rests with each institution. Also, the primary opportunity for effecting such integrity is located within the institution. No external agency can bestow quality or integrity on a program or institution—although they may be able to withdraw it. Experience has shown that efforts to improve program integrity or quality are most effectively done at the institutional level by those actually in the institution. After all, those who are intimately involved in the activities under question are in the best position to know what is and is not viable. Thus, the very process by which guidelines or other self-regulatory measures are developed can be important in building support for their subsequent acceptance and implementation. Indeed, one possibility for increasing the effectiveness of ACE self-regulation guidelines is to incorporate within the regular regional accreditation process specific review of the institutional implementation of the guidelines. This procedure would cement community recognition of the importance of such guidelines as well.

The key concept in this context is persuasion. Observation of, and compliance with, community standards will be truly effective only if those affected are persuaded of their reasonableness and merit. Grudging acceptance—motivated by fear of adverse consequences or the need to appear publicly correct—will inevitably eventuate in reluctant and superficial observation. In most areas of human behavior, imposed standards yield only short-term results. There is no reason to think that people in higher education are in these respects any different.

However, unless institutional efforts are made to promote effective self-regulation in areas and on issues of importance, reforms will indeed be imposed from outside the community. And then everyone will be poorer.

Notes

1. Chester E. Finn, Jr., "Trying Higher Education: An Eight Count Indictment," *Change* (May/June, 1984), p. 30.
2. For one helpful document, see *The Maintenance of High Ethical Standards in the Conduct of Research*, published in 1982 by the Association of American Medical Colleges. This statement contains recommended procedures for dealing with alleged research fraud.
3. *The Control of the Campus: A Report on the Governance of Higher Education*. (Princeton, N.J.: The Carnegie Foundation for the Advancement of Teaching, 1982), p. 66.
4. Ibid., p. 6.
5. Derek Bok argues that post-World War II bigness and complexity have created the necessity for universities to be much more deliberate and reflective about the self-regulatory dimensions of their social responsibilities. See his carefully argued *Beyond the Ivory Tower* (Cambridge, Mass.: Harvard University Press, 1982).
6. For a study about state higher education agency activity in this area, see John Bennett et al., "Academic Progression Tests for Undergraduates: Recent Developments," *Educational Record* (Winter, 1984), pp. 44–48.
7. For just such a prediction, see Lawrence R. Marcus et al., *The Path to*

Excellence: Quality Assurance in Higher Education (ERIC: Association for the Study of Higher Education, 1983).

8. See George Keller, *Academic Strategy: The Management Revolution in American Higher Education* (Baltimore: Johns Hopkins University Press, 1983), p. 23: "The American Association of University Professors has, since its founding in 1915, been principally a narrow protective league that guards faculty rights such as academic freedom and tenure rather than an encompassing professional association that insures professional standards, behavior, and obligations and censures or expels culpable members for fraud, abuses of intellectual freedom, incompetency, and gross violations of ethics."
9. See the essay by John B. Bennett and Shirley S. Chater, "Evaluating the Performance of Tenured Faculty Members," *Educational Record* (Spring, 1984).
10. See Elaine H. El-Khawas, "Accreditation: Self-Regulation," in *Understanding Accreditation*, ed. Kenneth E. Young et al. (San Francisco: Jossey-Bass, 1983), pp. 54–70.
11. Richard M. Millard, "Accreditation," in *Meeting the New Demand for Standards*, ed. Jonathan R. Warren (San Francisco: Jossey-Bass, 1983), p. 10.
12. The summary report of the National Commission on Higher Education Issues was issued in 1982 and is entitled *To Strengthen Quality in Higher Education*. See also the critical comments and suggestions about accreditation in Marcus et al., *The Path to Excellence*.
13. *To Strengthen Quality in Education*, p. 78.
14. Elaine H. El-Khawas, "Solving Problems Through Self-Regulation," *Educational Record* (Fall, 1978).
15. The monograph, by Elaine H. El-Khawas, was entitled *Management of Student Aid: A Guide for Presidents* (Washington, D.C.: American Council on Education, 1979).
16. Elaine H. El-Khawas, "Self-Regulation: An Approach to Ethical Standards," *Professional Ethics in University Administration*, ed. Ronald H. Stein et al. (San Francisco: Jossey-Bass, 1981), p. 59.

PART TWO
Self-Regulation and Institutional Relations

"Thy Firmness Makes My Circle Just" Professional Schools in the University

TIMOTHY S. HEALY, S.J.

IN THE PUBLIC EYE AMERICAN UNIVERSITIES are recognized by their professional schools. A "college" deals with the liberal arts and sciences and may be allowed one or two practical programs. A "university" is a galaxy of schools, including at least some of the professional ones—business, law, medicine, engineering, or public administration. In this there is nothing new, since the medieval university itself began as a gathering of professional schools with its original faculties of arts for training in statecraft, law, and medicine, and theology for training in churchcraft. There is thus no historic remove between the parent university and its professional schools, nor do we look for one. Within our walls, however, the pattern is more complex. American universities drew their English and thus medieval understanding of undergraduate colleges from Oxford and Cambridge. In the nineteenth century we grafted onto these colleges the German professional graduate schools. Like John Ormond's apple tree, the graft took over the stock, and the professorial graduate school has ever since been the dominant faculty. Devoted as it is to the arts and sciences, this faculty is, at the very least, suspicious about professional schools other than those that prepare for the profession of professing. There are several levels to this suspicion. The least suspect are two of the four original schools, law and theology. Deeper suspicions are held about the third of the ancient faculties, medicine, since most medical schools are given to high technology and are tied to a health care business called a hospital. About equally suspect are schools of business and public administration. Graduate faculties are even more leery of schools of dentistry, engineering, and social work, while suspicion bordering on dismissal is reserved for one of the newer additions to the university, the school of education.

Behind such suspicions lies a deep instinct that the steady growth of professional schools is capable of destroying the university so cherished by professors of the arts and sciences. The great rudder on its hull is its collection of classic departments, philosophy, history, science, literature, and the arts. These are the studies by which a university defines itself, these set the norms against which it judges itself, and these make up the irreducible core of its being. Philosophy distributes the university's terrain by describing and delimiting all other subject areas and also by judging their competencies. Within the university philosophy is the keeper of peace and order. It adds another dimension through its ethical preoccupations and looks beyond the university to the works of citizenship. In universities with a religious tradition, theology aids philosophy in its delimiting role and on its own ground points to another and more lasting citizenship.

History is needed to root both university studies and university people and lends all our contemplative activities the relief of time. Like philosophy it has an ordering function; it provides a bulwark against passion and immediate involvement; it is the great antidote to the deep distraction of relevance because it shelters the contemplative work of the university from the compromising demands of the immediate, the contemporaneous, and the urgent. For the busy world outside our gates W. H. Auden's advice, "take short views," may be good; in the contemplative world of the university, history guarantees the long views that both strengthen and clear the mind.

The sciences also move in that contemplative world. They

bring us a different kind of knowing than either philosophy or history; they work in an abstract world where clarity makes us aware of beauty, where investigation like contemplation is its own reward, and where both mind and heart are involved in the intractable reality of matter. Science protects us from idiot-savantry, the tyranny of theory, and the heresy that our intellectual constructs run the universe. In like manner the university needs its faculties of literature and the arts, since they teach us man's traditional way of organizing his understanding and experience. Like the sciences, the arts root us in matter, in the earth, in the duality of our being in mind and body. The arts share with the sciences the urge to poke and probe into the future. Like the sciences they involve us in a separate kind of knowing, one that goes beyond and outside the discursive reasoning of the academic intelligence. They lure us into the tangle, the thrill, and the engagement of symbolic learning.

Into this understanding of the way a university works the stern and practical focus of professional schools can fall with all the subtlety of a brick into a birdbath. Their isolation, their intensity, and above all their ties to outside authorities and economic pressures can make impossible the essential job of the university, in Alfred North Whitehead's memorable phrase, "the imaginative consideration of learning." John Henry Newman says: "There can be no doubt that every art is improved by confining the professor of it to a single study. But although the art itself is advanced by this concentration of mind in its service, the individual who is confined to it goes backwards. The advantage to the community is nearly in an inverse ratio with his own."[1] Behind that paragraph lies an Aristotelian understanding of human good that is mightily opposed to the post-Kantian confusion of the modern academy. Whatever reduces the reach of the minds of students and faculty is bad and counters the clear human good a university exists to foster.

Professional schools can be seen as working three great ills in any university. For both faculty and students they can deny its essential work of contemplation. Their reliance upon external bodies of practitioners can work to deprive the university of its greatest gift, its freedom. Finally, all professional schools by the nature of their work can be a block to the university's age-old dream of integrating its intellectual work.

A metaphor for all three dangers is the process of professional accreditation, which like the Seven Plagues of Egypt bedevil all complex universities. The general accreditation of colleges and universities is called "regional" and always looks at the institution as a whole. Accreditors arrive to evaluate general management, the library, the structure of the curriculum, the adequacy of budgetary arrangements, and then build their judgment on the university's own definition of its being and aims. The members of the regional accrediting teams are colleagues—administrators and professors from other but comparable institutions. The scope of their investigation is broad, and their purpose is to give what help they can to the health of the entire institution. Their reports and recommendations are ultimately submitted to another body of colleagues, faculty members from various departments and administrators in other universities and colleges in a given region. The whole process enjoys a kind of amateur status; nobody involved does accreditation all the time, nobody reports to any outside authority, and most evaluators are as much interested in learning from the process as in arriving at good judgments.

When we turn to professional school accreditation everything changes. The sponsoring body is most frequently the profession itself, and accrediting team members are all drawn from the same discipline, whatever institution they may come from. The norms they use have little to do with the general health of the institution; they are rigidly professional, are derived from the practice of the profession, and are acutely sensitive to the economic pressures that govern its marketplace. This narrow focus, with norms foreign to the university and canons built upon utility (and frequently upon greed) can make professional accreditation tear at the vitals of the university itself. Demands are made on behalf of one faculty for space, support, books, personnel, and salary that bear little or no relation to the health or growth of the institution as a whole. Professional accreditation aims at improving one school's status among the many schools of the university at whatever cost to the university itself. The American Bar Association, for instance, has its own arcane and stringent rules about course hours, teaching loads, and faculty–student ratios, nor is it at all averse to denying the university's independent control over its own budget and the share all its schools can have in it.

Professional accreditations frequently bring with them a kind of intellectual arrogance. The American Association of Collegiate Schools of Business insists that all business-related courses be under the control of the dean of the school of business, whatever havoc this may wreak in the adjacent and necessarily different departments of economics, international studies, and applied mathematics. The university's freedom to determine its own curricular structure is thus directly and stridently challenged. Many such accreditations have another, perhaps indeliberate, effect that can compromise the university's norms for the appointment, tenuring, and promotion of faculty members. It is hard for universities to tell the difference between professional accreditations and the worst kind of trade unionism when the principal thrust of a supposedly academic review is to raise salaries, expand faculty numbers, and perpetuate incompetence.

Such practices fly in the face of the university's immemorial understanding of itself, but they all too clearly reflect the dangers and ambiguities professional schools pose to their parent universities. Let us look first at schools of law. We need not deal with problems present only in law schools that are academically weak. Our worst law schools lose themselves and their students in technique, but it is not fair to draw conclusions from those that are bar prep academies. Nor are vaguer social suspicions much help since so many of them are founded on flaws in the school itself. One such is that all law schools are bastions of privilege, and the more competitive they are the higher the bastion. Some law schools can be and have been conservative anchors that serve as a drag on the university's own citizenship in the society it serves. On the other hand, the best of the nation's law schools, thanks particularly to their clinical extensions, are far from that parody of what a law school should be.

There are, however, serious reasons for the university's suspicion of law schools that have little to do with the intrusion and arrogance of the American Bar Association and a great deal to do with university's Aristotelian understanding of itself, that its highest work and its best gift to society is contemplation. Law schools are suspect because they can be filled with those who "turn the wheel and look to windward," who are so wrapped up in the giving and getting of professional credentials that they have neither time nor inclination to examine or understand the philosophical limits of their study or its historic roots. The law is a great human artifact, in many ways a work of art. It deserves long and loving looking at; in other words, it merits contemplation. To the extent that the sheer busyness of going to law school, the image shown in *The Paper Chase*, eliminates that contemplative urge, the law school is failing as a part of a university. To the extent that contemplation disappears, the minds and hearts of both faculty members and students are stunted and the joy they should find in the challenge and conquest of their work is wrecked.

Universities are ornery places and guard nothing so much as the second part of the image and likeness of God, their freedom. Like the law itself, that freedom is a thin shield against a world of violence and force that lies outside academic walls. Law schools in the United States are disciplined by the profession of law, indeed ultimately responsible to certain of its courts. The universities have accepted that, but their acceptance is now given with an increasing reluctance. Why this kicking against the goad? The answer is straightforward. Law schools, disciplined as they are by an external profession, can also be dominated by that profession and the university rightly regards this as a kind of intellectual death.

As has been eloquently pointed out by President Bok of Harvard, the social effect of this external dominance can be costly.[2] The academic effects, those internal to the university itself, are every bit as bad. The first is an overconcentration of mind and heart that is destructive precisely because it achieves concentration at the cost of too much elimination. The second is the imposition on the university of the adversarial posture of American law. In university terms, that begets a kind of competition that is unhealthy for individuals and destructive of institutions. Concentration and competition combine to make it impossible for students and at times faculty members to see the relevance of their discipline to other studies within the university or, more tragically, the necessary bearing of other studies upon the study of the law.

Precisely because overconcentration and the competitive urge isolate law faculties and law students, they also ill serve the law itself. An essential task of any university is to question assumptions; isolation usually breeds ironclad and unquestionable assumptions. These are bad enough when they are social, when, for instance, the prestige of great law firms is so unassailable that their works and days cannot submit to question. It is even worse when the assumptions are purely intellectual. In that case, orthodoxies are established that both inhibit debate and predetermine conclusions. The result is learning by rote and expounding by rule in a context that not only challenges learning but also distrusts and decries all imaginative contemplation.

Leaving aside the dictionary definition that a profession is a self-organized, self-policing, and self-fulfilling occupation, let us look at its deepest root, that it is meant to serve society. That leads us to the questions President Bok raises about the teaching of law in the United States. How effective are our law schools as tools for society's good? How realistically are law students taught to apply their professional skills to that same societal good? How deeply is the notion of service to society instinct to legal research, teaching, and learning? In the contemplative world of university subjects, as in the reflections of Cardinal Newman, one can easily talk of knowledge as its own end. The consolation may be offered to those whose intention it is to teach the law. The ambiguity of professional training within the contemplative university, however, means that no matter how we try to condition our conclusions we still have to see every professional school as an "instrument" for a social good which necessarily lies beyond contemplation. Any university worth its salt must maintain that however valid that external good may be and whatever claims and demands the profession makes on its behalf, the learning and teaching that reach toward it lie squarely within the university's contemplative tradition.

Let us turn now to a second professional school, the school of business. At the moment, business is probably the most popular single subject in American colleges and universities. Business schools are crowded with students and turn away far more than they can take. Because of that popularity and the growing number of students seeking undergraduate and graduate degrees in business, business schools and their parent universities have to deal with an unsettled new agenda. First of all, business schools are open to attack from jealous rivals in older and more established disciplines. Second, precisely because of their popularity and the demand for their seats, business schools can themselves develop the arrogance of power. Jealousy is fairly easy to handle, arrogance is a deeper problem.

The real danger that business schools pose is again that of any professional enterprise, that professionalism can destroy the nature of the university itself, in other words, subvert "the imaginative consideration of learning." It does not take much imagination to see three primrose paths up which business schools can amble, or perhaps in a better metaphor, three greasy chutes that yawn before them. Either the amble or the slide will make sure that business education divorces itself from the university and will, in a matter of decades, skid into the status of most of the nation's schools of education, isolated and unrespected, at their best peripheral, at their worst destructive.

There are several ways schools of business can divorce themselves from their parent universities. The first is to ape the world of business in structure and in process. Universities are not in the business of business. The second is to yield to the seductions of high technology and by doing so clone medicine's flight from the university. A third is to abandon the structures and studies that feed the human imagination.

Any of these moves, not to speak of all of them together, would be fatal for the long tenure of business as an appropriate university faculty.

Industry itself, its panoply, its corporate intricacy, its money, and its importance, has to be something of a siren for all schools of business. Universities, however, do not thrive in bear hugs. It took some centuries for us to shed the bear hug of the church, only to find another and stronger bear waiting for us in the state. Western universities, at least those in the northern parts of the Western world, have managed to stave off the state bear, more or less. It would be a shame if, having escaped him, we rushed straight into the clutches of a third bear, business and industry. Parallel to the ties between law schools and the legal profession, any business school needs the support of business and industry and must be both in contact and in sympathy with what they do. Business and the university should, in other words, be allies, but alliance can exist only when there is a certain difference between the allies, and when each knows and keeps its distance.

Universities are not hierarchical organizations and businesses are; only a short step separates the structure of what is studied from the rhythms and patterns of how it is studied. At their best, universities resist most authoritative structures. By nature, university faculties are a band of individuals, working at research and teaching as best they can and content to put their case only to the bar of collegial, student, and public opinion. Our students and our colleagues share our scholarship and are the only ones who can tell us the quality of our work. Nobody, particularly nobody in authority, gives many orders in universities, and none so given bear upon research and teaching. This truth about the faculty, and the way it organizes and sees itself also determines the way universities treat students. While universities are great at collecting gross results, averages, and other statistical information, in our heart of hearts they do not much matter to us. What does matter is the individual contact, the teacher in his classroom, the head-on-head between student and faculty member, the arc across which our learning bangs into the energy of the young. That interchange is more important for us than all the statistics, rules, and regulations issued by the Office of the Dean or Provost, all the fulminations of the President and the Board of Trustees or of anyone else on the good ground on which we serve. Only individuals grow, and that growth in mind and heart is the faculty's preoccupation.

Precisely because of the importance of that individual exchange, universities are essentially somewhat withdrawn, at times both cloistered and sheltered. The young must learn to use their minds and imaginations, and that can be done only where there is general absolution from consequence. The wildest ideas must have their day, even if the day lasts only long enough to shoot them down. By jumping and flopping the young learn to fly. Putting them too early "into the marketplace" in mind or body, for all the attraction it may have as clinical training, robs them of freedom and dulls their best gift, their imagination. No employer in an office or factory hires young men and women to dream. If, on the other hand, they do not use their time on campus to dream, the promise and the premise on which they are hired are both false.

In short, not only are we not hierarchically organized and responsive to authority, but in a deep sense, universities are profoundly anarchic institutions. We must continually explain that anarchy to our friends in business and, for that matter, to those in government. We are constantly told we should get ourselves organized, and that if "we got our act together" we could be more productive, more helpful, and above all more economical. It isn't so much that we know better, it's just that we know otherwise. Those outside the walls of the university never seem to realize that our anarchy is a kind of freedom, the kind of freedom that young minds need most to grow. Out of that growth comes our best hope for national and indeed industrial power.

The second waiting chute is an undifferentiated enthusiasm for and a promiscuous yielding to the blandishments of technology and to its underlying assumption that learning can be reduced to the metaphor of number and so limited to the comfortable rut of things. To read the daily press, the computer is going to solve all our problems, from the kindergarten up to the MBA. The university's cool and steady resistance not to the ease in learning that computers and other tools can bring us but to the notion that they represent some kind of salvific gift becomes more intelligible when we look at our brethren in the schools of medicine. So far into technology has modern medicine gone that it is now one of our hardest wrestles to teach medical students that tools, no matter how sophisticated, are no better than the men and women who wield them.

What I am urging is not only a defense of the university but a defense of the common humanity of its men and women. No university can ever allow tools, no matter how sophisticated and promising, to replace or, worse, take precedence over their makers and users. Whitehead states succinctly the problem of all technical education, and he indicates that its solution requires a very careful balancing of goods. "Technical excellence can only be acquired by training apt to damage those energies of man which should direct the technical skill."[3] That goes further than saying that prolonged, not to mention exclusive, attention to routine dulls the imagination. It also means that the young mind can get lost in a manipulative skill that, while requiring high intelligence, seldom calls forth the imaginative control needed to learn what lies behind both the machine and its use.

The corrective to this particular danger is to expose young minds to the principles underlying technology and its uses. Whitehead points out that if we teach this way, even a "routine" then receives its meaning and illuminates the principles that give it that meaning.[4] Attention to principles can render drudgery, even drudgery on computers, both bearable and harmless because the mind involved grasps its need, understands its principles, and knows where it is going. A quite incidental benefit of this kind of teaching is that it can carry students across and through the dullest parts of any subject we must cover. A solidly built imagination seems to have almost endless tolerance for hard work.

A third danger derives from the first two. In their urge to stay current and in their efforts to prepare the young for the intricacies of commerce and industry, business schools run a great risk of letting go of what it has taken the university a thousand years to learn, precisely those studies and structures that feed man's imagination and keep his soul alive. A symbol of this is the all too frequent divorce, particularly in graduate business schools, between faculty and students—in more practical terms, between research and teaching. The young need and love the excitement of what is new, untried, and daring. Even the whiff of the frontier gets their juices flowing, and the knowledge that a faculty member is working on new ground, in new ways, on new assumptions is an exciting stimulus that helps them see any academic discipline as alive and worth a man's mind. Faculty members in turn need the probing of energy, exposure to simplicity, and the bedevilment of youthful questioners. Obviously, freshmen cannot cope with the highest ranges of the university research but, if they are well trained, many seniors can. The real loss is to allow teaching chores to fall only upon those faculty members who are not at all or very little engaged in research. The university has learned well its rootedness in the teaching of the young and can help business schools retain it.

When it comes to curriculum matters, business schools must also learn restraint. Obviously, there is more to learn in any profession than the hours of classwork and homework can encompass. That, however, would be a poor excuse for banishing "the goodly trains of gods and goddesses" and focusing the time and energy of students on strictly professional courses that can be as sterilizing as they are sterile. The humanities have a natural and indeed significant place in what business schools teach. Minds devoted to commerce and industry no less than to the other pursuits of man need the ordering of both learning and life that Western man finds in the arts. One of the few known ways to discourage the young from acting like Richard III and the old from acting like Lear is to have them read both plays. Some knowledge of another language and another culture is one of the tricks we have learned to make certain that we have a straight view of our own.

In all these ways it is good for business itself that the business school incorporate the longer aims of the university.

Obviously, universities want and need to train leaders of commerce and of industry as they do for all other walks of life. But every university must also see its young in different guises; as tomorrow's citizens, husbands, wives, parents, and friends. No faculty within the university does its own job well unless it fulfills that longer vision the university has worked out over its centuries. Young men and women in Western democracies, thanks to 2,000 years of Judaism and Christianity, and thanks also to the freedom in which their countries let them live, come equipped with a mental circuit that translates their first question, "Is it true or false?" into a second, "Is it good or bad?" Aristotle said man was a philosophizing animal and that means he is an ethical one. As commerce and industry loom so much larger in our national life, and as indeed they more clearly determine our leadership even in international affairs, the greatest service that schools of business can render is to fill that leadership with men and women haunted by that second question.

Limiting this chapter to business and law is quite arbitrary. Much of what can be said about one professional school can be said about the other, as indeed many of these comments could just as well be made about medicine, engineering, journalism, or other professional schools. It might be helpful now to try to summarize the dangers that all professional schools by their very nature pose for the university as well as some of the steps that can and should be taken to counter them. Professional schools by their nature can work against the university's habit of contemplation, its freedom both internal and external, and its ancient dream of the unity of human knowledge.

Universities are essentially contemplative places and to that extent Cardinal Newman's insistence that knowledge is its own end is a given within any university. All university work also submits itself, both by custom and conviction, to a variety of philosophical and historical canons of inquiry, each of them meant to govern the contemplative pursuits of the university's departments. These canons are varied because all of us recognize that it is good to have more than one methodology to fall back on, at times to have conflicting ones. Our inquiry under these methodologies bears upon the facts of each discipline, the way these facts are used and organized, and the conclusions we draw from them.

The university's job is neither high journalism nor "contract research," because it also routinely questions the assumptions that underlie facts, processes, and conclusions. At the very least this job calls for an awareness of the regnant assumptions on any given piece of ground and some familiarity with their implications. It is quite possible for a journalist or a contract researcher to accept as an assumption that our relationships to Central America are to read strictly in terms of the present tensions that run from East to West. In university research and teaching, that assumption itself must be seduously put to the test. Both corporate behavior and the law that serves as its matrix are tied in the daily work of the world around us to the basic assumptions of capitalism. The university does not do its job if in analyzing and explicating that tissue of relationships it does not at the same time probe the assumptions that lie behind it. To the extent that we swallow assumptions whole and bother neither to identify them or put them to the proof, we fail in our jobs as a university.

The second good threatened by professionalism is freedom. Our defense of freedom is essentially round-about. It's all well and good for the president to mount whatever pulpit he can and proclaim his university as a free society, but it has to be free in its internal workings just as much as it must be free from external pressure. For that reason the university's habit of contentiousness is not merely a trick of the faculty mind but an essential part of its defense of itself. Universities thrive on conflict of ideas. An essential condition for such conflict is a carefully built and kept pluralism of persons and of personal views. I hasten to add that this kind of conflict and the taste for it does not equal chaos.

Conflict is eminently compatible with a strong and pervasive tradition, and the best of our universities have defended that compatability with great success. All such traditions are themselves of course open to probing realignment through the clash of ideas. There is no contradiction in a university supporting a variety of schools aimed at subsets of human learning, such as law, medicine, or business. They merely provide a more precise framework where contained conflict can run. All of us are bound by canons of civility and respect for each other, and thereby share in the common body of the university. We are also bound by sometimes quite arcane and ritualistic professional canons of conduct, debate, and discourse. Assassination is not one of the recourses of academic departments, or even of academic administrations. Provided we remain our contentious selves, our internal freedom in our professional as well as in all our other schools is likely to be as close to an absolute as it is possible to achieve in this vale of tears.

Our external freedom is more difficult and perhaps more complex. Western societies have left open a large terrain of freedom for their universities, leaving them free even to question the basic political assumptions on which those societies rest. It has been a long time since political coercion existed in American or British universities, and at least since World War II the same can be said of universities in the western part of the European continent. Obviously there is always political danger because we academics are paid to be bright not brave. James II knew this well when he surrounded Magdalen College with cavalry and the collapse of its dons before armed and immediate force was both predictable and pardonable. Bad as that was, a far greater threat to the university's freedom can come from its own subset or professional schools, particularly when those subsets are tied, as are business and law, to powerful and entrenched external bodies.

Earlier on this chapter dealt with accreditation as a symbol of the dangers that professionalism can pose to the university, but professional accreditation is a more worrisome phenomenon and much more than a symbol. There has been a growing university groundswell of resistance to the intrusions professional accreditations mount. It is based both upon administrative annoyance and the faculty's worry about the galaxy of unquestioned assumptions bar associations and other professional organizations outside the university are free to permit themselves. At times universities have suggested drastic solutions, like following the British lead and deprofessionalizing law studies altogether. So far these strong remedies have not been applied. That does not mean that our current net of relationships is acceptable or adequate, or that it is anywhere nearly enough concerned with the good of the universities themselves and above all with their academic and spiritual integrity. Resistance is shaping and shaping well. The universities would be well advised to make certain that it continues to do so.

The final threat professional schools pose is to the university's immemorial dream of the unity of all knowledge. In practical terms this dream derives from the fact that the knowers are themselves one, and that, like the faculty, the graduate and undergraduate students who come to us are full and autonomous human beings and must be treated as such. However, the dream runs farther than that and touches the very nature of the university itself in which the diversity of faculties and of studies profoundly influences the growth of the young.

Business schools in particular must labor to retain or regain their serious involvement with the liberal arts and scientific departments of the university. In some senses this is an obvious mandate upon undergraduate schools of business, and the best of them work to honor it. It seems, however, that the graduate schools are at greater risk in their slide away from the philosophical, historical, scientific, and literary preoccupations of their parent universities. It is all too easy for them to isolate themselves in the kind of sterile professionalism that in the long run will make them extraneous to the university itself. One cure is to fall back on the truism that a subject is "liberal" if it is taught liberally. Thus even the professional business curriculum can be instinct with history; can identify, acknowledge, and probe the philosophical and at times theological assumptions upon which it rests; and can be handled with a certain amount of care for style even if it manifests itself only in good English prose. Scientists have long since learned that part of their claim to fellowship in the intellectual community, no matter how abstruse and at times unintelligible to the layman their studies may be, is their ability to relate them to politics, to philosophy, and to economics and at the same time state them in intelligible language.

Law schools face a different problem. More and more bright undergraduates see the study of law as an integrator of their undergraduate studies. One of the most fascinating things in any democracy is the process of democracy itself, and as they contemplate it the young have a sure grasp that the law and lawyers are increasingly important in the conduct of our affairs, both personal and national. Many academics do not like to concede that the demands students make on them shape their work, but they do. Since that is so, America's law schools are in for a considerable reshaping just to bring themselves into line with the expectations their students carry into them. This reshaping is doubly important because in American academic structure the law is so often a cap for other professions. Any large law school class will have physicians, engineers, scientists, and even educators as students. They come to finish rather than to buttress their previous professional training. On the other hand, there are relatively few lawyers who go to other professional schools with the same purpose in mind.

In an ideal world a law school would be located in the dead center of any campus, allowing the profession thus to occupy physically in the university the same position it occupies practically in this democracy. In most instances that is impossible, and many law schools are famous for being islands unto themselves. This can be a dangerous and destructive luxury. Where they are physically separate it seems advisable that law schools should appoint as members of their own faculty historians, economists, and analysts of social reality. Where possible these appointments can be shared with an undergraduate college or a graduate school, but the sharing should be real. If the curriculum of law acknowledges the relevance and importance of none of these disciplines, then it ought to be reduced, as some indeed have suggested, to a year and a half of purely instrumental training, and written off as a university exercise. As Whitehead remarks, lecturing has been obsolete since the invention of movable type, and research can be better done in institutes devoted wholly to it. The purpose of pulling together the talents of faculty and students, of holding them together over a fixed curriculum and its corollary, a fixed course of time, must be something more than the dissemination of information, or even the much touted and cherished "legal habit of thought."

This chapter has dealt perhaps too much with the points of opposition between professional schooling and the parent university. It should close with some reflections in the other direction. Professional schools' membership in a parent university ought not to be seen as an accident, and indeed historically it is not. The university has had a thousand years to learn about itself and how it works best, and has in the process acquired a kind of wisdom. Out of that wisdom it has much to offer to any professional faculty, like a business school or, *pace* the ABA, even a law school.

A university's first gifts are structural. Any professional school will profit from the variety of studies, schools, and departments that the modern university contains. They come in all sizes and shapes, technical and verbal, ancient and new, and they involve every kind of knowing that the mind of men through the course of Western civilization has learned. Their variety of studies is matched by the variety of people they gather around them. A variety of races, creeds, and colors is easy, and is usually reproduced within the professional school. But the deeper variety the university offers is its collection of mind-sets, of habits of work, or styles, of fellowship, in short, of spiritual furniture. Newman's observation that merely bringing this many talented people together is a major part of any individual's education is profoundly true. Once brought together, all of these individuals are made welcome to a world that places a quite unrepentant accent on the human mind, on man as contemplator, and is never guilty of scouting or neglecting the dignity of ideas.

Precisely because these ideas are so strongly held and so clearly respected, universities are essentially contentious places, for all the civility in which that contention is wrapped. At times we are almost as civil as politicians, at times far less so. All of us know that we grow only by mental friction, and that difference, disagreement, argument, and debate are the current coin of our realm. The very rigor of that exchange imposes upon us a radical honesty in scholarship. Over and over again the university and its people submit their works, their conclusions, and even their dreams to analysis and comment. All the serious work of a university is continually subject to review by the "judicious, the censure of the which one must...o'er weigh a whole theatre of others."

Beyond the structural gifts the parent university offers to professional faculty members and students there are many more, all of them best gathered under the rubric of style. Universities have built into them the bequest of classics and of physics, an iron discipline of fact. They are deeply conscious of man's status as a "half-wit angel strapped to the back of a mule," but recognize, sometimes far more than professional schools do, the fit of all men's thoughts and dreams into the hard contours of a world of things. University style imposes a further discipline, the gift of historians. After almost ten centuries universities have learned a great deal, even from their own history. Much has been tried and much has failed, and every now and then there have been historic successes. The important point is not to cull the past but to be rooted in it, to understand that even the Creator's actions "ride time like a river." A further point of style in universities that speak either English or French is and always has been a care for language, a care that stretches even to owning academic speech as a form of art.

Finally, as it should be wherever the old and young are gathered, the university has learned over its centuries to see its people whole, even while it speaks mainly to their minds. We are preoccupied with citizenship not to endlessly reproduce ourselves (every teacher's temptation), but in the deep sense of Whitehead's vision that between us, out of the faculty's age and experience, and out of energy and generosity of the young, we are remaking this Republic in which we live. We are not fools enough to claim that we can either control or clearly foresee the shape of the future we hope to build in the minds and hearts of the young. If we do not know how the task will end, we do know how to do it; if we do not know where our reshaping will lead, we are conscious that reshaping is our job.

This chapter can well end with the words of Whitehead at the close of his essay on "Universities and their Function":

> the gift which the University has to offer is the old one of imagination, the lighted torch which passes from hand to hand. It is a dangerous gift, which has started many a conflagration. If we are timid as to that danger, the proper course is to shut down our universities. Imagination is a gift which has often been associated with great commerical peoples—with Greece, with Florence, with Venice, with the learning of Holland, and with the poetry of England. Commerce and imagination thrive together. It is a gift which all must pray for their country who desire for it that abiding greatness achieved by Athens:—
>
> > Her citizens, imperial spirits,
> > Rule the present from the past.
>
> For American education no smaller ideal can suffice.[5]

Notes

1. John Henry Newman, *The Idea of a University* (Oxford: Clarendon Press, 1976), p. 147.
2. Derek Bok, "A Flawed System," *Harvard Magazine* (May-June 1983), pp. 38–71.
3. Alfred North Whitehead, *The Aims of Education and Other Essays* (New York: Free Press, 1957), p. 96.
4. Ibid.
5. Alfred North Whitehead, 1957, *op. cit.*, p. 101.

Institutional Advancement and Funding

FRANK H. T. RHODES

Historical Perspective

With the founding of Harvard College in 1636 for the purpose of training Puritan ministers, America began a tradition of support for higher education that combined funds from the public treasury with those from private philanthropy.

It was a grant from the General Court of the Massachusetts Bay Colony combined with a personal gift from John Harvard, a graduate of Emmanuel College, Cambridge, that enabled those transplanted Englishmen, as Frederick Rudolph has noted, to "build themselves a college almost before they had built themselves a privy."[1]

Their action may seem impractical today, given the meager opportunities for elementary schooling and the more immediate needs of a new civilization in the wilderness, but it reflected a passion for knowledge and a profound conviction of its essential role in ministry and in life. An early Harvard pamphlet reflected that brave persuasion: "After God had carried us safe to New England, and we had builded our houses, provided necessaries for our liveli-hood, rear'd convenient place for God's worship, and setled the Civil Government; One of the next things we longed for, and looked after was to advance Learning and perpetuate it to Posterity."

So the Harvard idea was replicated in the College of William and Mary, founded by the Episcopalians at Williamsburg a few years later, and eventually in a host of other institutions, most of them small, church-affiliated and church-supported, throughout the new land.

It became a matter of community pride, if not practical necessity, in the expanding colonies to have a college nearby from which the community could draw its political leaders, lawyers, doctors, and ministers. And because such institutions were seen as serving the public good, they often received funds from the public purse despite their private and denominational roots.

As America developed from colony to country, education continued to enjoy the support of the nation's leaders. George Washington urged his fellow countrymen to "promote then as an object of primary importance, institutions for the general diffusion of knowledge. In proportion as the structure of government gives force to public opinion, it is essential that public opinion should be enlightened."

Thomas Jefferson concurred. "I know no safe depository of the ultimate powers of society but the people themselves; and if we think them not enlightened enough to exercise their control with wholesome discretion, the remedy is not to take it from them, but to inform their discretion by education," he said, and he went on to found the University of Virginia to implement his philosophy.

Yet it was not until the mid-1800s that higher education was seen as appropriate not only for training the very best doctors, lawyers, ministers, and civic leaders but also for meeting the more practical educational needs of farmers, mechanics, and merchants.

Through the Morrill Act of 1862, the states received funds from the sale of federal lands for use in establishing colleges of agriculture and the mechanic arts. Some of these land-grant institutions were to become preeminent state universities, while a few, notably Cornell and Purdue, retained their independence, using land-grant funds to supplement the private fortunes of their founders.

The influence of the Morrill Act was not confined to those

institutions receiving land-grant funds. By establishing higher education as relevant to the needs of the agrarian and industrial population, the Morrill Act prompted a major expansion of American higher education in general. Some 25 colleges had been chartered between 1630 and 1800, and another 44 had come into existence during the first three decades of the nineteenth century. Between 1860 and 1870, however, an incredible 175 colleges were chartered.[2]

The American system of higher education has evolved since that time to meet changing needs and opportunities, yet it has continued to draw support from both the state treasuries and private philanthropy because it has continued to serve the public good.

In the latter part of the nineteenth century, for example, the idea of the German research university, where faculty created new knowledge as they trained the next generation of scholars, was given life in America by Johns Hopkins University, an independent institution.

State governments followed this lead and were soon supporting university research, because such efforts were shown to be of practical value to their citizens. Almost every state had an equivalent of Cornell's Liberty Hyde Bailey, who won the confidence of New York agriculture—and state support for Cornell—by developing a spray to cure black rot in the vineyard of a state legislator and who was soon called upon to minister to a great variety of ills affecting New York crops.

Public and private higher education continued to evolve in the years before World War I, with the elective system pioneered at Cornell and Harvard becoming widely accepted and offering students more opportunities than either the old classical curriculum or the avowedly practical offerings of the land-grant institutions. No matter what one's interest, there seemed room within the fold of higher eduction to satisfy it.

But two world wars and a great depression limited the number of students able to pursue higher education until the middle of the present century, and it was not until the end of World War II, when thousands of veterans returned to campus supported by the G. I. Bill, that higher education in America came into its own.

Whereas a high school diploma had been a sufficient credential for most Americans before World War II, increasingly a postsecondary degree became necessary, and students flocked to campuses in record numbers.

The need for larger numbers of highly trained individuals was further brought home by the successful launching in 1957 of the Soviet satellite Sputnik. The Congress responded with the National Defense Education Act of 1958, which renewed a national commitment to education, especially in the sciences and foreign languages, from the primary grades through college.

The returning veterans were followed to campus by the children of the baby boom, and later by increasing numbers of minorities and women, whose interest in higher education had been kindled, respectively, by the civil rights gains of the 1960s and the women's movement of the early 1970s.

For the most part, public and independent higher education recognized the complementarity of their roles in meeting this unprecedented demand for higher education. The expanding public system provided accommodation for the growing number of new students, while the independent institutions provided distinctive programs particularly well-suited to the needs of certain students.

Public and independent institutions viewed themselves as partners in a noble effort to provide a university education to a far greater number of Americans than ever before. Respect was mutual. Statesmanship was the order of the day, with each sector supporting the other with the aim of strengthening the total system in all its expansiveness and in all its diversity.

The statistics bear out the wisdom of that partnership. In 1950, about 2.3 million students were attending American colleges. By 1983, some 12.4 million students were enrolled in a wide range of postsecondary institutions—public, independent, two-year, four-year, proprietary, graduate, and professional. Together, these institutions in 1982–1983 accounted for an annual expenditure of nearly $80 billion,[3] and in 1984–1985 expenditures were expected to reach $95.5 billion.[4] That places higher education on a par with transportation and ahead of communications and agriculture in its impact on the national economy.[5]

We have come very close, and much closer than any other nation on earth, to the Jeffersonian ideal of providing as much education to every citizen as he or she wants and is able to benefit from, and as a nation we seem to have accepted the maxim that if education seems expensive, one must ponder the price of ignorance.

An Era of Constraints

Yet much of the statesmanship that characterized higher education during the decades of growth has now given way to the pursuit of narrow self-interest as colleges, both public and independent, confront the realities of demographic changes, shifting student interests, and inadequate budgets.

The number of individuals in the traditional college-age group will decrease by 25 percent between 1980 and 1995 as a result of the baby bust that followed the baby boom years. The demographics are not merely pessimistic predictions by whimsical futurists; the people represented have already been born, and their scarcity has already had a major impact on elementary and secondary schools throughout the nation.

States in the Northeast and Midwest will be particularly hard hit, with New York, for example, expecting a 30 percent decline in its high school graduates between 1982 and 1992.

The population decline may be ameliorated somewhat by a higher rate of college attendance rate among high school graduates, by students who return to campus after some time in the work force, by students studying part-time, and by those in nondegree programs. Even if college enrollments do not decline in absolute terms, however, the changing nature of the student population will require new programs and services that will challenge the resources and resourcefulness of many institutions. Already there has been a marked shift in student interest into such high-cost instructional areas as engineering and computer science, and many colleges and universities have been hard-pressed to meet the demand.

Nationally, as many as 10 percent of the faculty positions in engineering remain unfilled because of a severe shortage of Ph.D. engineers and the reluctance of many with adequate training to work in academe, where salaries are generally lower and equipment often twice as old as in industry.

State support, for example, has lagged in recent years. Although both the federal government and industry have in recent months begun to address these problems, the demand for high-quality engineering programs in our colleges and universities can be expected to outstrip supply for several more years.

A larger number of part-time students and students who are combining education with ongoing careers are influencing the way in which instruction is conducted. Many institutions now conduct evening and weekend courses or use remote communications systems to link students at distant locations with the professor in the classroom.

As beneficial as many of these changes may be for the students involved, they do not come cheaply, and institutions in both sectors have been hard-pressed to secure the necessary funds.

Although state legislatures appropriated about $24.1 billion for higher education in fiscal 1983, state spending for students enrolled in public institutions has slipped nearly 8 percent, when adjusted for inflation, since 1978.[6] State spending for fiscal 1984 rose only about 5.5 percent, the smallest one-year increase in more than two decades.[7]

During the 1970s, institutions, both public and private, saw their endowments eroded by inflation and the vagaries of the stock market. And although inflation has slowed in recent years, endowments have not necessarily recovered. The purchasing power of endowments decreased 15.24 percent based on the consumer price index and 10.33 percent based on the higher education price index during the 1983–1984 academic year.[8]

Many campuses, facing tight budgets, have maintained their academic programs at the expense of their physical plants. Crumbling ceilings and leaky roofs plague not only the venerable buildings of established campuses, but also the nearly one-third of all college buildings erected, often hastily and without regard to energy conservation, between 1966 and 1972.

The National Association of College and University Business Officers has estimated that it would take roughly $30 billion nationally simply to catch up with the maintenance that has been deferred. The problem is most severe at independent institutions, where donors are often reluctant to provide funds for maintenance, but it affects public institutions as well.[9]

Funding Sources

Facing many of the same constraints, public and independent institutions increasingly are seeking support from the same sources—state and federal governments, foundations, corporations, and their own alumni.

Independent institutions now receive support from their state governments through such programs as New York's Bundy Aid, which provides funds to independent institutions based on degrees conferred in the previous year.

Many independent institutions also benefit from the so-called student choice grants, such as those made through New York's Tuition Assistance Program, which can be used by students at institutions in either sector. State grant programs of this kind provided more than $1 billion to students in 1983–1984, according to the National Association of State Scholarship and Grant programs.[10]

Still other independent institutions receive subsidies for high-cost instructional programs such as those in medicine and engineering or assistance in establishing major research facilities that will make the state more attractive to high-technology industries.

These independent institutions have argued, quite correctly, that they provide valuable educational services to the state at a cost far below that required to provide the same services at public institutions, yet they are placed at a substantial competitive disadvantage by the artificially low price (although not low cost) of education in the public sector.

Public institutions have argued, also quite correctly, that they need increased state support to maintain their low tuition in the face of rising costs and to finance new programs for nontraditional and part-time students, and those needing remedial help in order to succeed in a college program. Indeed, it is broad access to low-cost educational programs that has traditionally been one of public education's greatest strengths.

At the federal level, institutions in both sectors benefit from student aid programs. In 1980–1981, the last year for which complete data are available, public institutions received 60.1 percent of the Pell Grants and 53 percent of the campus-based grants awarded.

Yet both sectors also have felt the impact of reductions in student aid programs, primarily through the phasing out of Social Security benefits for education and restrictions on eligibility for Guaranteed Student Loans, which reduced the amount of aid from $18 billion in 1981–1982 to some $16.1 billion in 1983–1984.[11]

Both sectors are also competing, with almost equal success, for federal research dollars. Among the nation's top twenty research universities in terms of federal research support are an almost equal number of public and independent institutions. And in the public's mind, Harvard, Stanford, Berkeley, Michigan, Chicago, and North Carolina are known more for the high quality of their research than for the primary source of their support.

Foundations, corporations, and alumni, which once gave their support primarily to independent institutions, are now funding initiatives in the public sector as well. About 30 percent of all voluntary giving, including 40 percent of all corporate giving, now goes to institutions in the public sector.

The top ten institutions, in terms of voluntary support, in a recent survey were Harvard, Stanford, the University of Minnesota, Columbia, Cornell, Massachusetts Institute of Technology, Yale, and Princeton. When multi-unit systems were included in the totals, however, the University of California ranked above Harvard, with the University of Texas ranking third.[12]

The efforts by individual public institutions are as impressive as the aggregate numbers. The University of Arizona, for example, has obtained some $12 million from industry to bolster its programs in engineering, while Penn State is in the midst of a $200 million alumni campaign.

Negative Aspects of Competition

By and large, this competition is an indication of the resourcefulness, the enterprise, and the ability to adapt to changing conditions that has been a major source of higher education's strength in this country.

But it has also served to blur the distinctions between the sectors. As Clifton Wharton, with apologies to Gertrude Stein, said recently, "Public is public and private, but private is private and public. That's why public is public and private is private."[13]

Even more unfortunate than the confusion of mission is the open warfare that has erupted in many states as individual institutions use the tactics of professional lobbyists and pressure groups to push for their own advantage, sometimes at the expense of sister institutions both within and across sectors. This self-serving lobbying may well be destroying the broad base of public support that has been a foundation of higher education's strength and the basis for whatever claim to special privilege it once enjoyed.

The problem is particularly acute in New York State, which has the largest number of private colleges in the nation, together with two major state-supported systems, the State University of New York and the City University of New York. Combined enrollment in New York's independent institutions is more than 300,000 students while SUNY and CUNY have a combined enrollment of more than 500,000.

Moreover, New York State has been a leader in supporting both sectors through a variety of programs. The total annual budget for SUNY and CUNY is more than $2 billion while the state provides another $100 million a year to independent institutions through the Tuition Assistance Program, Bundy Aid, and other programs. Recently, the state has made a major commitment to its research universities, both public and independent, by helping to establish centers for advanced technology which serve the state's industries and other educational institutions.

Despite these initiatives and an overall growth in total expenditures for higher education, however, funding in New York State has not kept pace with per capita income or with trends in other states.

In 1974–1975, New York spent $11.30 per $1,000 of per capita income while in 1982–1983, it spent only $9.96 per $1,000 in personal income, a decline of 10.5 percent and enough to drop its standing from 24th to 31st in the nation in the percentage of per capita income devoted to higher education.

In 1974–1975, New York spent $63.50 on higher education for every citizen, placing it 14th in the nation in terms of such expenditures. By 1982–1983 it had dropped to 24th place, even though its expenditures per person had increased to $114.19.

The scarcity of resources has led to intense competition between institutions in the public and independent sectors in New York State, and a good deal of bitterness and suspicion as well. The situation in some other states is not dissimilar.

Appreciating the Strength of Our Dual System

The New York experience suggests that if public and independent higher education are to remain partners in a common effort to serve the public good, leaders of both sectors must recognize the strengths of the dual system and must also support initiatives, which, while sometimes difficult for individual institutions, can dramatically improve the effectiveness and responsiveness of the larger enterprise. The health of higher education as a whole demands that we strike an equitable balance between public and independent institutions in the nation.

A first step in achieving that balance must be to recognize the unique strengths of each sector, for neither has a monopoly on excellence nor is either alone sufficient for a vigorous and responsive system of higher education.

The strengths of public institutions are many, but two in particular stand out: broad access and low price. In the years following World War II, public institutions filled a need for which the resources of the independent sector were clearly inadequate, and so made higher education available to thousands of individuals who might otherwise have been excluded.

Between 1950 and 1980, enrollment in public institutions grew from 1.1 million to 9.4 million, largely because of the success of public community colleges, in which some 80 percent of these students were enrolled.

Many students at public institutions are women, members of minority groups, nontraditional, part-time students, some from low- and middle-income groups, who in the absence of a low-priced and broadly welcoming system of public higher education probably would not have sought higher education at all.

As our economy shifts away from the blue-collar jobs and becomes more service and information oriented, a highly educated work force may be our greatest natural resource. As Julian Simon has written, "Human ingenuity, rather than nature, is limitlessly bountiful (and) ... with knowledge, imagination, and enterprise, we and our descendants can muster from the earth all the mineral raw materials that we need and desire ... (for) our cornucopia is the human mind and heart."[14]

Because they are sustained primarily by the taxpayers, their appeal must be broad and their programs generally solid, orthodox, noncontroversial and as risk-free as possible. Public higher education is not the "generic brand" that some have claimed, nor is it colored in the "committee beige" that some have painted, but it does have a general consistency, if not a uniformity, that is both a characteristic and a strength.

The appeal of independent higher education is not nearly so universal, and not surprisingly its growth has been more modest. Beginning in 1950 with approximately 1.1 million students, it could claim in 1980 some 2.6 million students.

Still, even with their more modest enrollments, the contributions of the independent sector to the total higher educational enterprise are substantial. It has been estimated, for example, that if these independent institutions did not exist, taxpayers would have to spend some $2 billion to build comparable facilities at today's rates and would have to provide additional operating funds in excess of $2 billion annually.[15]

In many states, the independent institutions are the established leaders in providing high-quality graduate and professional education. In a recent year, for example, independent universities in New York State provided over 70 percent of all those graduating with Ph.D. degrees, over 74 percent of those graduating with first professional degrees in engineering; and over 68 percent of those graduating with the degree of M.D. This significant reservoir of talent contributes to the general well-being of the state at a cost far smaller than if these same individuals were trained at public institutions.

The value of independent institutions is not confined to their providing outstanding graduate-professional education or to their cost-effectiveness, however. Perhaps their greatest strength is their ability to undertake courageous experiments in substance, style, and context with the support of those citizens that share the institution's vision.

Many offer curricula, teaching styles, religious or ethical perspectives, and services that are suited to the needs of particular kinds of students. Their appeal is far from universal, yet when their missions are clearly defined and their programs are sound, they can serve certain students far better than public institutions.

Not everyone is suited to the great books curriculum pioneered by St. Johns University, where students take a common curriculum leading to a B.A. in the liberal arts. Not everyone would benefit from the work-study tradition of Antioch or the religious perspective offered by Notre Dame or Georgetown. Not everyone can excel in the competitive intellectual atmosphere of a Stanford or a Harvard or a Yale.

And not everyone does best at large or well-known schools. The heart of independent education in this country is the small college, often with a religious affiliation, that has set for itself a distinctive mission and that is uniquely suited to meeting the needs of a certain region or certain individuals within a region. Indeed, 75 percent of the private colleges awarding baccalaureate or graduate degrees have fewer than 2,500 students, and 75 percent of these institutions are affiliated with a church or other religious group.

The range of programs offered by these institutions is truly remarkable. Gary Quehl, president of the Council of Independent Colleges, has compiled an extensive list of such programs from which I cite just five examples:

—Alice Lloyd College in Pippa Passes, Kentucky, meets the needs of its Appalachian students with a special program on the politics, religion, economics, education, and ecology of the region.

—Central College in Pella, Iowa, emphasizes the study of foreign languages through a Cross-Cultural Communications and Perceptions Program. Students study one of seven foreign languages on campus and during a year or a semester abroad, and enrollment in foreign language courses is five times the national average.

—Berea College in Berea, Kentucky, charges no tuition but rather requires each student to contribute time and effort toward maintaining the institution.

—St. Andrews Presbyterian College in Laurinburg, North Carolina, has designed a new campus specifically to attract and serve handicapped students.

—Marylhurst College for Lifelong Learning near Portland, Oregon, is a Roman Catholic institution solely for older students. Its unusual curriculum is structured around four themes: self; other people and cultures; environment; the transcendent.[16]

Many of these programs would be inappropriate in public sector education, yet in their diversity, they reflect the diversity that is inherent in our culture. They provide a degree of choice that enriches not only the educational enterprise but also the life of the wider community.

Yet as beneficial and courageous as some of these experiments are, not all will be successful. Some major innovations have come from experiments in independent institutions, but so have a number of failures, and it is worth noting that the successes are often adopted by public institutions while the taxpayers are spared the cost of the failures.

One area in which this has been particularly true over the past decade has been in corporate support for university research. With the generous federal support of university research in the years following World War II, corporate support became confined primarily to certain applied work, particularly in engineering and agriculture.

Those interested in basic research, as most university investigators are, looked to the federal government for support that was free from the secrecy and pressure for results that was often expected by corporate sponsors.

With changing federal funding priorities and the emergence of high tech industries, where the line between basic and applied research is often blurred or nonexistent, universities and corporations found themselves intrigued by the possibilities of cooperative projects.

Yet to be successful, collaborative arrangements had to respect both corporate and academic cultures. They had to allow faculty to exchange information with their colleagues through publication in the open literature, for example, while protecting industry's proprietary interest in the results of the research.

Independent institutions, which entered into some of the most substantial early ventures with industry, have helped define the form of successful agreements and identify the boundaries beyond which academic freedom is endangered.

In addition to debate and discussion within individual institutions and corporations, agreements such as those between Exxon and MIT in 1979, between Hoechst AG and Massachusetts General Hospital in 1981, and between Monsanto and Washington University in St. Louis in 1982, have prompted a broader national discussion, and here, too, independent institutions have played a major role.

In March 1982, five university presidents, four of them from independent institutions, met with key industry representatives at Parajo Dunes, California, to discuss guidelines for university–industry cooperation. That meeting was followed in December 1982 by a much larger gathering of industry and academic representatives at the University of Pennsylvania.

From these discussions it has become clear that acceptable agreements can be negotiated when both sides retain their flexibility while recognizing each other's needs and goals. It has also become clear that certain kinds of arrangements, however compelling they may seem at first glance, are inappropriate in a university setting.

Harvard, for example, is a leader in the amount of corporate support it accepts for its research programs. Yet the university considered, then rejected as inappropriate, the suggestion that it go into business with its faculty to commercialize the products of university research. It has also been among the leaders in establishing guidelines for faculty involvement in commercial ventures, deciding, among other things, that individuals could not hold both faculty positions and executive positions in corporations.

In university–industry cooperation, as in curriculum reform, and many other areas of academic life, successful experiments undertaken in the independent sector have been incorporated into public institutions far more economically than if taxpayers had borne the costs of the failures along with those of the successes.

It is, by and large, the nation's selective independent institutions that have been particularly devoted to the liberal arts, that have been particularly concerned with the gifted students, and that have set the standards of excellence to which all—public and independent—can aspire.

It is because those aspirations have been transformed into

reality in both sectors that higher education has become such an important force in American life. California's Silicon Valley, Massachusetts's Route 128, and North Carolina's Research Triangle all owe their vitality to the proximity of high-quality research universities, public and private.

As other states attempt to foster centers of high technology within their borders, those with strong independent institutions, substantial resources, and augmented funds from the state treasury will have the best chance for success. The contributions of the independent sector here, as in training and public service, can only be seen as value added.

Actions Needed

The two systems of higher education in this country are complementary. Neither is capable of meeting alone all the needs and expectations of the nation, but together they form a system that is the envy of the world.

But today our dual system of higher education is under siege. The shrinking resources we all confront have generated the infamous zero-sum mentality, where it is assumed that if one institution gains, the others must inevitably lose. Statesmanship has given way to jealousy and intense competition.

Individual institutions in both sectors are seeking additional support from government, foundations, and corporations while disparaging their competitors in the press. In the process they are eroding the broad base of public support that higher education has enjoyed since World War II.

The continued health of higher education in this country depends not on competition but on cooperation that reaffirms the value of diversity. Independent and public, urban and rural, large and small, two-year, four-year, and graduate/professional institutions—all have contributed to higher education's success over the past three decades and all are important to its future.

Educational leaders, regardless of the kind of institution they represent, must renew their commitment to the system as a whole if we are to achieve a maximum return on this nation's investment in higher education. At a minimum, seven commitments will be required from our educational leaders:

1. We must be willing to support shrinking, redirecting, combining, or even closing weak institutions in both sectors so that limited resources may be allocated more productively. To date, however, the forces of the marketplace and the limitations of resources have been felt more keenly by independent institutions than by those supported through state appropriations.

We must also be more willing than in the past to share expensive research equipment, library resources, even faculty and students among institutions regardless of their status as public or independent.

A study conducted by William J. McKeefery a few years ago estimated that about one-fourth of the nation's colleges and universities are involved in cooperative arrangements, but cooperation between public and independent institutions accounted for less than 2 percent of the total. The potential for cooperation across sectors is five or more times the current level.[17]

2. We must undertake to build on our strengths, rather than sheltering our weaknesses. Both sectors should agree to establish new programs only with clear evidence of demand, only if the resources for the new programs are adequate, and only if the same people could not be served by building upon existing programs. Such rational planning is possible only if accurate statewide data are available.

3. We must insist upon certain minimal standards of quality in both independent and public institutions while striving for the highest quality in our own institutions.

A renewed emphasis on quality may challenge some existing programs. Open admissions programs, for example, have been a boon to many who because of economic circumstances or educational deprivation in their early years might not otherwise attend college. Yet we must ask whether existing colleges and universities are the appropriate places to redress the inadequacies in secondary preparation given the high cost of remediation and our limited resources. Granted there should be a second chance (and perhaps a third) for all, traditional colleges may not be the places best equipped to provide it.

It is significant that several states, including Ohio and California, whose public universities have traditionally maintained open admissions policies, now require successful completion of a specified college-preparatory program in high school.

And we must certainly demand that a college degree stand for something more substantial than a given number of hours spent sitting in class. The much publicized crisis in our public schools, where an alarming number of teachers have been found to be only marginally literate, points up our tragic failure here.

4. We must work together to preserve equality of access and choice across sectors, preserving and enhancing the institutional diversity and distinctiveness so essential to meeting the varied educational needs of our citizens.

We must especially encourage and nurture the flow of talented minority students into graduate and professional programs that will supply the future generation of faculty members. We have made substantial gains in recent years in attracting minority students to our undergraduate programs, but our record at the graduate level, especially in such fields as engineering and computer science, has been disappointing.

5. We must come to terms with the tuition gap between public and independent institutions so that price more closely approximates costs, which are roughly the same in both sectors. It would be unfortunate for both sectors if only affluent and lower-income students were able to enroll in independent institutions while middle-income students could never aspire to anything but public education.

We need a realistic tuition policy at our public institutions, coupled with state and federal student aid that will permit student choice on bases other than price. The pickets, threats, and political compromises that now characterize tuition decisions at some public institutions are no substitute for thoughtful state and institutional tuition policy.

6. Both sectors must work together to develop an acceptable pattern of public accountability that respects institutional autonomy.

All of us have learned that public monies, whether from federal or state sources, bring with them public responsibilities. Yet institutions in both sectors have a clear interest in ensuring that accountability has as its ultimate goal the enhancement of higher education.

Our state institutions already labor under the heavy hand of bureaucracy. In New York, for example, until recently every request for out-of-state travel by a faculty member of the State University unit had to be approved in advance by the department chairperson, the president of the campus, and the state deputy director of the budget. One fast reaches the point where the cost of compliance with the regulations far exceeds the savings in abuse and error that the regulations are intended to prevent.

We must also work to ensure that in the name of accountability we do not discourage internal responsibility and efficiency and impose a uniformity that negates the value of our dual system.

We in New York know all too well that state funding is a two-edged sword, for although independent higher education receives substantial support from the state, it is accountable to state regulators for, among other things, the number of full-time faculty employed, the number of minutes for which classes meet, the size of libraries, the location of branch campuses, the size of boards of trustees, the nomenclature of individual institutions, and the licensing and development of new majors and courses of study.

In a recent doctoral study completed at Stanford's School of Education, Kenneth Fulmer gave this advice to the State of New York: "While you have long asserted the value of a strong independent sector, you have eroded its autonomy more than most any state. Your intrusiveness may be destroying that which you want to preserve. Restraint is needed so that distinctiveness can be preserved."[18]

7. We must be tireless advocates for the long-term benefits that higher education provides, both for individuals and for the nation. Individual campus leaders must make

time in their schedules to serve as ambassadors for higher education generally, despite the more immediate demands of their own institutions.

They must also enlist the support of trustees, prominent alumni, and others in the effort. The chairperson of a private board who speaks out in support of increased appropriations for the public sector or the public trustee who champions a strong independent sector can be a tremendous force in advancing higher education generally, and in the process the leader's own institution is almost certain to benefit.

These are indeed difficult times for all of higher education, but universities are resilient institutions. Clark Kerr has pointed out that the sixty-six Western institutions that have survived since the year 1530 in forms that are still recognizable today include the Roman Catholic and Lutheran Churches, the parliaments of Iceland and the Isle of Man, and sixty-two universities. They have weathered wars, depressions, and revolutions because they have remained true to their high and noble founding purposes and have proven to each new generation their unique value.[19]

Yet unless we reaffirm the strength of our dual system, higher education may emerge from the current period of stress substantially less diverse, less credible, and less vital. We need informed and tough-minded leadership on each of the more than 3,000 individual campuses in this country which will have as its goal the strengthening of each campus, and, through it, the system as a whole.

The ultimate business of education, whether in the public or the independent sector, is the cultivation of the human mind and the nurture of the human heart, for as Alfred North Whitehead has written, "in the conditions of modern life the rule is absolute, the race which does not value trained intelligence is doomed."[20]

That awesome responsibility can best be fulfilled through a renewed commitment to partnership among this nation's educational institutions, both public and independent. If we can rededicate our energies to that broader purpose, while making our own institutions as good as they can be within the context of the mission we have defined for them, higher education can indeed emerge from the current period of stress strong and vibrant, the foundation of our national power, the basis of our economic strength, the source of our social well-being, and the bulwark of our cultural richness.

Notes

1. Frederic Rudolph, *Curriculum* (San Francisco: Jossey-Bass Publishers, 1977), p. 3.
2. Ibid., p. 60.
3. National Center for Educational Statistics estimate reported in *Chronicle of Higher Education* (June 1, 1983).
4. U.S. Department of Education estimate reported in *Chronicle of Higher Education* (Aug. 29, 1984).
5. Bureau of Economic Analysis, U.S. Commerce Department, reported in *World Almanac and Book of Facts* (1984), p. 109.
6. National Institute of Education, reported in *Time* (Sept. 5, 1983), p. 50.
7. *Chronicle of Higher Education* (June 1, 1983).
8. *Chronicle of Higher Education* (May 9, 1984).
9. *Time* (March 17, 1980), p. 62.
10. *Chronicle of Higher Education* (Jan. 4, 1984).
11. *Chronicle of Higher Education* (Jan. 25, 1984).
12. *Chronicle of Higher Education* (May 9, 1984).
13. Clifton Wharton, "Enrollment and Student Aid: The New Public–Private Clash?" (June 1, 1981).
14. Julian L. Simon, "The Scarcity of Raw Materials," *The Atlantic Monthly* (June 1981), p. 41.
15. Gary Quehl, *AGB Reports* (Jan./Feb. 1983), p. 10.
16. Ibid., p. 6.
17. William J. McKeefery, "Cooperative Arrangements Between Private and Public Colleges," American Association of State Colleges and Universities (1978).
18. Kenneth Fulmer, "The Effects of State Government on the Autonomy of Independent Colleges and Universities" (Research Abstract), Stanford University School of Education (1982), p. 15.
19. Clark Kerr, "Three Thousand Futures" (Final Report of the Carnegie Council on Policy Studies in Higher Education), *The Next Twenty Years for Higher Education* (1984), p. 9, n. 2.
20. Alfred North Whitehead, *The Aims of Education and Other Essays* (New York: Macmillan, 1929), p. 22.

Equity and Quality in College Education: An Essential American Priority

ROBERT H. McCABE

A YOUNG CUBAN REFUGEE WALKED ACROSS THE STAGE to receive his associate degree at the graduation ceremony of Miami-Dade Community College's Wolfson Campus. As he did, his father stood up in the back of the auditorium and shouted with pride and emotion, "Viva America!" The father saw clearly what so many of us in this country have learned to take for granted—that nowhere else would his son have had this wonderful opportunity to grow, to develop his talents, and to shape his life through education. That moment said more about what is good in American higher education than any I can recall. We have, through time, fostered the evolution of a system that places faith in the value of each individual and does not preselect those worthy of continued education. Our system recognizes that society benefits when the nation's human resources are fully developed. Our nation has been rewarded time and again when individuals from disadvantaged backgrounds, or those who matured later in life, became leaders or simply successful participants and contributors to the society. This approach has given America a major advantage over those nations that lose the talents of significant numbers of their populations by implementing tracking systems and making very early decisions on individual potential.

This is a time of rapid change in the nature of work, when ever-increasing percentages of jobs require the processing of information and thus basic academic competence. The American system of providing ongoing opportunity is now essential to the nation's economic and social well-being, as well as to our commitment to humanitarian goals. Yet there is currently a growing movement in the country to restrict access to higher education on the basis of childhood and teenage test scores or school performance records. In the emerging information age society, with new needs and challenges evolving constantly, it seems eminently clear that America must have more, not fewer, well-educated individuals. If we are to remain competitive as a world leader, all our human resources and potential must be developed. Any lesser effort would ultimately be destructive to our nation's future. This seems such a central and undeniable fact that it is difficult to understand the current support for actions that would severely curtail access to higher education. However, the changing attitudes toward education are a culmination of many events, including past failures of the educational system, disillusionment with social programs of the 1960s, and the broadly held belief that there has been a substantial decline in the quality of our educational institutions.

The Failures of Open Access

The period from the end of World War II through the 1970s can be described as the higher education "access revolution." Beginning in the mid-1940s, the industrial developments of the war effort were converted to peacetime uses and the demand for better-educated employees became insatiable. At the same time, the nation offered returning soldiers what was valued most highly—opportunity for higher education through the landmark G.I. Bill. The providential match between increased job opportunity and greater access to higher education fueled confidence in the ability of higher education to solve virtually any and all problems. The performance of the ex-G.I.s clearly demonstrated that test scores and high school performance were not the only predictors of success in college. American business hailed the noble experiment, as illustrated by the United States Chamber of Commerce pointing out the financial benefits that would accrue from the increasing number of educated individuals. The rationale was simple: college-educated individuals would find improved jobs and thus return more to the economy in increased taxes than it cost to educate them.

The opening of the doors to this new population in the 1940s only scratched the surface. With the growth of the civil rights movement, the doors to higher education continued to be pried open more fully and attention was focused on minority populations in a growing progression of actions to broaden access. However, progress toward the provision of full equity and opportunity was slow. To illustrate, when Miami-Dade Community College opened in 1960, it provided the first opportunity for a black person to attend college within 250 miles of Miami. This access revolution was fueled by the federal government through increased availability of financial aid and categoric aid for certain programs, but the bulk of the cost was borne by individual states which paid the operational and capital outlay costs for the remarkable expansion in higher education. During one ten-year period spanning the 1960s, more was spent on construction of higher education facilities than had occurred throughout all previous educational history. In addition, during the same period, operational expenditures increased by seven times and enrollment by three times.

Serious problems began to develop in the late 1960s. Schools and colleges, from kindergarten through graduate levels, struggled to adapt to more diverse and academically less well-prepared students. Those who thought of education as a ladder to success were surprised to confront students who viewed educational requirements for jobs as screens used to restrict opportunity. The anti-establishment attitudes generated by Vietnam and the Nixon years contributed to the mistrust of rules, questioning of virtually all imposed requirements, and a system built on the assumption that students knew best what they should do and what direction to follow, and that they, therefore, should be allowed virtually unlimited freedom to chart their own course through education. Concern was expressed that education should not be made punitive; thus individuals moved through all levels of the system with less guidance and lower expectations than had ever been the case in the past.

The urban community colleges had become the centerpiece in the expansion of higher education access and had the most diverse, least academically qualified student body. These institutions responded, often in radical ways, to the basic objective of helping students stay in school and complete degrees. Concern was primarily for the individual's feeling of well-being, gratification, and independence. Community college leaders talked of the "right to fail," and students were allowed to take any course desired because those students might know better than the professional staff what the prospect of success would be. An open-flow educational model evolved and, in many cases, virtually any course could be counted as part of a degree. It was argued, for example, that if a student received academic credits for a course in tennis, then ethnic self-expression or community work assignments should count as well. I even recall a publication describing fifty approaches to learning college English. In effect, a menu of choices was provided to find the method best suited to each individual for the completion of college English coursework, without common outcome expectations.

Returning Vietnam veterans added another problem in the 1960s. A significant number came to college disillusioned and discontent, and felt no obligation to take courses or to study. They argued that they were entitled to financial aid as repayment for the terrible experiences they had endured in Vietnam. In addition, in low-cost institutions such as urban community colleges, expanded federal grant programs provided many students with a payment in cash for living expenses after signing up for classes. In the free-flow operations of that period, a significant number of students simply signed up, collected their checks and went home, then came back to repeat the same procedure again the next term. In the community college, the unrestricted flow of students into any course expanded classroom diversity to such a degree that faculty were left with the choice of either having unacceptable numbers of failures and/or dropouts, or lowering academic expectations. There is also the strong probability that, over a period of time, faculty in community colleges and universities adjusted course assignments to match the time available for evening and working students. Gradually and systematically expectations were lowered in the community colleges stressing open-flow educational models and, in less dramatic fashion, evidence suggests that this happened throughout every level of education. Before being too quick to condemn these occurrences, one must remember the conditions that existed in the United States in the 1960s. The anti-authority attitudes, the drive for immediate rectification of centuries of prejudicial practices, and the hope of our minority communities that there would be significant and rapid change all fostered the events of that time. The opening of access to higher education and the emphasis on program completion, rather than on standards, did move more disadvantaged individuals through the system and onto the ladder of economic advancement. What was done may well have been right for that period. The problem has been that the mind set of many educators appears to be stuck in the 1960s, and this cannot be the basis for viable programs in the 1980s.

The National Assessment of Educational Progress (1981) reports that during the 1970s there was a 20 percent decline in the number of seventeen-year-olds able to interpret reading matter satisfactorily; scores on College Board examinations declined for 14 consecutive years before bottoming out in 1981; and a one-and-a-half school year decline in standardized test scores of American high school seniors had occurred over a six-year period, compounded by a further one-year difference for students in urban America. At Miami-Dade Community College, two-thirds of all entering students are tested as deficient in reading, writing, or mathematics; more than 90 percent of the black students tested are deficient in one of those skills while two-thirds are deficient in all three. Black students consistently test in the lower half of academic scores ranges, at a rate that is double their percentage of the population. Further, approximately 20 percent of white Americans and more than 30 percent of black Americans currently are not completing high school, and these figures are on the rise (American Council of Education and others, 1983). The net result is that both retention and standards of quality in American education have become unsatisfactory.

THREATS TO ACCESS

There is as near a consensus that education is not doing its job as the American public reaches on any issue, and the reaction of citizens and elected representatives has been both critical and punitive. The significant decline in federal and state support for schools and colleges during the 1970s strongly reflects this attitude. However, the reduction of funding has exacerbated the problem by making it more difficult to provide quality services and by making employment in education less attractive. As a result, we have seen the loss of some outstanding faculty and a dramatic decline in the quality of those preparing for careers in education. If the present issue of inadequate remuneration for faculty and other personnel in education is not addressed, there is little prospect for improvement. Education is a communications and interpersonal service, and dedicated, high-quality individuals are essential to build and maintain a quality system.

The nation is now moving through a period characterized by state legislatures taking decisions into their own hands and informing professional educators that they have not fulfilled their responsibilities. The objective is to ensure that changes occur, and the demand is for immediate action and visible, measurable results. Unfortunately, some of the proposed "quick fix" solutions have been developed without the benefit of advice from those who are most knowledgeable about education, nor have they been based on research, as would certainly be the case in any major decision reached by a business corporation. The current centralization of decision-making at the state level is designed to "force" change, and this has both negative and positive implications. Without doubt there will be change, and state actions will bring a focus to issues involving the schools and the promise of necessary additional support. In the end, education will probably move through a period of punishment to a period of receiving required support. However, there will also be an overreliance on standardized tests and trendy and counterproductive policies.

The major problems brought about by centralization are the introduction of additional layers of bureaucracy and the movement of critical decision-making further from the point of implementation—exactly contrary to the advice widely heralded by industry from the best-selling book, *In Search of Excellence* (Peters and Waterman, 1982). To illustrate, state legislatures are now becoming more involved in curriculum specifications. New high school requirements are being developed in California and course requirements for admission to higher education in Virginia are being implemented. Most sweeping in scope is the RAISE (Raise Achievement In Secondary Education) Bill passed by the 1983 Florida Legislature. Among other initiatives, this omnibus bill requires increased academic course requirements during the high school years, a positive direction. However, it deals only with curriculum, where it is overly specific, and thus it falls short of recognizing support and program concerns that must be addressed in order to have a successful program. In addition, the RAISE Bill called for the systematic elimination of developmental courses in colleges. The rhetoric sounded good—moving from a time of remedial to a time of quality education—but this would have removed one of the most important instruments to help students who begin with deficiencies to succeed. The decision to eliminate developmental courses through the RAISE Bill well illustrates the emotionalism currently involved in legislative educational decisions. This decision was made primarily because one high school principal testified that high school students were not doing better academically because they knew they could catch up later through developmental courses in the community colleges. This brought statements from legislators that the public should not pay twice for the same program, and that if higher hurdles were set, the students would learn to jump them. No data were collected, no analysis of programs was conducted, no forecast of impact was made. The commitment to this concept was decided on the spot. Fortunately, after a year of long hard work by educators, the 1984 Florida legislature moderated the provisions of the RAISE Bill on this issue.

The growing emphasis on standardized tests in maintaining standards is spreading throughout the country with actions being taken in California, New Jersey, Alabama, Texas, and Florida as well as many other states. Florida has been the leader in developing and instituting standardized tests, including one now required for high school graduation and one required for progress to the junior year in the state university system or for graduation with an Associate in Arts Degree from a community college. The major benefit of these testing requirements is that the important skills of reading, writing, and mathematics are clearly identified and emphasized, and educational institutions have no choice but to concentrate instructional programs in these areas. There are two major problems, however. First, the skills identified for testing are only a small subset of those that the educational programs seek to develop. Second, standardized tests *alone* are not the best measure of educational progress, and minority populations have historically done poorly on these tests. Studies consistently indicate that the best predictor of future academic success is a combination of grades in academic courses plus standardized test scores, and the second best predictor is grades in academic courses alone. Obviously, a standardized test cannot measure the student's motivation, level of commitment, or willingness to expend great effort in the learning process. The use of standardized tests as absolute requirements to pass from one educational level to another substitutes a two- or three-hour test performance for evaluations by faculty based on several full years of interaction with the students. The standardized testing movement is the clearest sign of public mistrust of education and will inevitably result in denying opportunity to many students who have the potential to succeed. Most important, measures that concentrate on objective standards without concern for program improvement are destined to reduce, rather than increase, the number of well-prepared individuals in our society, and this is a terrible waste of human resources.

Under the Reagan administration, the federal government has followed the more restrictive approaches of some states and is seeking ways to contract student financial aid. The emphasis of proposed restrictions is on those portions of the financial aid programs designed to provide access as opposed to those dealing with choice. Restrictions on the award of Pell Grants to limit the amount of time a student could spend in developmental coursework were already being considered in the summer of 1984. In addition, discussion has begun on what Reagan administration representatives term "priority students," that is, students with good prospects for success. These individuals argue that the nation can no longer afford the present level of expenditure for education and that if expenditures are to be cut, financial aid funds should be given to those students with the best potential to succeed. They emphasize that waste occurs when students without proper preparation are funded. Unfortunately, to the uninformed this sounds reasonable. It takes considerable effort to make the case that we cannot afford to fail to fully develop the talents of our citizens, that there is still not an equal starting place for all individuals, and that many of the "priority students" identified by the Reagan administration may have other opportunities available to them.

In recent years there has been a dramatic increase in federal student financial aid—Pell Grants and Guaranteed Student Loans. Many independent colleges and universities suffered severe financial difficulties in the early and mid-1970s. The indirect income from federal financial aid has evolved into an income subsidy that is a financial cornerstone for many independent colleges, and reduction of this support would threaten these institutions. At the same time enrollment-driven funding formulas have caused an overemphasis on enrollment in public colleges and universities. Unfortunately, the result has been to focus financial aid discussions on the impact on institutions rather than on the benefit to individuals. The debated issue becomes the distribution between public and independent institutions.

Emphasis on choice or priority students at the cost of access would be a disastrous step for our society. An increase in student financial aid is needed first to assure access to higher education for those with limited financial means, and second to expand the number of students who would have the opportunity to choose among institutions. The concept of reserving aid for priority students is especially distressing and contrary to the best interests of the nation. Yet in 1984 this concept is being actively discussed by the Reagan administration.

The Changing Nature of Work

We have entered a period of dramatic and systemic shifts in the nature of work in America, and are currently experiencing a rapid transition from less to more skilled occupations. Before World War II, 80 percent of all jobs in America were unskilled (Whited, 1982). With industrialization during and following World War II, there was significant decline in farm and farm-related employment, growth in manufacturing occupations, and increases in the number of professional and semi-professional jobs. By 1980, less than 20 percent of all jobs in America were unskilled, and agricultural employment had decreased to between 2 and 3 percent of all employment. We are now entering a period of transition from industrial fields to significant growth in computer and data utilization in all fields—a hallmark of the new information society. This transition is comparable in impact to the earlier transition from agricultural to industrial occupations.

In *Putting America Back to Work*, the American Association of Community and Junior Colleges (1982) estimates a continuing decline in manufacturing jobs over the next twenty-five years. The report indicates that the percentage of the American work force in manufacturing jobs was 41 percent in the 1950s; today it is 27 percent; and Peter Drucker of Claremont Graduate School in California predicts a continuing decrease to less than 5 percent within twenty-five years (p. 6). With more manufacturing jobs being automated, increasing numbers of occupations involved with high technologies, and the geometric increase in data and information processing, there is an obvious dramatic transition in occupations underway. Just as mechanization eliminated many unskilled jobs in the post-World War II years, developments in communications technology and the information explosion will certainly eliminate many semi-skilled jobs in the future. As new jobs are added, most will require more skill and involve information processing.

The dynamic growth of information technology has been the major force changing the American work place. At the outset, many in education completely misinterpreted the impact of new communications technology, and predicted that reading would become less important as other means of communication evolved. What has happened, in fact, is exactly the reverse; communications technology is rapidly becoming a part of everyone's work and home life, and is producing enormous amounts of information that must be read and interpreted. William Brazziel (1981, p. 50) has estimated that currently "the volume of scientific and technical information doubles approximately every eight years." In 1950, only 17 percent of all jobs in America involved information processing, while today 54 percent of all jobs are in information occupations (Klein, 1981, p. 15A). Currently more than half of all positions in America are in office occupations, and this figure will continue to increase in the future (Zorn, 1981, p. 17A). Thus, the level of communications skills necessary for employment has increased significantly. It is fundamental to recognize that, in the framework of present-day society, academic skills have become the most important vocational skills. The National Assessment of Educational Progress (1981, p. 5) reports on the need for such skills:

In a world overloaded with information, both a business and a personal advantage will go to those individuals who can sort the wheat from the chaff, the important information from the trivial. Skills in reducing data, interpreting it, packaging it effectively, documenting decisions, explaining complex matter in simple terms and persuading are already highly prized in business, education and the military, and will become more so as the information explosion continues.

Even during the highest levels of unemployment in 1982 and 1983, newspapers throughout the country were filled with employment opportunities in fields such as accounting, office careers, data processing, electronics, health care, and virtually all high technology areas. Unfilled jobs still exist in abundance, at the same time that we appear to be learning to live with higher levels of unemployment. The problem is inadequate information skills—there is virtually no area in the country with enough qualified persons to fill office occupation openings, and employers continue to complain of unsatisfactory communications skills among job applicants. In addition, in many areas of the country industrial and economic development is not being appropriately supported because the skills of graduates of our schools and colleges do not match the current needs of industry. Although the high-technology fields will not provide large numbers of new positions, the dearth of capable individuals to enter these fields is well documented. It results from a lack of both assessment and planning to meet regional educational needs, and the wide-scale problem of students who are inadequately prepared to undertake curricula in science- and math-oriented fields. Eva Galambos, in a report published by the Southern Regional Education Board (1980, p. 15), predicts the future in these fields:

> The signs in terms of demand are fairly clear: even with a continuation of past trends, the demand for engineers, computer and mathematics specialists, and other high technology manpower will exceed the supply.... In short, without deliberate action at all educational levels, if present trends are allowed to continue their own apparent course, then a serious shortage of high technology manpower may be in the offing.

Policy of Opportunity

There is no doubt that a serious problem exists in our society, nor that the American educational system has contributed to the problem and must now be looked to for the solution. Increased percentages of positions require strong information (academic) skills at the same time that attainment of these skills has declined at all educational levels, and dropout rates are rising. The obvious conclusion is that expectations in courses and programs must be raised, but at the same time there must also be more program completers. Many who are concerned with improving the quality of postsecondary education offer a simplistic solution to the problem, namely, to reverse the gains in access and limit admission to those who have demonstrated higher ability upon the completion of high school. These individuals have misplaced the emphasis on improving *institutions* of higher education, rather than improving education. Institutions would undoubtedly be of higher quality if only the best prepared were admitted, but what would be the impact on the nation? While raising admissions criteria is probably appropriate for some universities, such a policy applied to all higher education would be devastating to this country. The measurement of quality in the higher education enterprise should be based on the degree to which educational results meet the needs of society, and the American economy requires the fullest possible development of human resources and talent. Thus, access is an implicit factor in higher education quality. Limiting access would be a clear misreading of the mood of the American people. Although there is substantial disillusionment with the efficacy of some social programs, including those in education, this disillusionment is with the programs themselves and not with the great ideals of this nation nor the basic tenet of providing opportunity for each individual to fulfill his or her potential.

It is time to examine carefully the current environment and to redesign the postsecondary system, especially the community college, to become a positive force in improving our society. The effect of the changing nature of work in

America, along with a severe decline in communications skills of our youth, have resulted in a societal dilemma so serious that it can fairly be called a crisis. This decline in academic skills—precisely those skills most important for employability—leaves literally millions of Americans inadequately prepared and unable to gain employment, and thus unable to sustain themselves as productive members of the society. We have little alternative but to help each individual toward higher academic achievement as a basis for employability in the new information age.

The current situation can best be understood in the context of our minority populations. Early in the twenty-first century, minority populations will represent the majority in the United States. The birth rate decline has occurred almost exclusively among white non-Hispanics, and recent immigration has been substantially Hispanic and Oriental. There is a significant difference in the demography of the various age groups, with younger Americans being heavily minority and now being a majority of those enrolled in twenty-three of the country's twenty-five largest school systems (American Council on Education and others, 1983). In terms of wealth, education, and advantages, these minorities so heavily represented among our younger population are significantly disadvantaged as compared with the white non-Hispanic population. Thus the percentage of disadvantaged in our schools is growing rapidly at the very time that business and industry are requiring greater skills. There is little choice but to insure that these individuals gain the skills necessary to be constructive members of society and the work force.

As a pattern, the problems for black Americans are worst of all. With the centuries of systematic deprivation, the high hopes of the 1960s have faded into despair, frustration, and hopelessness. Widely anticipated improvements in conditions for our black population are being achieved at a painstakingly slow pace. The increase in academic skills required for employment today—the area where blacks as a group are at the greatest disadvantage—is making the plight even worse. In many poor black neighborhoods of our country, significant percentages of young children are growing up in single-parent families, typically a woman working at minimum wage. These youngsters have no basis for seeing a relationship between their futures and the academic courses offered in school. What importance can an impoverished youngster see in a seventh-grade English class? Yet that class, which builds the information skills so necessary for virtually all current employment, is absolutely essential for future success in life. As such youngsters learn through television how little their families have in comparison to others, they also want to possess things now and to have money now. Thus a part-time job in a fast-food chain—or any other means to obtain some resources quickly—becomes very attractive and far more important than school. Further, there is nothing in the context of the society in which they live that reinforces the importance of schooling. In effect, we have in place a set of conditions operating like an assembly line, producing one young person after another underprepared to participate effectively in the society.

Coordinate with the emphasis on quality in education, there are some disturbing occurrences in our country. For the first time since before World War II, there is a decline in high school graduation rates, and the sharpest decline is for blacks. A recent cohort study in Dade County, Florida, showed that only 42 percent of black students beginning the ninth grade were graduating from high school, and 54 percent of those graduates were women (Losak and Morris, 1983). Given the current unemployment situation of young black men, the impact of these statistics is alarming. There has also been a national decline in black enrollment in higher education over the last three years, reversing a trend of the previous fifteen years. Florida data show that two-thirds of all blacks in higher education are women. Further, there is a significant underrepresentation of Hispanics in American higher education (American Council on Education and others, 1983).

The problem we face is a dramatic decrease in the academic skills of our young people, especially minorities, at a time when those skills have become the most important occupational skills and the foundation for virtually all employment. If major efforts are not made to resolve this paradoxical problem, we face the frightening prospect of developing a permanent underclass of individuals who cannot fully participate or make any productive contribution. This would force millions to become a permanent burden on the society, and would leave American industry without the quality of employees necessary to compete in the international marketplace of the information age. The essential factor to understand is that the distribution of academic skills that was satisfactory a decade ago is clearly unsatisfactory today, and that educational policy and public support must address that issue directly.

A vivid illustration of our current circumstances is evident in my own community. With a booming economy based on international tourism, trade, and banking, some employers are actually paying bounties to employees who recruit a new, qualified employee—that is, someone with good communications skills who can process information effectively. At the same time, in an unreconstructed and hopeless Liberty City, thousands of unemployed young people hang out on street corners. The difference between remaining unemployed and being recruited vigorously for employment is based to a significant degree on the level of the personal information skills one possesses. How better could education help our country than by seeing to it that no new legions are added to those street corners, and that those who are motivated to improve themselves have the opportunity for education regardless of where they begin? Nothing could be done that would have more impact on improving our deprived communities than to improve the level of literacy, thus opening opportunities for existing jobs. Helping these individuals into good employment would provide them with the economic resources to help both themselves and their neighborhoods.

The Integration of Quality and Access

While it is clearly in the nation's best interest, in fact, an absolute necessity, to increase the number of individuals at high levels of educational attainment, the question remains:

is it possible to have both access and quality in the same institution? For the best answer one can look to the record of the open-door community colleges. Earlier sections of this chapter described the problems in education, and especially those in open-door community colleges, but there have been many successes.

Unfortunately, a problem that inevitably surfaces when student performance data are analyzed is the predilection on the part of researchers to "force fit" community college information into structures based on conditions in four-year residential institutions. It is reasonable, in a four-year residential institution, to measure success by the number of students who enter and the percentage of those students who complete two years of education two years later or four-year programs four years later. Students in these institutions are there for the single purpose of obtaining a baccalaureate degree, and they are principally full-time residential students committing all of their efforts to completing that degree. In addition, in most institutions with selective admissions policies, students begin, or at least are expected to begin, without academic deficiencies.

Because the characteristics of the student body in open-door community colleges are very different, evaluation based on the number of students completing an associate degree after two years of enrollment has little meaning. As little as one-third of the students begin full-time with the objective of obtaining a baccalaureate degree. Others enter programs of two years or less for direct employment, and many are there for specialized objectives, including career-oriented or other personal goals. Such students may take one or two courses and feel they have achieved their objectives, but no measurement of program completion would reflect this. The majority of community college students work, and many drop in and out of college. In addition, large numbers of these students begin with academic deficiencies and, with the changing policies in community colleges, are frequently required to take extra courses in preparation for standard college work. Kolstad (1981) affirms that college dropout studies fail to take into consideration the prolonged nature of many students' careers. At Miami-Dade Community College, for example, the mean number of terms of attendance for 1984 graduates was eleven semesters; more than half had begun their college work more than five years earlier. In addition, many students who are pursuing a baccalaureate program transfer to universities convenient to them without completing the associate degree. Transfer occurs, in many cases, after a full year of work and the amelioration of their academic deficiencies, or at the beginning of a fall term when they are near completion of the associate degree. For students with the baccalaureate as a goal, the award of an associate degree is of no particular concern. Typical studies undertaken by university researchers emphasize the percentage of entrants who graduate two years after admission, and draw the conclusion that dropout rates are staggering and that success rates are poor. Such data are misleading, inappropriate, and completely worthless to community colleges.

Other research compares the grade point average (GPA) of juniors who have transferred from community colleges to universities with that of native students. What is typically found is a drop in GPA in the first semester after transfer, followed by a leveling out or improvement in successive terms. This phenomenon is called "transfer shock" (Thompson, 1978) and is experienced when students begin at a new institution, regardless of the institution from which they transfer. In addition, the freshman class at four-year universities begins as a group with a higher level of academic preparation than those in community colleges, thus one would expect some advantage in GPA. With regard to Florida, Losak and Corson (1979) state that "when equated on ability before beginning their collegiate work, there is no significant difference in performance at the junior and senior years between community college graduates and those beginning their careers in the universities." Their study was done using grade point averages; however, the more important measure is the number of students who are successful, particularly those who might not have the opportunity to progress through higher education without the open-door community college.

There is considerable evidence suggesting that large numbers of students who would not have been directly admissible to universities when they began their college careers do succeed after completing community college programs and transferring to an upper-division institution. Data from the State of Florida provide the best information in this area. The State Community College Coordinating Board (1981) of Florida issued a report showing no significant difference in the percentage of community college transfer students with A.A. degrees and native state university students who were successful, that is, who had a GPA of 2.0 or higher after one term of the junior year. The native students were successful at a percentage rate of 78.51, while the transfer students were successful at a rate of 77.58 percent. This is remarkable given the difference in the level of preparation at the time these students began their work. Even more impressive is the fact that 46.14 percent of the community college transfer students had a GPA of 3.0 or higher, compared to 45.49 percent of the native students.

Since 1982, Florida has required a College Level Academic Skills Test (CLAST) for all students transferring to the junior year, whether they begin in a community college or a university. Effective in 1984, statewide common cutoff scores were instituted for CLAST. A report by Losak and Morris (1983) showed that the top half of the graduating students of Miami-Dade Community College achieved higher mean scores on all segments of that test than the university mean, and the top third had higher mean scores on all the tests than the students of any university. Most impressive was that one out of each six of these high-scoring students had begun at Miami-Dade with a requirement of taking developmental classes. With the establishment of common cutoff scores on CLAST, approximately one-fourth of all students in the state's universities and community colleges failed one or more subtests in the June 1984 administration of the test, thus confirming that this is a demanding examination (Florida Department of Education, 1984). However, Miami-Dade Community College data showed that 32 percent of the Miami-Dade students who passed all four subsections of

CLAST had begun with scores indicating academic deficiencies on the college's placement examination. In addition, 52 percent of those Miami-Dade students passing all four subtests on CLAST reported that their native language was not English (Belcher, 1984). Many of those students began their work with English as a Second Language preparation and would not be included in the students tested for deficiencies at admission.

All of us know of individuals who began college with limited academic skills and, often under the most difficult circumstances, went on to achieve success in many fields. Therefore, it should be no surprise that research data substantiate that it is possible to have high achievement in an open-door institution.

New Directions for Success

It cannot be denied that the problems of open admissions institutions have escalated in recent years. As we have seen, the academic preparation of entering students has declined and in urban areas the enrollment of minorities—those with the least academic skill and the greatest need for assistance—has increased dramatically as a percentage of the total enrollment. To illustrate, Miami-Dade Community College enrolls more minorities than the state university system of Florida, including 5 percent of all Hispanic students in American higher education. In addition, community colleges are working to eliminate the effect of practices developed in the late 1960s and early 1970s. Current problems also include important issues related to faculty. As faculty salaries have failed to keep pace with other employment fields over the years, more and more faculty members have sought additional part-time employment. This reduces the time they are available to provide the extra assistance necessary for students who are inadequately prepared or undecided about their goals. Many of the faculty have also come through the educational system since the late 1960s themselves, and thus do not have the well-developed background in writing, grading essays, and related areas that is required to prepare students adequately for information age careers.

Dealing with the dilemma of lower academic skills of entering students and higher expectations for program completion is an awesome task, and in many cases calls for full-scale reform of the educational program. However, our institutions must address these problems with a dedicated spirit toward new directions and with full understanding of the great importance of this work. Throughout the country there is evidence that community colleges are responding to this challenge and are already moving in new directions. Most important to understand is that simply raising requirements for admission provides an unsatisfactory solution for our country. It is essential that commitment to the open door be maintained, as the community college now stands as the pivotal institution in salvaging opportunity for the large numbers of Americans whose academic and occupational skills have not prepared them for effective participation in society. There could be no more vital or challenging responsibility. The community colleges have the capability to provide the necessary programs, but we will not be successful with practices of earlier years.

Because community colleges are the primary open access segment of higher education, and thus face the most substantive problems of underprepared students, there has been an emphasis on them in this chapter. However, virtually every college or university, to differing degrees, admits students with academic deficiencies, personal problems, minimal motivation, and inadequate resources. Thus, all institutions have a responsibility to be sensitive to these problems and design programs to help these students succeed. The frequently supported concept that when students enter college they should sink or swim on their own is unacceptable and unworthy of an institution of higher education. The result is the destruction of individual lives and the loss of human talent that is needed by our society. One great difference between American educational programs and the educational systems of other nations is our adherence to the belief in the worth of every individual, and a commitment to fully develop the talents of each. Our nation has been richly rewarded for commitment to this policy. All colleges and universities should share pride in our achievement and recommit themselves to provide programs to sustain that tradition.

Following are suggested program directions to integrate both quality and access effectively:

1. *Emphasis on Information Skills.* Information skills and learning skills have become of paramount importance in order to live productively and to obtain employment in our emerging information age society. Information skills are defined as the ability to read, analyze, interpret, apply, and communicate information. In order to adapt to the phenomenon of change—the most consistent characteristic of the information age—the ability to continue to learn throughout one's life is also essential. Every institution of higher education should have the objective of graduating students who have strong information skills and are skilled learners.

To achieve this end, there must be considerable change in our approach to instruction and a decrease in dependence on objective testing with computerized score results. Students at all educational levels are reading too little, and the data concerning writing skills are discouraging. Several community colleges have revealed similar results, namely, that students on the average had written only two or three papers during their high school years and that few had read as much as fifty pages per week (Losak and others, 1982). Unfortunately, the pattern in colleges is not much of an improvement, especially in the urban, commuter institutions. One suspects that course assignments have been adjusted to accommodate those who work and attend part-time, and that assignments have also been adjusted because of the lower performance levels of incoming high school students. The convenience of machine scoring and the emphasis on objectivity in testing have also contributed to less in-depth study and a lack of concentration on literacy skills. A reversal of these trends must be emphasized immediately, especially in open-door colleges.

The information skills policy instituted at Miami-Dade Community College in 1983 illustrates the new direction.

There is now a writing requirement in every course, and faculty in all disciplines are being trained systematically to deal with an increased volume of writing across the curriculum —from very brief classroom assignments to essay examinations and lengthy term papers. In addition, instructional objectives relating to information skills and learning skills are required to be built into every course. Students must take a percentage of work in sophomore level courses, and the faculty have increased reading expectations and have instituted higher level learning competencies and the application of information skills in those courses. However an institution chooses to address this problem, it must be done on a broad scale and must be integrated throughout the curriculum in order to change program direction and achieve higher standards.

2. *Provide a More Directive, More Supportive Program.* The tremendous increase in the spread of students' abilities and goals has been one of the factors that caused the breakdown in the open-flow model. The idea that students should "have an opportunity to fail," that is, be allowed to choose any courses they wished at their own risk, simply did not work. The resulting spread of abilities often precluded the establishment of an effective learning environment in classrooms, and did not afford either students or faculty the opportunity to succeed. Perhaps more than any other factor, this contributed to a decline in faculty morale and to the serious questioning of the efficacy of the system. Faculty commitment is essential to effective education, and must be regained.

A broad range of student abilities and goals does exist, however, and recognition of this should be a centerpiece in open-door college planning. Programs must be organized to provide direction and special assistance as required, in order that each student have the best opportunity to achieve. There should be a controlled student flow, carefully constructed so that students progress through the program based on their competencies and performance. In a more directive system, students with deficiencies are required to take necessary developmental work before proceeding to programs where the lack of skill could cause failure. Such a system also ensures that students are assisted in selecting courses and in maintaining reasonable loads. In addition, the curriculum should be aligned so that students who cannot complete a program will have gained skills and competencies that are useful in life. Given this type of directive system, faculty should be able to provide effective instruction within a narrower range of academic competence, thus increasing both faculty and student opportunity for success.

3. *More Service for the Less Prepared Students.* Over a period of time, institutions became embarrassed when students were unable to complete programs in a standard amount of time, or when they required developmental courses or other forms of special assistance. As a reflection of new attitudes in higher education, students should be informed at the outset that if they begin with deficiencies in academic skills, they must take longer to be successful. There is little prospect that a standard application of educational service will move a student who is four or five years behind in academic skills to the acceptable level within a standard period of time. Programs should be organized to allow students variable time for achievement of a program, a course, or even a unit within a course.

There must exist not only developmental courses but a system that will accommodate appropriate reduction in load for students experiencing difficulty (one of the few procedures that shows documented results). Many working students underestimate the amount of time that courses require and often enroll for more credits than can be handled successfully. This is especially true for underprepared students. The college system should provide necessary restrictions, advisement, and additional support service coordinate with coursework. There should be continued emphasis on the development of faculty skills necessary for effective individualization of instruction. Reduction of the academic range in classes will not eliminate individual differences. The thrust of the program must remain on assistance to individuals. College credits must be viewed as currency, and institutions must not award credits until course standards have been met.

Thus the fairly widespread practice of granting additional credits when students take longer to complete courses, or granting them easily, must be discontinued.

With the new techniques and discoveries of the teaching/learning process over the last several decades, the tools are now available to fully develop variable-time programs. In some states, revision of statutes or rules related to finance will be required in order to permit broad utilization of variable-time practices.

4. *Assuring Standards.* Standards in American education have declined at all levels. The open-door community college, however, receiving less prepared high school graduates and committed to help all, has been especially vulnerable. It is most important that student expectations be raised, and that degrees and certificates be awarded on the basis of demonstrated competencies, in order that they remain meaningful. In the future, most individuals will require some postsecondary education, yet society is demanding that funds not be expended where there is little hope of achieving a successful result. A student's first year at the community college may well become the deciding point as to whether the public will continue to pay for further education. The college should assume responsibility to assist individuals to succeed, and an ordered curriculum should be instituted to deal with reading, writing, and computational deficiencies first, so that all benefit from attendance. However, the colleges must also be prepared to suspend students if there is no evidence of reasonable progress.

5. *The Use of Communications Technology.* Most would agree that there is no short-term expectation for substantial increases in funding. Thus, individualization must be achieved within acceptable cost parameters and, without doubt, application of communications technology offers important prospects for attaining this goal. The economic aspects of the use of communications technology continue to improve, while the capability and cost of hardware are declining rapidly. The key consideration in utilization of this technology is that responses and advice for students, which are dependent on many factors, can and should be developed

with great care. Since the results will be utilized in many similar circumstances, the development cost may be shared, or amortized, over many students. This allows more time and care to go into the preparation of responses, with cost-effectiveness maintained, than would be possible with responses designed for a single student.

It also appears that faculty are now ready to use communications technology after years of resistance. Computers and other communications devices have become an integral part of all of our lives. It would be most unusual not to use them in the field of education, which is a combination of communications and human interaction. A recent study of Florida community college faculty (Cook and Toback, 1981) showed that the highest interest in new instructional techniques—49 percent—was in the application of computers.

To illustrate the use of computers for individualization of instruction, all students at Miami-Dade Community College receive information about their current academic progress approximately six weeks into each term. In addition, computerized instructional systems serve in more than one hundred courses, especially those with large enrollments. Ninety-three percent of our students have expressed appreciation at receiving this personal computerized information, and recent studies show that students improve performance, increase completion rates and GPA, and lower suspension rates when they are informed early of performance deficiencies and avail themselves of needed special assistance.

6. *Economic and Institutional Planning.* The changes that must take place in the educational program of open-door colleges in order to provide variable-time programs, to recognize individual differences, and to integrate the use of communications technology clearly indicate the need for a different configuration of service from the traditional institution. Institutions cannot regard all of the new elements merely as additions to the standard format; this has long been a stumbling block to advances in education. Rather, they must think in terms of reconfiguration of costs, based upon substantial change and reorganization of the educational program. Only this type of planning will result in meaningful

change and provide any real opportunity to bring about effective reform in our current dilemma.

There must be an overall institutional plan and commitment that involves careful ordering of educational experiences and that is more directive, more controlled, and more supportive of the students. Each department should fulfill its unique role and develop its programs in support of the total. There is little prospect for success, even with the excellent work that might develop in individual departments, if it is not part of an integrated system. The current diversity of the students, their lack of academic skills, and the requirement for greater competency for graduates demand full college reform.

7. *Services for Superior Students.* With the goal of an increased focus on achievement in the open-door colleges, it is important that these institutions not become places for only those with poor academic skills. Yet, overwhelmed by the problems of the underprepared and the task of providing support for them, the community college and other open-door institutions have, over a period of time, neglected superior students. These students represent one more aspect of our total diversity, and they can be well served. The superior student is an important asset, not only to other students, but also in building and maintaining a positive public attitude toward the open-door colleges. Many institutions are implementing creative new programs for these students, and a number of community colleges now enroll more than 30 percent of the top 10 percent of high school graduates.

8. *Leadership with High School Programs.* Seventy-five percent of high school graduates enroll in postsecondary institutions within seven years of high school graduation and, in some areas, more than half eventually enroll in community colleges (McCabe and Skidmore, 1982). High schools must recognize that most students require preparation for postsecondary enrollment, and that all need a foundation of strong academic skills in preparation for employment and for a life of productive participation in our society. For large numbers of Americans it is too late to begin improvement of academic deficiencies at the community college level. The

colleges and high schools should work together in order to bring about necessary curricular change before enrollment in the postsecondary system. It is time for someone to take the leadership in bringing about close cooperation with high schools and, more important, in beginning to convince the community and parents of the increasing need for higher levels of education and to be both more supportive and more demanding of the schools. Community college leaders are in an ideal position to undertake this responsibility.

Summary

Improvements in the quality of education must be accomplished together with maintenance of opportunity. Critics of American education have emphasized the advantages of Japanese education, and it is true that greater expectations do exist at many levels in the Japanese system. Yet that system reflects other problems; for example, the incidence of personal problems highlighted by suicide rates is startling among students in Japan. The United States continues to produce individuals who have the ability to think creatively and to apply knowledge more effectively. Other countries, believed by many to have educational systems superior to ours, still show great interest in imitating the American system and continue to send their young to our country for higher education.

America is a unique amalgam of cultures and requires a uniquely American educational system. This nation has become the greatest nation in the world, principally by its commitment to help all individuals develop their potential to the fullest extent possible. That great tradition should not be discarded or ignored simply to be able to brag about standards. Rather, higher expectations must be systematically introduced at each level of education in a progression over a reasonable period of time. There are sufficient examples of success in combining quality and access to encourage us to improve our approaches and programs, and to continue in that direction. Expanding requirements of the information age and the need for virtually all individuals to have strong information skills leaves no other acceptable choice.

We must recognize that our nation needs the productivity and fully developed talents of all our people, and we must continue to make every effort to provide opportunity for individuals who are motivated to self-improvement, regardless of their age or educational status. We are indeed "a nation at risk" because of the forces shaping American education as we enter the information age. However, the risk is present not only because standards in the schools have slipped but also because a significant percentage of our population withdraws from the educational system with a totally inadequate level of preparation. We must strive for educational quality based on compassion, full understanding of the teaching and learning processes, a dramatic improvement in the support of education by the public, and the raising of expectations at all levels.

In guiding educational policy, our goal should not be simply to improve American colleges and universities, for this could be done easily by restricting admission to only those guaranteed to be successful. Institutions of higher education should be seen as instruments in the service of the people, and excellence in education should be defined in terms of improvements in educational services that contribute positively to the improvement of society. Toward that end, our goal must be to establish educational policies that will permit access for all who are motivated to learn, concurrent with a raising of standards for program completion. The challenge is great, but full integration of both quality and equality can and must be achieved.

References

American Association of Community and Junior Colleges and the Association of Community College Trustees. *Putting America Back to Work* (Washington, D. C.: American Association of Community and Junior Colleges, 1982).

American Council on Education, Forum of Educational Organi-

ZATION LEADERS, AND INSTITUTE FOR EDUCATIONAL LEADERSHIP. *Demographic Imperatives: Implications for Educational Policy.* Report of the forum on "The Demographics of Changing Ethnic Populations and Their Implications for Elementary-Secondary and Postsecondary Educational Policy" (June 8, 1983).

BELCHER, M. "A Cohort Analysis of the Relationship Between Entering Basic Skills and CLAST Performance for Fall 1981 First-Time-In-College-Students" (Miami, Fla.: Miami-Dade Community College Office of Institutional Research, #84-22, 1984).

BELCHER, M. "Initial Transcript Analysis for a Sample of Students Who Failed Two or More Sections Versus Sample Who Passed All Four Sections of the June 1984 CLAST" (Miami, Fla.: Miami-Dade Community College Office of Institutional Research, #84-21, 1984).

BRAZZIEL, W. F. "College-Corporate Partnerships in Higher Education." *Educational Record* (1981, 62, 2), pp. 50–53.

COOK, J. AND TOBACK, D. "Teaching Methods, Strategies and Techniques Used by Florida Community College Instructors." Unpublished study (Boca Raton, Fla.: Florida Atlantic University, August 1981).

DEPARTMENT OF EDUCATION. "Percent of CLAST Examinees Meeting 1984–86 Standards on All Four Subtests." Data provided by the College Level Academic Skills Program (Tallahassee, Fla.: Department of Education, July 1984).

GALAMBOS, E. C. *Engineering and High Technology Manpower Shortages: The Connection with Mathematics* (Atlanta, Ga.: Southern Regional Education Board, 1980).

KLEIN, W. "To Get the Right People for Future Jobs, Schools, Employers Must Work Together." *Miami News* (April 8, 1981), p. 15A.

KOLSTAD, A. "What College Dropout and Dropin Rates Tell Us." *American Education* (Aug.–Sept., 1981), pp. 31–33.

LOSAK, J. AND CORSON, H. "Community College Graduates Fare Well" (Miami, Fla.: Miami-Dade Community College Office of Institutional Research, #79-20, 1979).

LOSAK, J. AND MORRIS, C. "Highlights of CLAST Results for October 1982 Testing at Miami-Dade Community College" (Miami, Fla.: Miami-Dade Community College Office of Institutional Research, #83-04, 1983).

LOSAK, J. AND MORRIS, C. "Projected Impact of Entry and Exit Testing in Secondary and Postsecondary Education" (Miami, Fla.: Miami-Dade Community College Office of Institutional Research, #83-32, 1983).

LOSAK, J., MORRIS, C., AND SCHWARTZ, M. "High School Preparation as Viewed by Academically Underprepared College Students." *The College Board Review* (Fall 1982).

McCabe, R. and Skidmore, S. "The Literacy Crisis and American Education," *Junior College Resource Review* (Los Angeles: ERIC Clearinghouse for Junior Colleges, Spring 1982), p. 4.

National Assessment of Educational Progress. *Reading, Thinking and Writing: Results from the 1979–80 National Assessment of Reading and Literature.* (Denver, Colo.: National Assessment of Educational Progress, Education Commission of the States, 1981).

Peters, T. and Waterman, R. *In Search of Excellence* (New York: Harper & Row, 1982).

State Community College Coordinating Board. "Community College Student Performance in Florida Universities" (Tallahassee, Fla.: State Community College Coordinating Board, 1981).

Thompson, J. "The Growing Role of Community Colleges." *Journal of College and Student Personnel* (January 1978), pp. 11–15.

Whited, C. "There's a Lesson for Educators in 3R's Crisis." *Miami Herald* (Jan. 19, 1982), p. 2B.

Zorn, E. "Why Can't Johnny Log On?" *St. Petersburg Independent* (Aug. 18, 1981), p. 17A.

The Politics of Accreditation and the Role of COPA in Self-Regulation

C. GRIER DAVIS, JR.
ROBERT H. STROTZ

ACCREDITATION IS A UNIQUELY AMERICAN PHENOMENON. The tradition of self-regulation by voluntary accrediting groups grew up at the turn of the century, through the concern of school principals and college presidents to evaluate the quality of secondary and higher education, and through efforts of the medical, legal, and other professions to improve the educational standards in programs prerequisite for practice. The first movement resulted in the formation of regional accrediting agencies to evaluate institutions, the second in specialized accrediting agencies to evaluate professional programs. Over the years, accreditation has played a critical and positive part in quality assessment and institutional enhancement for higher education in the United States.

During the past several decades, the primary threats to accreditation have been problems that derive from federal regulation and specialized accreditation and that politicize the accrediting process. In order to ensure the health, integrity, and diversity of American higher education, the academic community must cooperate in defending and supporting accreditation and its self-regulatory character. In recent years, the Council on Postsecondary Accreditation (COPA) has taken a vital leadership role on behalf of accreditation as a critically important form of self-regulation.

Problems in Accreditation

In 1982, the Carnegie Foundation published *Control of the Campus*, which examined the full range of current trends that threaten autonomy in the governance of higher education. Two of those trends have serious implications for the tradition of voluntary self-regulation through accreditation: expanded government influence over both institutional and specialized accreditation; and continued intrusion by some professional associations through the process of specialized accreditation.

These two issues, which were identified as important to accreditation more than two decades earlier by W. K. Selden (1960), give every evidence of being perennial concerns in the future. Both issues represent a shift of focus from the most fundamental questions addressed by accreditation (What constitutes educational quality? To what degree is that quality manifested in institutions or programs under review?) to essentially political questions (Who will determine the definition and evalution of educational quality? For whose benefit will such reviews be made?).

Milton Friedman's *Capitalism and Freedom* (1962) laid out the classic argument that government intervention into the free market does not effectively separate competence from incompetence in efforts to protect the public. Nevertheless, the history of the United States since World War II has been increasingly characterized by government encroachment in the nongovernmental sectors. In the case of education, the Tenth Amendment to the Constitution delegated all matters, including accreditation, to the states and the people. However, with the exception of New York, most states took a limited role in regulating colleges and universities until the 1960s. Since that time, declining resources, pressures for accountability, and consumer protection movements have resulted in an often duplicative variety of state agencies and coordinating boards that regulate institutions of higher education.

The Constitution does not establish a direct role for the federal government in education. Nevertheless, since World War II, federal special-purpose programs, which are created under the Constitution's general welfare clause but channel funds to colleges and universities, have also brought increasing federal regulation of higher education. In particular, both state and federal regulations have misused the traditional status of accreditation as a nongovernmental means of educational self-regulation.

Accreditation originated as a process of voluntary self-regulation. However, to the extent that specialized accreditation has become linked to state licensure of practitioners and institutional accreditation to eligibility for certain state and federal funds, accreditation is no longer truly voluntary. This change in the status of accreditation is a reflection of the larger shift in our society from voluntary to government support of many cultural and social needs. For accreditation, the main question now would seem to be whether the accrediting agencies and the educational institutions can effectively join forces to combat governmental influence and restore the traditional character of voluntary self-regulation. However, some, who assume that maintaining or even expanding the present regulatory scope of accreditation as a quasi-public process is the only bulwark against further direct government regulation, stand Friedman's argument on its head and ask instead whether accreditation should be voluntary.

Kaplin (1975) took a middle position, describing the concept of a triad in the governance of postsecondary education. Under this concept, provided that the state governments were able to achieve greater consistency in their regulation of postsecondary education, federal and state governments and nongovernmental accrediting agencies could serve complementary roles not only in improving educational quality but also in eliminating fraud and addressing other regulatory issues. This supposedly ideal concept is considerably removed from the actual situation, which is characterized by a host of very real problems.

To cite a central example, the institutional eligibility process of the Department of Education requires both state licensure and accreditation. Yet some postsecondary institutions, although incorporated by the state, are neither licensed nor accredited, and many more have one but not the other. In fact, private colleges and universities, in order to avoid state agency intrusion, often argue that institutional accreditation should be accepted in lieu of state licensing. However, exemption from state licensing or insufficiencies in state authorization have conferred a quasi-public status on accreditation by default and encouraged the federal government to propose inappropriate policing functions for the accrediting agencies. Although the number of states that report some licensing authority for degree-granting institutions has increased during the last decade, the future possibility of the triad functioning in a manner acceptable to all parties seems unlikely.

One aspect of federal influence over accreditation also served to exacerbate misuses of the specialized accreditation process by professional associations. Once federal law had called for the Commissioner (now Secretary) of Education to publish a list of accrediting agencies, tremendous pressures were generated for the proliferation of such organizations. Institutions or programs that were denied eligibility for federal funds sought membership in existing agencies or, failing that, created new accrediting associations. As a result, the primary purpose of some such organizations was not accreditation per se but lobbying for member interests both with governmental bodies through the state and national political process and with academic institutions through the accrediting process.

Pressures toward proliferation already existed because of the rapid postwar development of new technologies, especially characteristic of the allied health fields. Practitioners of new occupations such as these tend to view federal listing, state licensure, and specialized accreditation in terms of prestige and recognition as a profession. Indeed, there has been a tendency for such professional associations, old as well as new, to use the specialized accrediting process inappropriately. Although such associations have a legitimate concern that practitioners receive the necessary education, this end is often used to justify attempts to dictate curricula or obtain special privilege. Despite wide acceptance of the argument that licensure protects the public, professions act in a questionable manner when they seek a requirement that practitioners be trained only in institutions or programs having the association's approval. In these and other instances, professional organizations may intrude upon institutional prerogatives and misuse accreditation.

To understand better the politics of accreditation, it is necessary to begin with a definition that is generally acceptable throughout the educational community. The Council on Postsecondary Accreditation, which is the organization founded to coordinate accreditation, has described the essential elements of such a definition in its *Policy Statement on the Role and Value of Accreditation* (1982).

> Accreditation is a status granted to an educational institution or a program that has been found to meet or exceed stated criteria of educational quality. In the United States accreditation is voluntarily sought by institutions and programs and is conferred by nongovernmental bodies.
>
> Accreditation has two fundamental purposes: to assure the quality of the institution or program and to assist in the improvement of the institution or program. Accreditation, which applies to institutions or programs, is to be distinguished from certification and licensure, which apply to individuals.
>
> The bodies conducting institutional accreditation are national or regional in scope and comprise the institutions that have achieved and maintain accreditation. A specialized body conducting accreditation of a program preparing students for a profession or occupation is often closely associated with professional associations in the field.
>
> Both institutional and specialized bodies conduct the accreditation process using a common pattern. The pattern requires integral self-study of the institution or program, followed by an on-site visit by an evaluation team and a subsequent review and decision by a central governing group. Within this general pattern the various accrediting bodies have developed a variety of

individual procedures adapted to their own circumstances. Increasingly, attention has been given to educational outcomes as a basis for evaluation.

This statement helps bring into focus the problems that arise when the accreditation process is politicized. Although the statement gives equal importance to an institution's or program's self-regulation as a means of self-improvement, the external uses of accreditation emphasize only the final decision that results from on-site peer evaluation. Although accreditation is voluntary and nongovernmental, there are strong financial, social, political, and perhaps even legal pressures upon institutions to accommodate external uses, such as determining eligibility for government funding and professional licensing. Nevertheless, these problems are complex and grounded in a lengthy history. Therefore, the options available for addressing these problems cannot be adequately understood apart from an examination of their context.

Federal Regulation

Among the various problems arising from expanded governmental influence over accreditation, none are more important than the conflicts surrounding the U.S. Office (now Department) of Education. An excellent review and analysis by Charles Chambers of problems regarding the federal government and accreditation, in *Understanding Accreditation* (1983), provides the basis for a brief summary. Central to these problems is a dilemma that arose in the period after World War II. If the federal government used no criteria of educational quality for participation in its programs, fraud and abuse on the part of questionable institutions would be inevitable. If the federal government granted funds to some institutions and withheld funds from others on the basis of its own criteria, that action would be construed as unconstitutional and perhaps the first step toward a centralized ministry of education.

Under the first G.I. Bill of 1944, the Veterans Administration (VA) was given authority to approve institutions or use state lists of authorized institutions without regard to any established criteria. As a result, scandals developed, especially among the technical schools, often lacking both accreditation and licensure. When the second G.I. Bill of 1952 was passed, Congress asked the states, on behalf of the VA, to conduct an approval process for postsecondary institutions, and the U.S. Office of Education (OE) to publish a list of nationally "recognized" accrediting bodies that could be considered "reliable" in evaluating educational quality. Because state approval did not rely on prior accreditation, the role of OE was limited and the federal government was not involved directly in the process of quality evaluation.

The publication of the first list by OE nevertheless dramatically changed the nature of accreditation. The newly founded National Commission on Accrediting (NCA) declined to provide OE with such a list because its own agenda involved limiting the number of specialized accrediting bodies. However, when the federal list appeared, including the newer specialized accrediting groups that were the target for limitation, NCA lost its role as a monitor of accreditation and made the expedient political decision to recognize all accrediting agencies listed by the federal government.

The second major change in the relationship between the federal government and accreditation resulted from the National Defense Education Act (NDEA) of 1958, which Congress passed in response to the scientific challenge of the Soviet satellite Sputnik. Unlike the G.I. Bills, the NDEA gave OE responsibility for administering the program funds. The NDEA program, which excluded proprietary institutions, was open for eligibility to institutions of higher education that were public or nonprofit, authorized by the state of location, and accredited through an organization determined by the Commissioner to be a reliable authority. Eligibility entitled an institution to apply for funds, which were then awarded on the basis of an OE review of the proposal. Therefore, OE program funding became a two-phase process, with accreditation as a requirement only in the first phase.

For this purpose, the Commissioner continued to use the list originally prepared for the VA.

The contradictions of this new situation emerged through a new version of the old dilemma. If an institution was to be eligible for federal funds, it had to receive accreditation from a recognized accrediting body. If alternate routes to eligibility were allowed by the federal government for church-related or other institutions not voluntarily submitting to accreditation, the federal government was again assuming the unconstitutional role of evaluating educational quality. The Commissioner sought a way around this dilemma by the so-called three-letter rule (the equivalent of accreditation being conferred by letters to attest that transfer credits were accepted at three accredited institutions). Subsequent legislation also empowered him to make eligibility decisions in consultation with an advisory committee. However, because the higher education community was unhappy with these alternatives, a compromise was found. Through an ironic reversal, the regional associations' candidate status, which had no guarantee of final approval, was accepted by OE as "satisfactory assurance" of eventual accreditation.

The Higher Education Act of 1965 produced the next major change in the role of accreditation and its relations with the federal government. The requirements for eligibility were altered in two important ways. First, because the Great Society programs were aimed at educational opportunity, vocational and technical programs in both community colleges and proprietary institutions were accepted for eligibility. With the accrediting agencies for the proprietary business, correspondence, and technical institutions now on the Commissioner's list, students at accredited proprietary institutions were eligible for guaranteed loans. Moreover, since such benefits were viewed as entitlements, the OE second-phase review was essentially pro forma.

Second, although state authority was necessary in order for educational institutions to operate and offer degrees, no specific state agency approval was required for program eligibility. As a result, a greater burden was placed upon the accrediting bodies, in effect converting them into quasi-public agencies. Under the circumstances, the regional accrediting bodies chose to broaden their membership, including community colleges and vocational schools. However, with the growing importance of the accrediting bodies came increased pressure for new organizations to be included on the Commissioner's list. Finally, in an action that Chambers calls one of those instances "when a critical turning point comes... sharply into focus," the Commissioner's newly reestablished advisory committee identified one of its functions as "safeguarding the *right* of the legitimate accrediting groups to be recognized" (Chambers's emphasis).

Traditionally, accrediting bodies had derived their prestige from service to their membership. In this new statute, national recognition was adopted as a requirement for inclusion on the Commissioner's list. By the end of the 1960s, the dependence of OE on accrediting bodies to determine eligibility had transformed this relationship. If OE was now protecting the rights of the accrediting groups and conferring prestige through the Commissioner's list, then OE could also set the criteria and require application for acceptance on that list. Although the established accrediting groups objected that they were only submitting information, the newly formed groups found it far easier to comply with these regulations than to gain recognition through years of service.

Through their regulations, OE not only subverted the statutory requirement that the listed accrediting bodies be nationally recognized but also assumed the role of NCA in defining the nature and functions of accreditation. In 1974, new OE regulations again exceeded the statute and redefined the responsibilities of accrediting groups to include: fostering ethical practices, protecting the interests of students and society, and involving representatives of the public in decision-making. Although the regional accrediting associations adopted a statement opposing the use of accreditation to enforce federal social policy, the newer accrediting groups that owed their status to OE were either less vocal or compliant. However, when OE in 1976 proposed legislation that would have encoded the social policy regulations of 1974, the newly formed COPA was able to organize the postsecondary community into successful opposition.

COPA's defeat of this proposal in effect confirmed the 1952 statute—that accrediting bodies were responsible for establishing institutional eligibility only on the basis of quality evaluation. Moreover, in 1978 the Commissioner responded to the concerns of the postsecondary community by issuing new OE regulations that held strictly to the statute. During the 1980 reauthorization of the Higher Education Act, in the spirit of the general movement toward deregulation, the Carter administration proposed to remove the accreditation requirement and accept for eligibility any institution with state authorization. Although this proposal was not passed into law, as the trend toward deregulation has continued under the Reagan administration, the relationship between accreditation and the federal government has remained in a state of uncomfortable balance. Nevertheless, given the unequal weight of the two partners, it is not surprising that COPA has recently made a decision to oppose the use of its own recognition process as a prior requirement to federal recognition, preferring to leave accreditation as a persuasive, not a mandating, factor in determining eligibility.

Specialized Accreditation

The second major problem area under consideration, specialized accreditation, clearly overlaps with that of government regulation. The Commissioner's list initially recognized those specialized accrediting groups that NCA hoped to curtail and subsequently expanded its number fivefold, encouraging the proliferation of new groups. The other governmental source of status and prestige for the professions and specialized occupations is state licensure. As in the case of the Commissioner's list, when state laws require an individual candidate for license to graduate from an accredited program or institution, the accrediting organization for that profession becomes a quasi-governmental agency, which may then become involved in the enforcement of government regulations. Moreover, this authority subverts the voluntary nature of accreditation and creates undue leverage for the accrediting agency in its dealings with educational institutions.

An obvious source of tension between specialized accrediting bodies and institutions is the question of whose interests are being served by accreditation. Although institutional accreditation evaluates the educational quality of the institution as a whole, specialized accreditation judges the educational quality of a single program that has the limited objective of preparing practitioners for a profession. By its nature, specialized accreditation is oriented toward the interests of the profession. As a result, institutions object that some specialized accrediting groups attempt to dictate curricula and seek special privilege, interpreting criteria rigidly and focusing on such specifics as faculty salaries, teaching loads, and facilities. Institutions further complain that proliferation multiplies the burden of accreditation in terms of time and money.

Although some educational leaders, especially university presidents, have argued that only institutional accreditation is essential, COPA's *Policy Statement on the Role and Value of Accreditation* reaffirmed the position that specialized accreditation is necessary in order to provide public assurance regarding the educational quality of professional programs. Although this statement suggests an ideal of collaboration between two entities with legitimate concerns about educational quality, the political issue remains unresolved. When there is disagreement, who is the final arbiter of quality—the institution or the profession? Although the new focus upon educational outcomes may eventually provide a common perspective on this issue, some degree of continued tension seems inevitable in light of divergent interests between the two parties and governmental erosion of accreditation as a voluntary system.

The main goal of a professional organization is not just to improve the educational program or institution, but to advance the status of the profession and its practitioners. In achieving this goal, established professional associations often view accreditation as a secondary tool, supplemental to licensing by state agencies and certification by voluntary professional organizations. Only the newer specializations, which are struggling to establish credibility, regard accreditation as a tool of equal importance. Furthermore, institutions often have little choice against inappropriate demands by the accrediting body because the process is no longer truly voluntary. For the health fields and certain other professional areas, federal funding depends upon accreditation. For the health fields, law, engineering, and several other professions, a degree from an accredited program is the route to licensure in numerous states. Under these circumstances, the decision not to seek accreditation means loss of funds, loss of students, and in some cases, perhaps even loss of the program itself.

Because of historical priority, professional eminence, and numerical dominance, medicine and the other health fields provide perhaps the best subject for a more detailed examination of specialized accreditation. According to Robert Glidden's article on specialized accreditation, in *Understanding Accreditation* (1983), the first of such efforts were undertaken to improve the then lamentable condition of medical education. Although twenty-six states had already instituted medical licensure by 1900, the previous efforts of the Association of American Medical Colleges (AAMC) and its predecessor had fallen short of adequate reform. After its reorganization in 1902, the American Medical Association (AMA) took the initiative, first to develop a rating system and subsequently to join with the Carnegie Foundation of New York in an evaluation of the medical, legal, and theological professions. The Flexner Report, as it became known, made a series of recommendations—notably the teaching of basic sciences by full-time faculty and the association of medical schools with universities and teaching hospitals—that resulted in the elimination of almost half of the existing medical schools and influenced the shape of modern medical education in the United States.

The initial process of accrediting medical education set an example followed by many other professions. While state agencies, associations of professional schools, and the professional association all took actions aimed at reform, the professional association became dominant. Although some elements now identified with accreditation were missing (for example, self-study), a pattern of voluntary self-regulation was established. Finally, the reform produced identifiable gains in terms of educational quality, but not without generating tension between the profession and the institutions. However, it is also appropriate to ask who benefited from this new process of self-regulation.

The standard histories (for instance, Richard Shryock's *Medicine in America* and Rosemary Stevens's *American Medicine and the Public Interest*) place the initiation of licensure and accreditation in a larger context—the medical profession's consolidation of its authority over health care during the late nineteenth and early twentieth centuries. In this period, the medical profession not only improved medical education but also eliminated or restricted competing forms of health service (midwives, folk doctors, homeopathic doctors, chiropractors, and osteopaths) and gained the respect of the public. According to the standard explanation, the primary motivation for this change in the profession was desire to improve the quality of medical care, and the necessary means was utilization of advances in modern science and technology. However, a recent study by Paul Starr, *The Social Transformation of American Medicine* (1982), characterizes this transformation of medicine into a powerful self-regulating profession as the story of a special-interest group establishing an economic monopoly.

Considered within this broader context, the higher standards that resulted from the accreditation of medical education can clearly be said to have benefited the public, but the profession benefited no less. Demonstrably, the medical schools and their host institutions also benefited. The argument in favor of specialized accreditation on the basis of social need is most justifiable for medicine and the other health fields, but less so for other professions or occupations not directly involved in public health or safety. However, in any given field, the health fields included, specialized accrediting and state licensing are likely to exist because of political power (or historical accident) as well as systematic assessment of benefits to the public.

An article by Corrine Larson on regulation of the professions, in *Understanding Accreditation* (1983), argues that recent trends (proliferation, geographic mobility, fragmented delivery systems, changing public attitudes, and governmental pressures for accountability) are moving toward a more organized system for regulating professions. Although state licensure has been a vehicle for growth of the professions, some states have recently developed new licensing criteria for a "sunrise" process to evaluate requests in terms of public protection, disciplinary uniqueness, functional overlap, and economic impact. Most states have already developed a "sunset" process to review existing regulations for usefulness and necessity. Both processes are intended to ensure that licensure is less restrictive in terms of educational and employment opportunities, more responsive to consumers, less political, and more rational. Progress has been slower in developing information systems to match comparative levels of competence with specific occupational credentials—systems necessary in order to improve policy regarding both entry into the professions and recertification through continuing education or other means.

Larson projects the implications for accreditation of both sustained and recent trends in terms of three possible scenarios. In one version, current conditions would get worse. Specialized groups would continue to control the licensing process, gain designation as the only acceptable accrediting body in a given area, and use this quasi-governmental authority to impose requirements upon postsecondary institutions. Therefore, accreditation would become less voluntary, and institutions of higher education less autonomous. In a second version, recent trends would cause the professional movement to consume itself, creating an era when all would be professionals, and no profession would have monopolistic control. In a more positive version, recent movements toward reform, including those supported by COPA as discussed below, would provide professions with a role definition based on proficiencies, state licensing boards with a frame of reference in terms of functions, and postsecondary institutions as well as accrediting bodies with a common perspective regarding professional education. However, Larson concludes that, unless some such purposeful linkage is achieved among these competing interests, specialized accreditation will continue to be a source of conflict and divisiveness.

COPA and Reform

During the first eight years since its establishment, COPA set as a major priority to deal with problems regarding federal regulation and specialized accreditation. Increased federal influence over accreditation was an important factor in the formation of COPA and a target for successful opposition organized by COPA, as detailed above. In a recent paper on the accreditation of health profession schools, Richard Millard (1984) has surveyed the ways that COPA has dealt with the problems of proliferation and undue influence in specialized accreditation. Although COPA has endorsed the need for specialized accreditation, it has worked against unnecessary duplication and excessive demands or costs. Nevertheless, COPA functions not as a policeman but as a coordinator within the postsecondary community.

The issue of proliferation is raised by the mere fact that COPA recognizes thirty-seven specialized associations, approximately half in the health fields, including the Committee on Allied Health Education and Accreditation (CAHEA), which coordinates sixteen joint review committees representing various subfields. However, COPA has actually reduced the number from forty to thirty-seven and has discouraged many potential new members. The ability of COPA to control proliferation is obviously limited by the voluntary nature of COPA's recognition process, by other forms of recognition such as state licensing and federal listing, and by the fact that many institutions permit groups not recognized by COPA to evaluate programs. Therefore, COPA has also taken other initiatives: an interagency cooperation policy and guidelines, which encourage accrediting groups to employ joint or phased reviews and institutions to coordinate accrediting activities under a designated liaison officer; and a major project funded by the Ford Foundation to develop a common accreditation data base, which would also be compatible with the Higher Education General Information Survey (HEGIS) and the financial self-study guides of the National Association of College and University Business Officers (NACUBO).

COPA's ability to combat the undue influence of accrediting agencies is also limited. COPA's policies are binding on its member accrediting bodies in only two areas—recognition and coordination. COPA can dismiss those agencies that do not comply with its general standards, such as self-study and site visitation, but it cannot dictate the specific standards of any agency. While rejecting any implication of criticism against all specialized accrediting agencies, COPA is taking corrective measures through its recognition requirements, which specify that an accrediting body "develops and interprets its criteria to allow and encourage institutional freedom and autonomy" and "examines and evaluates institutions and programs in relation to operational goals of the total institution and to educational outcomes." However, COPA's power to ensure reasonable accrediting standards is hortatory rather than statutory and based upon the principle of self-regulation rather than of legal enforcement.

One of the most important results of COPA's recent reorganization was to provide institutions with their own assembly and a role inside COPA, which must now be viewed not just as a trade association for accrediting bodies but as an organization responsible for all of the main interests in the accreditation process. One of the past difficulties in seeking a coordinated approach to accreditation problems has been a lack of involvement on the part of certain major universities. However, the Committee on Institutional Cooperation (the Big Ten universities plus the University of Chicago) has just issued *Accreditation: A Statement of Principles* (1984), which sets out criteria essentially in accord with those of COPA. That document, which asserts that "even the strongest universities have an obligation to do their part to make accreditation work," is a significant statement of institutional commitment.

Conclusion

For more than three decades, the politics of accreditation has centered mainly on the issues surrounding federal regulation and specialized accreditation. In recent years, COPA has played an increasingly effective role in self-regulation by defending the voluntary nature of accreditation against government encroachment and by encouraging cooperation between the institutions and the professions in the specialized accrediting process. These issues also point up the contradictions inherent in COPA as an organization that is expected both to advocate and to monitor the accrediting bodies while protecting the institutions from exploitation. However, these problems must be on the agenda of any organization that would provide national leadership for accreditation. In order to succeed, COPA must have the active support of all the institutional accrediting associations, the major specialized accrediting associations, the most important national associations of postsecondary education, and the most influential colleges and universities.

References

CARNEGIE FOUNDATION FOR THE ADVANCEMENT OF TEACHING. *The Control of the Campus: A Report on the Governance of Higher Education* (Washington, D.C.: Carnegie Foundation, 1982).

CHAMBERS, CHARLES M. "Federal Government and Accreditation." In *Understanding Accreditation: Contemporary Perspectives on Issues and Practices in Evaluating Educational Quality* (San Francisco: Jossey-Bass, 1983).

COMMITTEE ON INSTITUTIONAL COOPERATION. *Accreditation: A Statement of Principles* (Evanston, Ill.: CIC, 1984).

COUNCIL ON POSTSECONDARY ACCREDITATION. *A Policy Statement on the Role and Value of Accreditation* (Washington, D.C.: COPA, 1982).

FLEXNER, A. *Medical Education in the United States and Canada: A Report to the Carnegie Foundation for the Advancement of Teaching.* Bulletin No. 4 (Boston: Updyke, 1910).

FREIDMAN, M. *Capitalism and Freedom* (Chicago: University of Chicago Press, 1962).

GLIDDEN, ROBERT. "Specialized Accreditation." In *Understanding Accreditation: Contemporary Perspectives on Issues and Practices in Evaluating Educational Quality* (San Francisco: Jossey-Bass, 1983).

KAPLIN, W. A. *Respective Roles of Federal Government, State Governments, and Private Accrediting Agencies in the Governance of Postsecondary Education* (Washington, D.C.: COPA, 1975.).

LARSON, CORRINE W. "Trends in the Regulation of Professions." In *Understanding Accreditation: Contemporary Perspectives on Issues and Practices in Evaluating Educational Quality* (San Francisco: Jossey-Bass, 1983).

MILLARD, RICHARD M. "Whither Accreditation in the Health Professions?" *Educational Record* (Fall 1984).

SELDEN, W. K. *Accreditation: A Struggle over Standards in Higher Education* (New York: Harper & Row, 1960).

SHRYOCK, RICHARD. *Medicine in America: Historical Essays* (Baltimore: Johns Hopkins University Press, 1966).

STARR, P. *The Social Transformation of American Medicine* (New York: Basic Books, 1982).

STEVENS, ROSEMARY. *American Medicine and the Public Interest* (New Haven: Yale University Press, 1971).

PART THREE
Self-Regulation and Academic Inquiry

Intercollegiate Athletics

DEREK BOK

"The powerlessness of our educational leaders to originate, and their failure to adopt, effectual measures for evolving order out of the athletic chaos over which they nominally preside, constitutes one of the marvels of our time."
    United States Commissioner of Education, Report for 1897–1898.

"My feeling has been for many years that the university presidents and the faculties of many institutions have just walked down the halls and looked at the ceilings. They didn't want to see anything."
    Joe Paterno, Football Coach, Pennsylvania State, 1981.

IN JANUARY 1983, AFTER DECADES OF INDIFFERENCE AND NEGLECT, more than one hundred university presidents converged on the NCAA convention in San Diego, bent on passing new rules to strengthen academic standards in big-time college sports. Three days later they dispersed, having secured all of their legislative goals. At last, presidents had bestirred themselves to demand real reforms in intercollegiate athletics. Why did they finally intervene? What did they accomplish? And what remains to be done in order to reconcile athletics with the proper aims of educational institutions?

These questions would be incomprehensible to educators in any other country of the world. Only rarely do universities abroad offer more than modest recreational programs for their students, let alone reap revenue and glory from the exploits of their athletic teams. But America is different. Its universities are unique in their efforts to please many constituencies—prospective students, donors, legislators, the general public. Each of these constituencies contains many ardent sports enthusiasts. As a result, when universities started to grow rapidly a century ago, they soon began to cater to these interests by fielding teams and playing each other in front of large public audiences, first in football and then in other sports as well.

The growth of intercollegiate sports aptly illustrates the strengths and weaknesses of a constituency-oriented system of higher education. With enthusiastic support from students, alumni, and even government officials, our colleges have developed athletic programs that have brought great satisfaction to thousands of athletes and millions of spectators. Few aspects of college life have done so much to win the favor of the public, build the loyalties of alumni, and engender lasting memories in the minds of student-athletes. And yet, the very success of intercollegiate athletics and the passionate enthusiasms they arouse create a constant tendency toward excess, pushing the search for winning teams to extremes that threaten to harm the lives of student-athletes and compromise the integrity of universities as serious educational institutions. And so it is that university presidents find themselves in the strange position of having to regard athletics as a serious ethical challenge.

The Long Parade of Problems

The earliest crisis in intercollegiate sports was a crisis of violence. From the minds of inventive coaches came the flying wedge and a succession of other ideas for winning football games. The equipment worn by players at the turn of the century was no match for these techniques, and serious injuries multiplied. In 1905 alone, eighteen students died of injuries, and 149 others were badly hurt. President Roosevelt himself called upon university presidents to stop the bloodshed and threatened to have the government intervene if they failed to act. The result was the formation of a new association —which eventually became the National Collegiate Athletic Association (NCAA)—to formulate rules that would minimize injuries.

After determined efforts, the injuries and deaths diminished. Nevertheless, as crowds grew larger and intercollegiate rivalries increased, a more intractable problem arose in the form of clandestine efforts to recruit able athletes who could ensure a winning season. Recruiting had already begun in the 1880s. By the turn of the century, one heard complaints about the "tramp athlete," a skillful player who moved from one college to the next without actually enrolling as a student. Collective action eventually put an end to these roving mercenaries. But evidence repeatedly came to light of questionable methods of recruiting talented athletes and rewarding them with easy jobs and other favors. Unlike the tramp athlete, illegal recruiting did not quickly disappear.

If the NCAA has failed to stop illegal recruiting, it is not for lack of trying. No problem has more consistently engaged the organization over the years or evoked a wider variety of remedies. Fantastically elaborate rules have evolved to regulate recruiting by coaches and alumni. Various penalties have been devised—from monetary fines to bans on TV appearances. The NCAA has even hired secret investigators to question high school stars for evidence of irregularities. At times, certain forms of improper behavior have been exorcised by the simple expedient of declaring them legal—as the NCAA did, first by allowing recruiting itself and then by legitimating athletic scholarships in the early 1950s.

Yet recruiting violations still go on. A study in the early 1970s by a committee of coaches concluded that "only" 12 percent of the member schools cheat—and many consider that figure an understatement. A 1974 investigation by the American Council on Education revealed a wide variety of transgressions ranging from altering high school transcripts and admissions test scores to offering prospective students private apartments, automobiles, and payments for nonexistent jobs. In 1983, the basketball coach at Notre Dame openly charged that the going rate for basketball stars was $10,000 per year, with much more allegedly given to outstanding halfbacks and quarterbacks. By 1984, the executive director of the NCAA was declaring publicly that the situation was virtually out of control.

Bad as they are, recruiting violations rarely infect the basic educational functions of the university. In recent years, however, media attention has begun to concentrate on a new problem. Articles have appeared describing the admission of academically unqualified athletes who are kept eligible by one trick or another until their eligibility runs out, whereupon they leave without ever graduating. Sportswriters have seized on one lurid episode after another to dramatize the problem. A football player from UCLA was criminally charged and sentenced to take remedial classes when the judge discovered that he could not read. After a basketball star was expelled from the University of Minnesota for failing grades, a court reinstated him on the grounds that he had been recuited with the implicit understanding that he would be coming to play and not to study. Seven former students at a California state college settled out of court after suing on the ground that the school's basketball program had kept them from studying or receiving a degree and thus had harmed their employment prospects.

Although such cases were doubtless not unprecedented, several developments in the 1970s made them much more common. For some years, NCAA rules had prohibited member schools from admitting athletes whose academic grades and test scores made it unlikely that they could pass their courses. In 1973, however, this rule was abrogated, ostensibly because of pressure to admit disadvantaged students but also to ease the way to recruit more outstanding players. Thereafter, recruited athletes simply had to have a 2.0 high school grade average without regard to the nature of the courses taken. Only 5 percent of all students interested in attending college fail to meet that test.

In the ensuing years, large numbers of athletes enrolled in universities without being able to meet the normal admissions standards. Thus, a report from the University of

Southern California revealed that 330 athletes were admitted as special cases during the 1970s without the participation of the Admissions Office. Most universities with "big-time" programs had negotiated similar dispensations to allow them to enroll substantial numbers of unqualified student-players every year.

Once having accepted these marginal students, member schools seemed to feel little or no obligation to assist them with the formidable task of completing their education. Until 1982, the NCAA rules merely required a student-athlete to "enroll" in twenty-four units each year; nothing was said about actually going to class, let alone taking exams or receiving a passing grade. In these circumstances, many coaches discouraged their charges from allowing course work to interfere with the athletic program. Athletes were encouraged to take the easiest courses.[1] Worse yet, many of the students admitted as exceptions had little chance of passing even if they had been given every encouragement to try. Thus, of the 330 marginal student-athletes admitted by the University of Southern California in the 1970s, only 12 percent managed to graduate. According to the *Chicago Sun Times*, in 1984 not a single member of the vaunted University of Houston basketball teams had received a diploma since 1969. Entire conferences, such as the Big Ten and Southwest, were reported to have graduated fewer than one-third of their senior basketball players in 1982, and many more who entered as basketball recruits presumably dropped out before their senior year.

Despite these revelations, those who support the status quo sometimes dismiss such reports as isolated examples that should not be used to discredit current practices as a whole. Such apologists often point to an NCAA study of forty-six colleges suggesting that athletes as a whole graduate at a rate significantly higher than nonathletes while even football and basketball players graduate at approximately the same rates as nonathletes. Such claims must be interpreted with a liberal dose of salt. For one thing, such surveys normally include only those colleges that agree to participate. Thus, the results are not necessarily representative of truly "big-time" schools, where separate admissions practices for athletes are common and the competitive pressures are most intense. Another point to bear in mind is that athletes have various advantages that should make it easier for them to graduate. For one thing, the reason most cited for leaving college is financial need, a problem that rarely afflicts athletes since they almost always receive a grant to cover all or most of their expenses. For another, players in many big-time athletic schools tend to choose easy majors (such as physical education) to a much greater extent than nonathletes. Finally, 20 to 30 percent of all students graduate from colleges other than those in which they were originally enrolled. Athletes, on the other hand, rarely transfer to other colleges because they lose at least a year of eligibility and may lose their athletic scholarship as well. As a result, studies of graduation rates from individual colleges substantially understate the rates at which nonathletes actually receive a college degree. All things considered, then, it is likely that big-time athletics actually makes deep inroads on the graduation rates of participants.

The President's Predicament

In the face of such problems most presidents have reacted with remarkable indifference. Few have troubled to investigate the extent of the problem on their own campus by asking to review the graduation rates of athletes in major sports or to examine the admissions folders of freshman football and basketball recruits. Such neglect seems hard to comprehend. What could be more offensive to the ideals of an educational institution than to admit substantial numbers of unqualified students every year, pay them to subject themselves to an athletic schedule that often reaches thirty-five and forty hours a week, and then abandon them without a degree or any serious preparation for a career after their eligibility expires?[2]

Some presidents may have been ignorant of the extent of these problems on their own campus. But ignorance is often selective, responding to deeper imperatives that turn the conscious mind away from dilemmas that seem unpleasant or impossible to resolve. In big-time athletics, the imperatives are not hard to find.

To begin with, athletics matter—sometimes passionately so—to important members of constituencies vital to the welfare of a university. Many presidents say that their "athletics mail" exceeds their correspondence on any other subject. Students, alumni, legislators, important donors all include strong sports enthusiasts. In some institutions, the pressures are so intense as to leave a president little choice. The late Bear Bryant, for example, once observed: "The only president who's ever been fired at Alabama was against football. Any new president cuts his teeth on it, and he better be for it. Because if he's not, they won't win, and if they don't win, he'll get fired."

Universities that fit this description may be in a minority. In other institutions, however, the pressures are less obvious but still effective. No one can prove that losing teams or battles with coaches will lead to lower alumni donations, student disaffection, or diminished appropriations from the state. But few presidents are anxious to put the matter to a test by launching a crusade to expose and eliminate athletic abuses.

These inhibitions are reinforced by a nagging realization on the president's part that his powers to remedy the situation are limited. Recruiting abuses and illegal payments to athletes are clandestine and hard for a president to uncover, especially if he has few allies to help him carry out the search. Worse yet, athletics are competitive, and it is hard for any school to deemphasize recruiting and tighten admissions and eligibility standards without putting itself at an intolerable disadvantage against its conference opponents and traditional foes. As one president put it, "Cutting back on an institution's level of commitment is about as feasible as world disarmament. One doesn't do it alone unless one is willing to accept the consequences—in athletics, probably a lower level of competition or abolishment of programs altogether."

Occasionally, a single institution has the determination to take bold steps. Robert Maynard Hutchins buried a famous football program at the University of Chicago. The Catholic fathers in charge of the University of San Francisco terminated a successful basketball program after they found it impossible to control recruiting abuses. Understandably, however, these cases are the rare exception.

The Possibilities for Reform

Regardless of the difficulties facing the president, athletic abuses remain an ugly blot on the record of scores of well-known colleges and universities. All the evidence, moreover, suggests that the prevalence and seriousness of these abuses have steadily increased over the past several decades. As a result, it is important to examine what university presidents can accomplish, individually and collectively, to limit the corruption without intolerable sacrifice to themselves or their institutions.

If most presidents are constrained in their athletic policies, none is truly helpless. Yet the variations in presidential discretion are immense. Many Division I schools have modest admissions standards for their regular student bodies, and are happily free of severe pressures to dominate athletically every year.[3] For such institutions, it is possible to recruit adequate teams without making huge concessions in admissions policies or admitting students who cannot hope to graduate. At the other end of the spectrum, a very few selective schools, such as Notre Dame or Duke or Stanford, have sufficient attractions for athletes that they can escape recruiting scandals, avoid gross compromises in their admissions standards, and achieve graduation rates for their players that equal the high rates for their student bodies as a whole. Nevertheless, surprisingly few selective schools can aspire to such achievements, and still compete in the big time; there are simply not enough genuine scholar-athletes to go around.

Most Division IA schools, therefore, find themselves occupying an awkward intermediate positon. They do have admissions standards of at least moderate rigor. But their drawing power is not sufficient to stock their teams with highly talented players who meet—or even nearly meet—their regular requirements. For these institutions, the practical choices have been either to wink at drastic concessions to the normal entrance requirements or to move out of the big time.

In any institution, however, a president can take at least some important steps toward a more defensible athletic program. Responsible chief executives can begin by educating themselves and their boards of trustees about the facts of the athletic program. What are the high school records and national test scores of athletes in the major sports? What academic programs do they take? How do their graduation rates compare with those of the student body as a whole? What special measures are taken to help them succeed academically? Painful though the revelations may be in some cases, they are the essential prerequisite for progress. Athletic abuses breed on inattention and on the vast temptation to persuade oneself that big-time athletics and sound academic standards can somehow be reconciled. Unless the president and the board confront the true facts, there is scant hope that they will use whatever discretion they have to keep some semblance of standards and avoid the shameless exploitation of athletes.

The second step for presidents to take is to communicate personally with coaches and alumni that violations of the rules will not be tolerated, that strict penalties will ensue, and that effective procedures will be instituted to investigate complaints of wrongdoing. These measures, at least, are feasible in virtually any institution, for only rarely will coaches or alumni leaders dare to disagree with a policy of adhering to the prevailing rules.

A third step is to review the instructions and the expectations communicated to coaches and the athletic department in order to remove intolerable pressures to cheat or undermine academic standards. It will hardly do for a president to proclaim high standards while his subordinates press the athletic director to increase ticket sales and television revenues. Nor will it help to rail against recruitment violations if coaches believe that their jobs depend on winning almost all of their games. These petty hypocrisies and inconsistencies thrive on presidential indifference. Progress toward decency can never come unless a chief executive takes the time to learn the facts, talk with the coaches, and sit down with the athletic director to develop a clear and realistic set of expectations within which coaches and other athletic officials can function. Only then can a president hope to do an adequate job of lifting academic standards to the highest point permitted by the practical constraints that bear upon the institution.

A fourth step is to place the athletic program under real academic supervision. Most universities do have faculty representatives and athletic committees composed of professors. Through presidential neglect, however, many institutions have allowed these assignments to become the preserve of sports enthusiasts who either willingly cooperate with prevailing practices or are easily duped by the athletic department. To remedy this situation, a president might begin by asking a provost, dean, or a trusted respresentative to chair the athletics committee and report regularly about its work. Faculty representatives should be rotated periodically and should be supervised by appropriate academic authorities. The admission of athletes, including all waivers of the rules and special cases, should be clearly under academic control, preferably by the regular admissions office, instead of remaining in the hands of the athletic department. Coaches should be paid by the university and not, directly or indirectly, by alumni. Finally, the athletics committee or some suitable academic authority should be charged with developing and administering a suitable program for advising and tutoring athletes who need help to continue making satisfactory progress toward a degree.

The fifth and last step should be for the president to develop academic goals for the athletic department and then take steps to monitor progress personally until the stated objectives are achieved. In the last analysis, only the president can decide how far admissions standards for athletes can be raised or what graduation rates seem attainable without exceeding the practical constraints on the institution. And ultimately, the president must communicate goals to the athletic department and the admissions offices—and personally keep watch on the progress achieved—in order to give these objectives the authority they need to stand up against the constant pressure to relax the rules in the interest of winning games.

Although these measures can produce appreciable progress on the vast majority of campuses, we have seen that there are practical constraints that limit the extent to which most institutions can exceed their athletic competitors in lifting academic standards. For most institutions, therefore, major reform will require a collective effort, both at the level of the athletic conference and within the NCAA.

If all the presidents of a conference would agree to reform their athletic programs, much could be accomplished. The presidents might decide that recruited athletes should meet reasonable admissions standards (for example, that members of each team should achieve median high school grades and test scores no more than one standard deviation below the median for the student body as a whole). Schedules could be limited to restrict the length of season and avoid excessive travel during term time. Presidents could agree to cap recruiting budgets or even reduce them. Conceivably, athletic scholarships could even be eliminated or limited to simple tuition grants.

Such reforms would quickly create an environment in which athletic abuses could be minimized. Graduation rates for athletes would rise dramatically. Conflicts between athletics and academic work would diminish. Even recruiting might grow less intense, though opportunities would still exist for secret payments, summer jobs, and even forged transcripts.

For a number of conferences, such measures seem feasible. The Ivy League took this route many years ago. In recent years, it has encouraged other schools to follow suit in football and hockey so that most of its games outside the League can now be played against schools with a similar philosophy. For these institutions, such a path offers a way to overcome the worst aspects of high-pressure athletics while preserving traditional rivalries and a vigorous level of competition.

Despite these advantages, many schools will find this approach impractical. In some conferences, academic differences between members are so great that it is hard to find much room for agreement on minimum admissions standards. Obviously, it is hard to fashion a rule requiring minimum high school grades and test scores that will set a meaningful standard and still prove equitable in a conference—such as the PAC-10 or the Southwest Conference—where average College Board scores vary by more than 400 points between the academically strongest and weakest members. Limitations on recruiting may be hard to achieve where some members have strong national alumni networks that help them attract students while other members lack such assistance. Strong local rivalries that matter to alumni may also inhibit some of the members from reaching conference agreements if the neighboring opponents do not belong to the conference or play by its rules.

The strongest impediment to effective conference agreements, however, is undoubtedly rooted in a reluctance to give up the attractions of big-time, national athletics. Many writers place the blame on television, and TV revenues have undoubtedly fattened the rewards of athletic prominence. But other temptations are almost as great. Some presidents believe that athletic success can raise a school's visibility and attract more student applicants. Others are convinced that donors feel more warmth toward their alma mater when her teams attract national attention. Still others look at attendance figures for Ivy League games and conclude that the financial costs are simply too great, even apart from losing TV contracts. Whatever the reason, only two or three presidents in a conference need decide not to cooperate in order to destroy any hope of agreement.

For these reasons, widespread reform is unlikely to come without an effort by the NCAA to establish minimum standards for all. As a vehicle for reform, however, the NCAA is something of a mixed bag. Its obvious strength resides in the comprehensiveness of its membership and its experience in dealing with the peculiar problems of athletics. Its weaknesses are no less apparent. Because it is all inclusive, it numbers schools of such contrasting philosophies and circumstances that agreement on common standards is often difficult. For obvious reasons, its annual conventions (where the rules are made) are dominated by athletic directors and faculty representatives—sports enthusiasts all. As a result, though Article 2 of the NCAA Constitution states that a "basic purpose of this Association is to maintain intercollegiate athletics as an integral part of the educational program and the athlete as an integral part of the student body," the organization has paid scant attention to this goal while athletes and athletic programs have drifted ever further from the ideal. Finally, the permanent staff exercises considerable authority and, like all bureaucracies, has a keen eye for maintaining its power. For the NCAA, this entails being responsive to the wishes of the athletic officials who populate the conventions and committees along with a constant effort to preserve the television revenues from which the organization derives the bulk of its financing.

The Presidents and the NCAA

How to bring about significant academic reform through such an institution? This was the question that confronted a group of Division I presidents who hastily convened in 1982 after a flurry of embarrassing media exposés. In the course of several meetings, the presidents decided on a short-term strategy containing both a substantive and a procedural component.

The substantive initiatives came first and included two proposals. The first sought to bar from varsity competition all freshmen who entered college with less than a 700 composite score on the College Board exams (SATs) or with a high school grade average below 2.0 in a program that numbered at least eleven academic courses, including three years of English, two years of math, two years of science, and two years of history and/or social science.[4] The intent of this proposal was to identify academically marginal students and to insist that they have an initial year in which to establish themselves academically before undergoing the pressures and distractions of varsity competition. The second substantive proposal was to require all athletes, as a condition of eligibility, to have successfully completed in the preceding year twenty-four units of course work leading toward a recognized academic degree. The point of this proposal was to increase graduation rates by requiring athletes to make steady academic progress toward a degree in order to remain eligible.

The committee of presidents put these initiatives before the 1983 NCAA Convention and met a surprisingly warm reception. Coaches and athletic directors were sensitive to media stories of deplorable lapses in academic standards. They welcomed an effort by the academic leaders of their institutions to take responsibility—especially through proposed rules that seemed to treat the member schools equitably. Amid this general support, the proposals passed overwhelmingly.

Only one small group of institutions protested the initiatives—and protested vehemently. The historically black colleges saw in the new eligibility rules an effort to impose standards that would fall with disproportionate weight on the black athlete. Blacks have traditionally scored less well on standardized tests than whites. For the SATs, it quickly came to light that slightly more than 50 percent of all blacks (but only 14 percent of whites) were achieving less than the 700 score required by the new rule. To Joseph B. Johnson, president of Grambling State University, "a message has been sent to black athletes across this country. There's just too many of you on America's athletic teams." Added Benjamin Hooks of the NAACP, "The latest attack by an institution—the NCAA—to penalize the victims of years of deprivation and discrimination in the segregated school system, through the untrammeled use of testing instruments with inherent cultural biases, is another example of blaming the victim for the crime."

In retrospect, these criticisms seem overstated. Despite much talk of the new rules "excluding" blacks, the rules in fact did not bar their admission—or even curtail their four years of athletic participation—but simply prevented them from beginning their varsity competition before they had spent a year studying at the university. Far from victimizing them, the new rules sought to protect blacks with marginal academic records by giving them a chance to establish themselves academically before being subjected to the thirty-five or forty hours per week required of many varsity teams. Since 70 percent or more of black athletes were failing ever to graduate from college, according to sociologist Harry Edwards, some such protection seemed clearly in order.

Yet black leaders also objected that the freshman eligibility rule simply penalized the student without fixing responsibility on the university to intensify efforts to educate its players and cease exploiting them to achieve athletic prestige. Such criticisms overlooked the companion rule intitiated by the presidents which required each athlete to complete twenty-four units each year toward a recognized degree in order to remain eligible. This rule completely reoriented the incentives for athletes and universities alike. Before 1982, coaches had little reason to care whether athletes ever graduated or successfully completed course work toward a degree. Now, the athletic department could not keep its players eligible unless they managed each year to make significant academic progress. Indeed, no athlete could complete the four years of eligibility without fulfilling most of the work required to graduate. Of course, players could still enroll in the easiest majors. But most universities would be reluctant to dilute entire degree programs simply to serve their athletic interests. Hence, the new rule, if not perfect, still went a long way to engage the university in caring about the academic progress of its athletes in order to secure its athletic aims.

A more telling explanation for the opposition of black leaders was expressed by Harry Edwards, perhaps the leading black writer on athletic issues. In his words, "The core issue in the Rule 48 controversy is not racist academic standards or alleged efforts by whites to resegregate major college sports, so much as parity between black and white institutions in the collegiate athletic arms race." What Edwards meant was this. For most universities, students with less than a combined score of 700 on their college boards would definitely be marginal cases academically. In the historically black institutions, however, and in a number of predominantly white colleges as well, the median score for all students hovered around 700. As a result, many more freshman athletes would be initially ineligible at these institutions than at most other colleges.

For a variety of reasons, it is far from clear that even this result would ultimately damage black colleges athletically. Even so, Edwards's point served to uncover a definite weakness in the new standard. At most universities, the rule managed to identify marginal athletes who would run grave academic risks by plunging immediately into a big-time varsity program. Nevertheless, such students could hardly be deemed "marginal" if they enrolled in colleges where a majority of the student body entered with records that were similar or even less promising. Black college presidents could also make a strong case that their institutions were remarkably successful in motivating and graduating a high percentage of their students despite their lack of initial qualifications. Some adjustment, therefore, seemed clearly justified for such schools, and efforts were soon underway to develop a suitable compromise. All in all, however, the new rules undoubtedly marked a great step forward in protecting vulnerable student-athletes while encouraging players and school authorities to pay closer attention to academics instead of slighting their classwork to succeed on the playing field.

Having gained these substantive advances, the university chief executives turned to procedural reforms. Recognizing that the corrosive pressures of big-time sports are constantly in operation, they sought to create a permanent place in the NCAA structure for presidents to influence rules and policies governing athletics. Achieving this goal was not a simple matter. NCAA officials, as well as coaches, were quick to point out that university presidents could play a decisive role by simply exercising their prerogative to come to conventions as the official representatives of their institutions. But this possibility was illusory. Beset by many other demands on their time, individual presidents had no reason to attend conventions. They could not know if enough of their colleagues were coming to make a difference. They would have to sit through hours of debate on matters of no practical concern to them. As individuals, their voices would be lost in the sea of other delegates. Some other mechanism was required to secure their participation.

By far the best alternative was to create a representative body composed of presidents elected for limited terms. No chief executive could devote several days a year every year to athletic problems. But most presidents would agree to serve for a few years as the elected representative of their fellows in a body that could deliberate and propose reforms.

Accordingly, the concept of an elected presidents' committee was endorsed, not only by the ad hoc group of presidents but also by a select committee commissioned by the NCAA to study athletic abuses and, ultimately, by the NCAA itself. A controversy then ensued over the powers that such a body would wield. The ad hoc group took the view that a committee of presidents should be able to enact binding rules on policy matters affecting the academic standards, financial stability, or integrity of the university, subject to being overruled only by a mail-ballot vote of all the member presidents. The NCAA predictably shrank from awarding such powers to an untried body and opted instead for making the committee advisory to the convention. Eventually, the NCAA won support from a majority of the convention delegates. But the delegates did adopt a proposal put forward by the presidents to ensure that the committee members would be selected independently by member presidents without risk of control by the NCAA officialdom. The net result was that the presidents gained a permanent voice in the official counsels of the organization. Although the voice would be advisory only, one could predict that proposals on academic issues by an officially elected group of presidents would carry great weight with the convention delegates and that the member presidents would quickly demand a stronger voice if the committee's recommendations on important issues were disregarded.

A Future Agenda

Armed with this influence, the presidents now need to decide how to use it to best advantage. The issue is difficult. Although many initiatives are possible, few of them hold real promise while many are likely to prove unproductive, divisive, and even destructive for the authority of the commission. At this early point, one can only sketch some of the steps the new commission is likely to take, and add a few words of caution about some other possibilities that are temptingly attractive but probably unwise, at least at the onset.

As a practical matter, it is quite possible that the Commission's most important role will not be to propose new reforms but to protect existing standards from being undermined. Already, critics of Proposition 48 are beginning to gather their forces to back amendments that would severely weaken the new rule. As the impact of the regulations becomes more evident, the opponents are likely to grow in strength, using the concerns of the black colleges to clothe their arguments in the garb of civil rights. It will take a strong, articulate commission simply to cope with these attacks and resist any reforms that do not truly serve the educational needs of athletes and the academic standards of the member institutions.

If the Commission can successfully ward off further assaults on academic standards—and that is a big "if"—its most urgent new initiative should be to perfect Propositions 48 and 56, since, properly implemented, these rules will accomplish more than anything else the NCAA can do to help counter the academic exploitation of athletes. To begin with, the commission should encourage the negotiations currently under way with the historically black colleges to amend the rule on freshman eligibility so that it will respect the special circumstances of these schools and the few others like them. In addition, the commission should propose more effective rules to enforce the academic progress requirement, recognizing that this rule can accomplish more than any other NCAA initiative to increase the graduation rates of athletes and to interest players and athletic officials alike in the educational advancement of the student-athlete. At present, the NCAA is empowered only to investigate on a complaint from another school, and few schools are likely to know how well opposing players are faring in the classroom. A far more effective solution would be to empower the NCAA to conduct audits on a spot-check basis to ensure compliance. Only a few such audits each year, backed by the threat of publicity and proper sanctions, should suffice to induce the vast majority of schools to abide by the rules.

As a final step, the commission will undoubtedly wish to work informally to encourage the NCAA staff to publicize the new rules among colleges and high schools. Aside from requiring minimum grades and board scores, the new freshman eligibility rules require every student athlete to take at least eleven academic courses, including three years of English and two of math, science, and social science. In addition to helping student-athletes prepare for college work, these requirements could do a great deal to bolster high schools in strengthening their programs and reducing the number of insubstantial electives that have proliferated so widely in recent years. None of these benefits will be fully achieved unless the NCAA makes sure that the rules are well known throughout the high schools of the country.

These steps should do much to diminish exploitation and increase the graduation rates of athletes. But if such progress does not occur, other measures will be worth considering, Through formal or informal means, the commission can publicize the graduation rates of athletes from member schools and thus bring pressure to bear upon the least successful schools. With sufficient ingenuity, schemes could be developed to take away athletic scholarships from schools in which the graduation rates of athletes fall below predetermined norms. Presidents could also back measures to require delinquent schools to offer a fifth-year athletic scholarship to help their players continue in school after their eligibility expires. Through measures such as these, the NCAA could put increasing pressure on its members to attend successfully to the education of athletes.[5]

In addition to these steps to encourage academic progress, the commission has indicated interest in limiting the number of contests and the length of the season for more sports. This interest is well taken. Pressure constantly arises to lengthen schedules, add games, and expand postseason tournaments and playoffs. Already, the baseball season of many colleges exceeds eighty games, while ice hockey and tennis include thirty or more contests, and basketball is close behind at twenty-eight. Now that big-time programs can consume thirty-five and forty-five hours a week, the length of season has an obvious significance to a school's academic program. Players will have fewer weeks to prepare for exams. In addition, as playing seasons spread beyond a single semester, athletes are likely to respond by scheduling easy academic programs throughout the entire academic year, with further damage to the quality of their education.

Tournaments and playoffs, both national and for individual conferences, add substantially to the season and are so absorbing as to leave most participants with little power to concentrate on classwork. In addition, they greatly augment the temptations and rewards of national athletic prominence and thus make it harder for conferences to agree on stringent measures that would safeguard academic standards but might put the conference members at a disadvantage nationally. Unfortunately, the playoff process has proceeded so far—with even the NCAA itself dependent on TV revenues from the basketball championships—that there is little prospect for improvement. But the commission can at least be alert to the dangers involved and keep the present situation from growing worse.

Several other tempting possibilities come to mind for the commission that may prove questionable on closer analysis. Pressures will surely arise, for example, to have the presidents enter the controversy over the use of television revenues. This issue has come to be highly controversial. By and large, the NCAA has acted as a moderating influence to spread television revenues more widely by preventing a few teams from dominating the airwaves. The NCAA has also sought to limit the number of televised contests in order to minimize the risk of taking audiences away from contests at smaller schools and thereby jeopardizing the financial viability of their programs.

Recently, the larger schools have begun to rebel at such treatment, and the NCAA program for televising football games has been struck down as unconstitutional by the Supreme Court. Apart from its legality, the program was also vulnerable to increasing competition from cable television. Major changes, therefore, are clearly in the offing. In an ideal world, one can readily discern certain TV policies that could help to moderate the excesses of big-time athletics. Television revenues could be spread as widely as possible to minimize the temptations to win at all cost, as by resorting to shady recruiting practices and the admission of academically underqualified student-athletes. Or a large portion of the revenues could be earmarked for some academically worthy purpose, such as financing a fifth-year academic scholarship for all student-athletes who have successfully completed more than two-thirds of their classroom requirements for a degree.

If the occasion ever arises, such proposals might be advanced on a trial basis to see if they can muster wide support. Failing such approval, however, the commission would be well advised to stay clear of the television controversy. If the major athletic powers cannot agree to share revenues widely or direct them to some worthy academic purpose, the dispute will simply degenerate into a contest over dividing up the spoils. Such battles have little to offer to the worthier goals of higher education, and the commission would be wise to avoid getting caught up in the conflict.

Another danger zone involves the continuing struggle over the proper organization of the NCAA into divisions. Originally, divisions were designed to group institutions according to the intensity of their athletic programs. More recently, the nature of these groupings has provoked acrimonious controversy as divisional status came to determine access to larger and larger television revenues. In theory, at least, divisional structures based on academic criteria could help to bring about athletic reform, since it would be easier to agree on common standards if the group making the rules were more homogeneous scholastically. But this possibility seems fanciful as a practical matter. The roster of established athletic powers is studded with schools that are academically weak along with those that are very strong. At this late date, it is hard to imagine what could persuade these institutions to divide themselves along academic lines. Thus, disputes over divisional groupings are bound to turn on money and prestige rather than standards. As such, the controversies are likely to be acrimonious and divisive, and the commission will need to take care to avoid being embroiled in such disputes, at least until its status and prestige are firmly established.

A final area for intervention is the familiar brier patch of recruiting abuses. Unlike academic standards, recruiting is hardly a subject that has suffered from neglect. Indeed, the rules have become so intricate that only experts can master them, and the subject is scarcely one in which the presidents are particularly knowledgeable. As a result, if chief executives choose to intervene, they run a grave risk of simply adding further complexity to an already overregulated subject. In these circumstances, the commission would do better to conserve its energy for more promising issues unless abuses begin to occur for which obvious remedies are available and the NCAA consistently refuses to act.

Conclusion

Recent events have brought university presidents to their best position in a quarter century to strengthen academic standards even in the most prominent athletic schools. Whether the presidents capitalize on this opportunity remains to be seen. Perhaps the greatest danger lies not in failing to make good use of the new commission but in looking to the NCAA to accomplish too much.

In reality, the NCAA is too vast and includes too varied a membership to do more than set minimum standards—and these at a modest level. One of the least appreciated virtues of such standards is that they make it possible for individual conferences to go further without excessive sacrifice to their athletic ambitions. Thus, once the NCAA's new rules on freshman eligibility become operative, conferences could begin to consider whether they might adopt their own rules embodying a somewhat more rigorous and realistic definition of the marginal student-athlete. Once rules on academic progress are in place, conferences could start to think about schemes to publicize the graduation rates of their athletes, or to take away athletic scholarships from schools with rates below some predetermined norm, or to share television revenues to finance fifth-year scholarships for athletes who are close to graduation.

Similarly, effective rules at the NCAA and conference level should ease the way for individual presidents to make efforts to strengthen academic standards on their own campuses without threatening to place their institutions at an intolerable competitive disadvantage. Thus, NCAA reforms do not provide a valid reason for presidents to relax and wait for their representatives on the commission to "handle the problem." On the contrary, the NCAA initiatives help to remove a common rationalization for doing nothing. Presidents need to ponder this fact carefully, or in the end the athletic problem is a moral problem in which they are the most prominent moral agents. In the name of money, visibility, popularity, and other shabby gains, many well-known universities have compromised their admissions policies, cheapened their curricula, and, worst of all, sacrificed hundreds of young people on the altar of athletic success, leaving them with no degree and little preparation for productive careers. Until now, many presidents could argue, with understandable conviction, that there was little they could actually do to remedy matters. In the future, that excuse will be much less convincing, and the ethical challenge many university leaders face will suddenly become immediate and real.

Notes

1. *Sports Illustrated* reports that Bernard Madison, a basketball player at Montana State, was enrolled in a program that included courses entitled Basketball Fundamentals and Techniques, Basketball Philosophy,

Physical Conditioning, Wrestling Theory, General Biology (health), and Safety with Hand Power Tools. John Underwood, "The Writing Is on the Wall," *Sports Illustrated* (May 19, 1980), p. 43.

2. A colorful example of a distressingly common practice is the following description by a basketball recruit of the well-known Jerry Tarkanian when he coached at California State, Long Beach. "How can you be a *student*-athlete if during the month of December you're on the road 25 days out of 31? Since I couldn't go to my classes, my professors didn't know who I was. I was a phantom. The athletic department filled out my forms. I had no choices as to what courses I was taking. The big brainwash was that Tark said, 'We're third in the country. We're going to beat UCLA.'" *People Magazine* (March 12, 1984), p. 97.

3. At present, approximately 57 percent of all public colleges and 42 percent of all private colleges have virtually no minimum requirements for admission.

4. A 700 test score represents a modest way of defining the marginal student at most institutions. For example, in one study of 2,000 athletes over a ten-year period at Oklahoma State University, researchers found that only 18 percent of those with scores below 700 ever graduated [Purdy, Eitzen, and Hufnagel, *Social Problems* (29, 1982), p. 439]. Nationwide, only approximately 17 percent of all those taking the College Board exams score less than 700.

5. One measure that is probably not worth pursuing is to declare all freshmen ineligible for varsity athletics. While this rule would have the virtue of equal application, most studies fail to show a convincing correlation between grades and athletic participation among college freshmen as a whole. As a result, it has been hard to mount a convincing argument for forcing all freshmen to give up intercollegiate athletics or for requiring colleges to undertake the added expense of providing freshman teams.

The Nature and Integrity of the Undergraduate Degree

JERRY W. MILLER

CREDENTIALS—DEGREES, CERTIFICATES, AND DIPLOMAS —awarded by colleges, universities, and other postsecondary institutions are the symbols used to capitalize the value of education beyond the high school. Whether the postsecondary education enterprise retains its prominent role in society and continues to thrive depends on maintaining the confidence of those who use the capital it produces.

There are disturbing signs that segments of society are losing faith in college and university credentials as certifying basic relevant academic skills. Complaints are being heard with increasing frequency that college graduates lack skills historically associated with the award of baccalaureate and associate degrees. As a result, formal processes external to insitutions are beginning to be established to check the integrity of undergraduate credentials awarded by accredited institutions.

In addition, the controversy—now spanning more than half a century—regarding the proliferation and requirements of specialized accrediting agencies continues to simmer. Continually at issue is whether all accreditation requirements are inherent in quality education or whether at least some of them serve the interests of the profession and faculty more than they do the commonweal. Top-level academic administrators continue to question the cost-effectiveness of much of specialized accreditation and whether it is needed in many fields.

There is ample evidence that postsecondary institutions and the nongovernmental self-regulatory processes that serve them need to tone up credentialing standards and processes. This chapter will review some of the traditions, meaning, and uses of academic credentials, while exploring these problems about the integrity of undergraduate credentials. It will conclude with some suggestions for action by institutions and the self-regulatory and service agencies that have historically attended to standards of quality and related issues.

Awarding of Credentials: Traditions, Processes, and Purposes

A brief review of the institutional and academic values and processes for establishing and enforcing standards and the roles of licensure and accrediting mechanisms is necessary to establish a context for an action agenda. The discussion will center on the award of undergraduate degrees, but the traditions, principles, and processes at issue are also relevant for certificates and diplomas even though they are less comprehensive in meaning because they do not require a base of liberal/general education.

FUNCTIONS AND STRUCTURE OF A DEGREE

It is a bit dangerous to generalize about the functions and structure of undergraduate degrees. The different emphases on values, religious heritage, and preparation for employment and responsible citizenship vary significantly depending on whether there is public, religious, or independent control of the institution. In most institutions, it depends as well on the predilections of faculty. Moreover, requirements for college credentials, both in content and in standards to be achieved, have traditionally been largely matters of institutional prerogative and have been fiercely defended as such. In addition to the fact of diversity in types and sponsorship of institutions, degree titles themselves number over 1,600, and their number grows each academic year as new specialities requiring formal postsecondary education emerge in the workplace.

Undergraduate degrees have many meanings, and serve a variety of functions. Among them are: (1) qualification for advanced study; (2) qualification for employment and delivery of services; and (3) recognition for personal development —an educational and social accolade for persevering in a program of rigorous study.

Colleges and universities appear to have mixed emotions about their credentialing responsibility. The meaning and integrity of a degree and what it certifies about the holder are explicit discussion items in curriculum committee meetings and faculty senate sessions on graduation requirements and admissions standards. Yet, when pressed externally, institutions seem very reluctant to get overly specific about the skills certified by a degree and for good reason. An American Council on Education Task Force on Educational Credit and Credentials in a 1977 report put the meaning of a valid credential, including a degree, in clear perspective:

> The possession of a valid credential is evidence that the holder has qualifications which, in the view of the issuing authority, entitle him to authority and confidence within the area certified. The credential is not a guarantee that every person credentialed will perform satisfactorily or that any credential holder will perform well in every situation. It merely indicates that those people who hold the credential tend to deliver adequate services with substantial more consistency than those who do not hold the credential. Given the difficulty of defining and assessing the requisites for delivery of complex and highly refined services, credentialing cannot be expected to provide absolute protection to society. It has social utility because it increases the likehood that satisfactory services will be delivered.[1]

Throughout the history of American higher education, degrees have certified with a high degree of reliability abilities and characteristics that distinguish college graduates as a group from noncollege graduates, especially in the area of basic academic skills. The credentialing function of colleges and universities, therefore, must be carried out with care because it has great import for graduates and nongraduates alike. The preface of the ACE Task Force report noted:

> Educational credentials are used to label people according to educational accomplishment, thus dramatically affecting how far the door of opportunity opens, if it opens at all. Not only do educational credentials affect the image other people hold of a person, but they also affect the person's self-image. Consequently, the role of postsecondary education in credentialing educational accomplishment is laden with troublesome, complex questions.[2]

The social significance and importance of the credentialing responsibility of colleges and universities is so great that a sound argument could be made for adding it as the fourth general purpose of higher education along with research, teaching, and service. Certainly, higher education cannot conduct its credentialing function in an irresponsible manner and expect to continue to enjoy the confidence and support of society.

In thinking about current quality and certification issues in higher education, it is helpful to consider the basic components of associate and baccalaureate degrees and their significance in projecting the meaning of the credentials.

General/Liberal Education. Rhetoric regarding general/liberal education can be boundless and discussion concerning it is certainly invigorating to the true academic. Such discussions also probably illustrate best the value higher education and society place on educating the whole person, for the purposes and goals of general/liberal education are as lofty as its results are immeasurable. The fact that there is a constant stream of rhetoric on the importance of general/liberal education, including a great deal from chief executive officers of multinational corporations, does confirm the allure and magnetism of a higher calling for college and university education. Higher education in general remains committed to the pursuit of general/liberal education goals and remains undisturbed that it lacks conclusive evidence that its graduates have achieved them. Similarly, society in general has supported the notion that colleges and universities through general/liberal education should strive to graduate men and women with distinguishing attributes: lettered, analytical, reflecting high moral and ethical values through responsible citizenship and service to society; leaders in commerce, the professions, government, the church, and community.

As a consequence of the belief in their value, general/liberal education courses have usually comprised from 25 to 50 percent of the requirements for undergraduate degrees. While it is impossible to certify the ideal characteristics listed above or the inherent aesthetic, political, or spiritual values, colleges and universities consider it important to assert through the award of the degree that graduates have been exposed to certain bodies of knowledge and to a breadth of essential information and ideas. Still, although the general/liberal education component of the degree probably correlates well with the attributes and values listed or alluded to above, it does not predict future performance to the extent normally associated with other aspects of earned degrees. Moreover, because of wide variances in general/liberal education curricula among institutions and their differing missions, a high degree of commonality in educational outcomes for this component of the degree should not be expected. In a pluralistic society, common outcomes for this part of the degree may not even be desirable.

Area of Specialization. The area of specialization, or major, ranges in number of courses from one-quarter to three-quarters of the total requirements. Although not all majors are directly related to a specific job, the area of specialization is the one component of the degree where institutions are certifying in the strictest sense of certification: those awarded the degree are expected to possess knowledge, values, and skills that correlate highly and reliably with satisfactory performance on the job. To illustrate, journalists are expected to be able to interview, research, and write; teachers are expected to know their subject matter, to be able to organize and teach it effectively, and to manage the classroom experience.

Curriculum specializations have grown rapidly in recent years. And, the likelihood is that as the economy and the need for human services becomes more complex, job-specific curricula will continue to expand dramatically. Given its historical role in certifying occupational proficiency, higher education will be looked to for expansion of its job-related programs and certification functions. Occupational specialties requiring a substantial body of knowledge and erudite skills have invariably turned to higher education to enhance their status through formal college-level study and certification as a requirement to enter the field.

Greater commonality of educational outcomes among institutions is likely regarding the specialized components of degrees. Lack of commonality of curricula and educational outcomes in many job-related fields has given rise to pressures for specialized accreditation. This is especially true in occupations that have strong or aspiring national associations which seek to use specialized accreditation as a means of establishing a professional identity for those already in the field and to limit entry-level employment to those who meet their definition of being qualified.

Electives. Generally, there are only minimal requirements for courses students take in the elective component of the degree: they must be college-level in rigor and content, and there must be enough such courses to round out the total number required for the degree after the general/liberal education and specialization courses requirements have been met. The theory undergirding the elective component of the degree—students should be allowed some latitude to pursue special interests—works against this aspect of the degree certifying anything except the overall requirements of a specified number of college-level courses for graduation. However, some students do use the electives to earn a "minor" in a particular curriculum or discipline, which may provide a significant additional dimension to the meaning of their degrees in terms of job-related certification.

Other Requirements. Other aspects of degree requirements merit brief mention because they have an impact on the meaning of the credential. One example is the residency requirement—the stipulation by most institutions that a certain amount of the total courses required for a degree must be taken at the awarding college or university. In theory, this assures that the degree awarded reflects unique requirements or characteristics of the conferring institution. It also provides some assurance to the institution that courses it accepts in transfer meet its quality standards. Another example is the requirement by a limited number of institutions of senior theses or comprehensive examinations in the major or basic academic skills. One other factor that constructs a floor under the meaning of the undergraduate degree is a required grade point average, usually a "C" average on all courses applied to meeting graduation requirements.

Basic Academic Skills. There is a substantial consensus in higher education and among those who employ its graduates that the college-educated person should be proficient in reading, writing, and speaking English, have the ability to apply mathematics as required in high-level jobs, and exhibit analytical and reasoning skills associated with college-level study. While difficult to define wiith great precision, these threshold characteristics are nonetheless the accepted marks of a college-educated person. Accordingly, basic academic skills have long been central to the traditional meaning of undergraduate degrees. They are also considered vital to adequate performance for persons employed in upper-level management and in high-tech and complex personal services environments. They remain the core of the body of comprehensive abilities assumed and expected to be certified by undergraduate degrees regardless of which institution awards the credential.

College curricula generally have not been purposely designed to assure that graduates have a broad range of basic academic skills. Instead, an acceptable level of basic academic skills, those normally associated with a solid secondary school preparation, are traditionally required for admission to college-level study. As a student progresses through a program of study for a degree, the abilities are expected to be honed and extended to a level significantly higher than when the student first entered the institution. Unfortunately, current problems no longer make these expectations reasonable for students in many institutions.

INTRAINSTITUTIONAL PROCEDURES FOR QUALITY ASSURANCE

In keeping with the belief that institutional autonomy produces educational and social benefits, American colleges and universities have enjoyed great latitude in areas critical to quality undergraduate education: the design of curricula, the appointment, retention, and promotion of faculty; determination of necessary learning resources; establishment of grading standards and graduation requirements; and, in independent institutions, control of admissions standards. Many public colleges and universities have their admissions requirements prescribed by state legislation, but they can, through the forceful application of grading standards and graduation requirements, within a short time quickly weed out those whose secondary school preparation leaves them unqualified to benefit from college-level instruction.

The critical areas listed above underlie a basic tenet of faith regarding quality in higher education: students qualified to benefit from college-level instruction, studying in a well-designed curriculum taught by qualified faculty and supported by vital learning resources, and meeting predetermined grading and graduation requirements will earn degrees that communicate and certify abilities and characteristics predictive of successful performance on the job and as citizens after they leave the campus as graduates.

Assuring the competency of graduates in most colleges and universities is currently almost totally dependent on the course structure. Given the traditions of the faculty member being king or queen of a virtual "iron curtain" classroom, assuring the competency of graduates now rests firmly in the hands of individual faculty. Those who instruct decide how closely they will adhere to the curriculum plan, what are acceptable standards for student achievement in a given course, and what procedures they will use for evaluating learning outcomes. Faculty also certify whether the student has attained the standard and at what level by assigning a grade.

A few institutions modify to some extent the dominant role of the individual faculty member by requiring senior theses and comprehensive examinations as a check on the course structure as the sole means of certifying learning outcomes. These practices are relatively rare among institutions, however.

It is interesting to note that for admissions purposes colleges and universities have long been squeamish about relying totally on the course structure as a means of certifying student accomplishment and abilities. First, results of college admissions tests are used to qualify judgments that otherwise would have to be made on the basis of high school courses satisfactorily completed and cumulative grade point averages—certainly a tacit recognition of the weakness of the course structure as a reliable means of certification at the secondary school level. Second, graduate and professional schools factor in test results such as the Graduate Record Examination and the Law School Admissions Test in evaluating the undergraduate records of applicants because college courses passed are not believed to be a sufficient basis for judging qualifications to undertake advanced study—another tacit admission of the lack of faith in the course structure's reliability for certifying learning outcomes.Yet, most colleges and universities appear comfortable in relying solely on the course structure for certifying the knowledge and skills required for the associate and baccalaureate degree.

EXTRAINSTITUTIONAL PROCESSES FOR ASSURING QUALITY

Two formal external review systems have a bearing on the integrity of undergraduate degrees. One is governmental authorization to exist, which, except in all but a few select cases, involving federal charters, comes in the form of a state government charter or license to operate. Yet, state government requirements are so minimal and so uneven among the states that they serve mainly to help weed out the fraudulent institutions of the degree-mill variety. Thus, state regulation in toto has minimal effect on assuring the value of degrees.

It has been left to the second external review system, nongovernmental accreditation, to provide the primary assurance to society-at-large that colleges and universities operate programs of quality and award degrees only to those who have earned them. Perhaps the most concrete evidence of the advantage nongovernmental accreditation enjoys over state governmental regulation is the fact that the federal government has chosen accreditation as the principal means an institution has available to establish eligibility for federal funds.

Nongovernmental accreditation comes in two forms: institutional, in that the agency vouches for the total institution and all its offerings; and specialized accreditation of a particular curriculum or program preparing practitioners in special fields such as law, medicine, elementary and secondary school teaching, or forestry. The Council on Postsecondary Accreditation, a creature of the accrediting agencies and associations representing governing boards and chief executive officers of colleges and universities, legitimates nongovernmental accrediting agencies through a recognition process. COPA, which also has public representatives on its Board of Directors, publishes a list of recognized agencies to guide institutions in inviting accrediting agencies to their campuses and to assist the general public and government agencies who make choices among institutions and programs on the basis of accreditation.

Institutional accreditation has the lead role in speaking to the integrity of undergraduate degrees. In brief, institutional accreditation examines the organization of the college or university, its processes for making decisions on key academic matters, the organization of its curriculum and graduation requirements, and the availability of resources to carry out its mission. To date, institutional accreditation has involved itself very little in examining the quality of student work and learning outcomes expected to be certified by the award of a degree.

In designing curricula and establishing graduation requirements institutions also have to be cognizant of the requirements of professional voluntary certification and state licensure programs. Graduates often have to pass these examinations to practice in their chosen fields or they often gain substantial advantage even if certification or licensure is not required. Often, eligibility to sit for the examination is tied to specialized accreditation—giving the profession important-leverage in forcing commonality of curriculum and presumed learning outcomes on an interinstitutional basis.

Except for obtaining governmental authorization to exist, institutional compliance with external requirements is in one sense voluntary; in another sense it is not. Institutions can operate without accreditation, but only a handful have been able to do so and to thrive as part of the postsecondary education industry.

There have been numerous strident critics of nongovernmental accreditation since it became the dominant method of external assurance of quality and integrity of institutions in this century. It does not take a great deal of brilliance or insight to produce valid criticism of any evaluation system that has one foot firmly planted on pluralistic values and the other on subjective judgment. But the critics should not be condemned, for their criticism has given rise to productive change in accreditation. And, accreditors, who often feel the sting of their critics, should take comfort and pride in the fact that few responsible leaders within or outside higher education would argue to replace nongovernmental evaluation with a governmental process, be it federal or state.

Label it fact, national pride, or American arrogance, it is reasonable to assert that American postsecondary education is the world's best in terms of both quality and access. Institutional latitude to respond to educational needs and freedom to experiment with new programs, methods and delivery of instruction, and new services are the major reasons American postsecondary education can make such a claim. These essential institutional freedoms and rights that undergird quality are buttressed and protected by society's dominant reliance on intrainstitutional and nongovernmental interinstitutional means of self-regulation for higher education and not by governmental regulation and control.

Two Disturbing Problems for Self-Regulation

Institutions solidify their claim to self-regulation and minimal outside review even by nongovernmental agencies primarily by establishing impeccable reputations for quality and integrity. The postsecondary education industry preserves the privilege of self-regulation by acting responsibly and quickly to protect societal interests that otherwise would need to be guarded by state and federal government. Preservation of this privilege is enhanced when problems that loom are identified and dealt with promptly. Denial of the existence of an obvious problem and refusal to address it can only erode the confidence now enjoyed by postsecondary education's system of self-regulation.

Since they came to the fore in this century, postsecondary education's voluntary nongovernmental self-regulation mechanisms and agencies have moved as the need arose to provide assurances to society regarding quality. The latest effort came in the 1970s when the nontraditional education movement and emphasis on serving adult students grew in intensity.

Responses came in several forms and involved faculty and academic administrators from a broadly representative group of accredited colleges and universities. Under the aegis of the American Council on Education, an evaluation system for establishing credit equivalencies for formal military courses was strengthened and expanded to courses offered by business and industry for their own employees. Testing programs to measure learning attained in extrainstitutional settings were expanded and improved. The Council for the Advancement of Experiential Learning, with the assistance of the Carnegie, Ford, and Kellogg foundations, developed portfolio procedures for faculty to use in evaluating experiential learning that otherwise had not been validated. Accredited institutions developed external programs that improved the social equity of credentialing college-level learning.

A policy statement issued by the Board of Directors of the American Council on Education emphasized that these new responses had important dimensions other than protecting the integrity of college and university credentials. They improved the social fairness of certificates and degrees used as credentials to qualify for employment, and they assisted in the proper placement of students in educational programs. The statement noted that teaching students what they already know is both stultifying to them and wasteful of educational and personal resources.[3]

These responsible actions by higher education in the 1970s assured the continuing validity of college and university credentials and were helpful in assisting colleges and universities to respond to the educational needs of a new clientele. A similar response is required in the 1980s to at least two problems that merit attention.

BASIC SKILLS

As mentioned earlier, there is disturbing evidence that some accredited colleges and universities are awarding degrees to students who fall short of competence in the basic academic skills expected of degree recipients. Evidence of the scope of the problem is too extensive to be ignored. External testing programs to measure basic academic skills are being imposed on accredited colleges and universities. Georgia, Florida, and California have testing programs that affect all degree-seeking students at substantial numbers of institutions. Eighteen states now require teachers to pass the National Teachers Examination (NTE) in order to enter the teaching profession in those states. The primary concern in imposing the NTE is the adequacy of the basic academic skills of prospective teachers. The Department of the Army in 1984 announced, then rescinded, a requirement that ROTC cadets would have to pass a basic academic skills test before receiving a commission as an officer, because it could no longer rely on the baccalaureate degree to certify college-level academic skills needed to be an effective officer. The Army policy was rescinded because it had a disproportionate impact on minorities, but spokesmen noted that the Army could not rescind the problem. Complaints regarding the basic skills of graduates are growing from others who hire the products of colleges and universities.

The trend toward a multiplicity of externally imposed testing programs is likely to continue unless institutions and their associations move quickly to convince the public anew that degrees can be relied upon for certification of college-level academic skills. Tax and philanthropic support and student aid programs could ultimately be at risk if growing numbers of the industry's constituencies question the validity of degrees. College and university students, the great majority of whom see a college degree as an investment that will yield future earnings, may be lost to other educational providers who can offer more narrow but also more meaningful job-related credentials.

The above scenario, if it occurs, will affect institutions differently. Selective admissions institutions whose reputations are substantially independent of collective higher education will not suffer; they more likely will prosper because their degrees, viewed as valid credentials, will have real value in the marketplace. But the great mass of institutions, whose reputations are generally undistinguished as places of superior quality and whose services are sought in restricted geographical areas or by a narrow constituency, would suffer as degrees in general lost their credibility.

Although it is critically important for higher education not to award degrees to people who do not have the requisite knowledge and abilities, solving the problem of basic academic skills is not as simple as repairing the defects in the certification sieve. Higher education must change its curricula and services to help students develop the requisite abilities so they can qualify for valid degrees.

The national goal of providing postsecondary educational opportunity to all those who can benefit by it combined with the disrepair of elementary and secondary school education have contributed to the basic academic skills problem at the higher education level. Many institutions in recent years have embraced the philosophy of open admissions, and many public institutions have been mandated by state laws to admit all high school graduates, regardless of their secondary school preparation program.

In addition, the drop in the number of traditional college-age students has left the survival of many institutions dependent upon the enrollment of students who, in previous years, would not have qualified to study at the college level. In brief, economic incentives for all but the selective admissions institutions run counter to the enforcement of high academic standards.

While these phenomena were occurring, relevant curricula changes across postsecondary education failed to keep pace. Apparently, neither did certification processes and procedures change, considering the spate of complaints about the basic academic skills of college graduates.

Recent reports on American education have spurred a definite trend toward tightening the requirements for admission to college. Increased emphasis on the secondary school courses in mathematics, English, science, and foreign languages is evident in most new requirements. Moreover, there seems to be a strong move in tightening standards and returning to the basics all across elementary and secondary education.

In time, these trends—if they are sustained—will undoubtedly ease the basic academic skills problem at the higher education level, but the interim poses a dilemma for postsecondary education.

College and universities face the problem of dealing with the long-term effects of poor elementary and secondary school preparation unless they want to tighten up their graduation standards solely by tightening up their admissions standards. Such an action would affect minorities, disproportionately curtail enrollments severely, and deprive millions of prospective students of a postsecondary educational opportunity essential for their own welfare as well as that of the nation—hardly an attractive or viable educational or public policy alternative.

SPECIALIZED ACCREDITATION

Two long-standing questions regarding specialized accreditation continue to dominate: how much specialized accreditation is enough, and the relevancy of the standards to producing competent graduates.

Proliferation of legitimized specialized accrediting (that is to say, COPA recognized agencies) was admirably controlled in the last decade, but COPA now faces a spate of recognition requests from agencies already organized with standards and processes in place. And, distressingly for COPA and the effectivensss of self-regulation in postsecondary education, agencies now requesting recognition are already accrediting programs on many college and university campuses. Given the likely rapid growth of occupational specialization, COPA's task of limiting specialized accreditation to agencies serving a clear social purpose that is not being served adequately by institutional agencies is formidable indeed.

COPA and its supporting presidential associations have made some progress in addressing the problem of relevancy and fair application of specialized accrediting agency standards. Firm and artful negotiations with the American Bar Association have generated improvements in law school accreditation. The COPA recognition process and its efforts to work with accrediting agencies show promise of improving the face validity of accrediting requirements as well as relationships between agencies and institutions.

As the budget noose draws tighter, it is likely that the cost-effectiveness of specialized accreditation in general and in certain fields in particular will increasingly be questioned, raising anew the old issue of whether specialized accreditation serves a useful social purpose, and if so, whether the agency's requirements are educationally valid. Mere mortals probably can never devise a scheme that will prevent clashes between the yearning for total institutional autonomy and the interests of professional groups and their aligned faculty on campuses, but the long-term health of self-regulation is worth a serious effort.

In placing the blame for the problems of specialized accreditation, it is not fair to point the finger solely at the agencies themselves or to expect COPA alone to perform the herculean task of producing order and tidying up the accreditation landscape. Colleges and universities also contribute to the problem.

COPA's effectiveness as an accreditor of the accreditors is rooted in institutional support of its activities. COPA's leverage is its recognition process and the list it publishes to advise institutions of agencies that meet its requirements. To the extent that institutions invite nonrecognized agencies onto their campuses, COPA's effectiveness is undercut and self-regulation in higher education is dealt a damaging blow.

Institutions err in two ways. The administrations of some institutions are ill-informed about COPA's critical role. A new president of one complex institution learned on taking over the job that the central administration had no list of programs accredited by specialized agencies and had played no role in inviting the agencies to visit the campus. Other institutions know of COPA's role but fail to support it because they see advantage in being able to advertise accreditation by an agency even though it is not on the COPA recognized list. It should, as a matter of fairness, be pointed out that leaders of many specialized accrediting agencies are just as interested as institutional administrators in cleaning up accreditation problems, and they are working actively through COPA to do so.

Suggestions for Consideration

The greatest source of useful remedies for the two problems addressed above is likely to be found on the campuses and in the agencies tasked with the responsibilities of assuring quality. But, the national-level perspective may also provide workable suggestions for consideration by those in places of responsibility, both on the campus and in the voluntary associations.

BASIC SKILLS

Colleges and universities should reexamine their curricula and processes for developing, honing, and credentialing the basic academic skills associated with the award of undergraduate degrees. The reexamination should consider the following:

1. Establishing a diagnostic testing program to determine the level of basic academic skills of entering students, and using the results to determine whether instructional policies and programs are properly designed to produce the basic academic skills. Some institutions, for example, are finding that they must place substantial emphasis on developing communications skills and, as a cooperative effort among faculty in several disciplines, are emphasizing writing across the curriculum—no longer relying on a student passing a couple of freshman English courses to satisfy the basic skills requirement.

2. Establishing a comprehensive basic skills examination program to measure the communications, analytical, and reasoning skills of students before they are awarded the associate degree or are advanced to upper-division standing. In many institutions, especially those with large and diverse student bodies, it appears no longer practical to rely on a student traversing course requirements as an adequate basis for awarding a credential. Under practices that prevail in most institutions, few checks are made to determine whether the prescribed curriculum content is being taught and there is virtually no peer involvement in determining and checking on grading standards applied by the instructor who teaches, evaluates, and certifies. The inevitable results are disturbing variances in curriculum content for sections of the same course as well as variances among the evaluation and grading policies and practices of the cadre of instructors who teach multiple-section courses. A comprehensive examination program would in most instances bring greater consistency in standards and therefore greater assurances that the degree actually certifies the basic academic skills.

A critical look at the adequacy of the course structure for

certification purposes for the basic skills will lead colleges and universities to reexamine their reliance on the course structure as the sole certification device for all components of the degree. A comprehensive examination for the electives component of the degree is impractical and not required in terms of an institution's certification responsibilities. A comprehensive examination for the area of the specialization, or major, would be reasonable, but is perhaps unnecessary if faculty will become more involved with their peers in the evaluation and certification process.

Faculties and academic administrators need to know that their colleagues are indeed following the curriculum plan, or else planning becomes fatuous. Methods that are useful and are likely to find receptivity with faculty are the development by an academic unit of a question bank covering essential concepts, skills, and knowledge and the grading of final examinations by two or more faculty. Such procedures make worthwhile the time devoted to debate on curricula and graduation requirements. They will also in due time result in improved curricula, evaluation procedures and policies, and testing skills of faculty.

3. Institutional accrediting agencies should take special steps to evaluate the adequacy of institutional processes and policies for credentialing basic academic skills as part of initial and periodic reevaluation of institutions. As society's principal agents for assuring the integrity of credentials awarded by colleges and universities, institutional accrediting agencies should consider special steps to assist institutions in developing credible policies and procedures before the basic skills issue reaches the crisis level.

SPECIALIZED ACCREDITATION

The Council on Postsecondary Accreditation, since it replaced the National Commission on Accrediting and the Federation of Regional Accrediting Commissions of Higher Education, has skirted the key question regarding specialized accreditation in its recognition criteria and processes:

when is it in the interest of society to conduct program accreditation and when it is not? Instead of dealing with that question, COPA has relied instead on making a judgment whether an applying agency has gained wide acceptance among institutions and other appropriate groups as a principal concern in awarding recognition.[4]

The time is at hand, because of the large number of new agencies aspiring to conduct specialized accreditation, for COPA on behalf of higher education to consider a new approach to dealing with agencies concerned with educational quality and standards in their sphere of interest. The time is also at hand for a new concept for dealing with these legitimate interests. In developing a workable concept, these factors should be recognized: (1) agencies have a legitimate and natural interest in standards of educational quality and in the integrity of credentials awarded by colleges and universities in their respective fields; (2) many of these agencies can render assistance to institutions, thereby serving their own self-interests as well as those of society; but (3) the contributions of these agencies do not have to follow uniformly in every instance the characteristics of specialized accreditation. Two examples at opposite ends of the specialized accreditation continuum—medicine and art—illustrate the point.

The relationship between quality educational preparation of medical practitioners and the protection of the public's health and safety is hardly debatable. The only route to becoming a physician is successful completion of formal study in a medical school, followed by passing a licensure examination and completing an internship before practicing without supervision is allowed. Specialty certification often follows because of the intense need to protect the public. There is substantial consensus on the desirable knowledge base and skills required to be a competent physician. Assurance through specialized accreditation that graduates of medical schools have had quality educational experiences and have met prescribed educational requirements is a key element in the total approach to quality assurance for medical services. It is recognized that institutional accreditation alone in this instance is not adequate.

Preparing to enter the field of art is quite different from becoming a physician. Art skills and values can be learned in many settings and from many sources. Graduation from an accredited program is not a uniform requirement for employment for practitioners of art. There are many successful artists who have never studied art in a college or university art department. Aesthetic judgments regarding art, among the highly educated and even among artists themselves, vary widely. Most educators will agree that certain benefits accrue to society as a result of the existence of college and university art curricula just as there are benefits that result from curricula in philosophy, political science, and history. Yet, philosophy, political science, and history are not served by specialized accreditation whereas art is, with basically the same processes and procedures (though with differing requirements, of course) as medicine.

Many agencies that aspire to COPA-sanctioned specialized accreditation can make a stronger case than the field of art that their accreditation is needed to protect the public health and safety or otherwise serves some pressing social need. Thus, unless COPA begins to fashion a new concept for regularizing agencies' relationships with institutions, colleges and universities can expect to be inundated with costly and time-consuming visits by specialized accreditation. Moreover, failure to exercise some sort of reasonable birth control for accrediting agencies could do serious harm to the concept of voluntary self-regulation.

To cope with the problem, COPA should consider developing a scheme for categorizing agency-institutional relationships along the following lines:

1. *Level One Recognition.* Agencies awarded this COPA status would be those whose programs of specialized accreditation are clearly related to the protection of the public's health and safety. Agencies granted level one recognition would be expected to engage in all the present processes related to specialized accreditation: publication of standards, requirement of a self-study, conducting of a site visit, *publication of a list of accredited programs,* and periodic evaluation of accredited programs.

2. *Level Two Recognition.* Agencies awarded this COPA

status would be those whose evaluation programs have no direct relationship to the protection of the public's health and safety. The agency's program, however, would be judged to serve one or more other useful social or educational purposes such as the identification of programs of superior quality. Because of the lack of a direct tie to protection of the public's health and safety, the evaluation program of the agency would have different characteristics: publication of standards, self-reporting by the institution on whether it meets the standards with auditing on a sampling basis by the agency, *publication of a list of approved* (as opposed to accredited) *programs*, provision of consulting services, and conducting of site visits at the option of the institution.

3. *Level Three Recognition.* Agencies awarded this COPA status would be those with interests in curricula not related to the protection of the public's health or safety or where the situation did not merit publication of a list of "approved programs." The agency could, however, provide useful services by publishing guidelines for program development and self-study, making consulting services available to institutions, and by otherwise engaging networks of institutional representatives in program improvement activities. Level three recognition would be in keeping with the concept of self-regulation guidelines that have been developed in recent years under the aegis of the Office of Self-Regulation Initiatives of the American Council on Education and found to be very useful by institutions.

Notes

1. Jerry W. Miller and Olive Mills, eds. *Credentialing Educational Accomplishment* (Washington, D. C., American Council on Education, 1978), p. 9.
2. Ibid.
3. Ibid., p. 235.
4. Robert Glidden, "Specialized Accreditation." In *Understanding Accreditation: Contemporary Perspectives on Issues and Practices in Evaluating Educational Quality* (San Francisco: Jossey-Bass, 1983).

Potential Conflict of Interest Issues in Relationships Between Academia and Industry

ELISABETH A. ZINSER

COOPERATION BETWEEN UNIVERSITIES AND CORPORATIONS is not a new phenomenon in American society. Corporations began to fund university research long before World War II, making modest contributions to applied research (Bok, 1982). After World War II several prestigious research universities participated in the development of new industries that were based upon discoveries in engineering, physics, electronics, and chemistry. The federal government increased research support to universities in the 1950s; thus corporate support became a smaller proportion of the budget for academic science (Bok, 1982). Because scientists concentrated on federal grant activity, they had less contact with industry. By the 1960s, campus unrest and various ideological differences be-

NOTE: The material in this chapter is based, in part, upon my thesis research while a Sloan Fellow in the Massachusetts Institute of Technology School of Management. I wish to thank Dr. Stanley Finkelstein, my thesis adviser; Drs. J. Buchert, A. Charles, P. Friedman, and B. Schiwek for editorial assistance, and Ms. M. Mokris for manuscript preparation.

tween some academics and industrialists led to strained relationships.

Several trends emerging during the 1970s brought these partners into closer association once again. First, scientific discoveries in a number of fields spawned capabilities for new high technologies, such as the emergence of recombinant DNA biotechnology. Second, American industry encountered unprecedented pressure from foreign competition, a weakened economy, floundering productivity, and escalating costs. Access to new technology from university-based research became urgent for industry once again. Third, higher education encountered increasing financial pressures associated with enrollment declines; waning federal support in relation to inflation, greater competition for limited resources, and the rising cost of research; and growing obsolescence in research equipment. Universities looked again to industry for assistance and for cooperative endeavors. Fourth, the increasing gap between faculty salaries and those of counterparts in industry led to more liberal consulting practices for faculty sought by industry for their knowledge. Fifth, increasing pressure for career-driven educational programs and a concomitant disenchantment with higher education curricula influenced some corporations (and other noncollegiate organizations) to offer credit-based and professional development programs. Some institutions of higher education responded by establishing linkages with corporations to offer such educational programs in the industry setting, ensuring a level of academic standards comparable with campus programs. These developments, among others, contributed significantly to the burgeoning interest in collaborative research and education between industry and academia, an interest so widespread as to become a hallmark of the 1980s.

Controversies have emerged along with this renewed and intensified interest in cooperative activities between business/industry and institutions of higher education, and faculty members. The realities of today's economy, higher education, scientific advancements, and high technology industries point to more complex arrangements than in the past.

Significant research activity is no longer confined to the major research universities. Thus, firms seek easier access to the knowledge explosion through a wider variety and higher number of institutions of higher education, many with little experience in such cooperative ventures. Some universities have begun to approach the transfer of technology with a new interest in acquiring returns on the commercialization of their discoveries in the form of shared equity rather than relying solely upon traditional royalty arrangements. As a consequence of such trends, institutional and national policies concerning ties between academia and industry are in a state of reassessment and redefinition.

The high technologies of the 1980s are emerging from fields that are both new to the commercial world and different from earlier developments (for example, engineering). Biotechnology offers an interesting illustration. Molecular biology and its biotechnologies have ventured into the commercial world almost exclusively from the academic laboratories, with little complementary capacity or expertise in the industrial sector. Discoveries from basic research in this area are proliferating with unprecedented speed, and potential applications become readily apparent. The field deals with the processes of life and health, attracting public attention to safety and ethical considerations as well as to the question of public versus private rights to the resulting intellectual property. Scientists associated with the medical fields, who have historically been seen as apart from the worldly nature of business, have now become the unlikely champions of free enterprise.

While the issues surrounding contemporary corporate–university connections are not wholly new, they have taken on a unique character. At stake are potentially long-term solutions to problems of stable funding for education and research activity and an accrual of human capital as well as new products (and processes) that may keep American industry ahead of foreign competition, maintain domestic standards of living, and protect the vitality of democracy. At risk, however, may be the very integrity of American higher education, if the proprietary needs of industry jeopardize academic values of free exchange of knowledge and a longstanding commitment to basic research and inquiry for its own sake. Without fundamental research in the academic community, unfettered by concern for immediate commercial value, the discoveries and technologies of the twenty-first century are unlikely to appear.

Public support will always be the foundation of the nation's strength in education and fundamental research. Lewis M. Branscomb, vice-preseident and chief scientist at International Business Machines, has said, "Should corporate contributions to academic research double or even treble, they would still support only a small portion of the total academic research effort. And such support would be concentrated in selected fields. The implication is clear. If the present level of academic research is to be maintained, the principal burden will continue to fall on the public purse, federal and state" (Association Council for Policy Analysis and Research, 1984, p. 11). Industrial support will not replace this capacity, but it can contribute greatly to America's competitive edge in economic development as well as to international harmony.

A clearer definition of relationships between industrial and academic communities is needed as a foundation for informed collaboration and the design of concomitant policies. This chapter will outline a framework for understanding the variety of relationships known today, and will review some of the issues that may raise conflicts between the university world and the corporate world. These concepts will then be related in a discussion of risk–benefit analysis as a means of establishing mutually beneficial relationships while preserving the integrity and autonomy of each party.

The Nature of University–Industry Relationships

Comprehending the diversity of university–industry connections requires consideration of at least four factors about a given relationship: (1) the parties or agents in the relationship; (2) the scope of participation; (3) the purposes of the connection; and (4) the structure of commitments or obligations made in the agreement.

PARTIES (OR AGENTS)

Scrutiny of the agents in university–corporate relationships suggests five classifications. First, a university and a firm may interact (directly or indirectly) through a faculty member *as an individual.* The role of the faculty member may be that of consultant, founder, investor, board member, or part-time employee. Such relationships may be established with or without direct participation from the parent institution, but the university is at least an indirect partner vis-à-vis the faculty member's obligations to the academic community. Second, a university and a firm may interact *as principals,* establishing a direct agreement. Third, academia and industry may connect through the facilitative role of a government agency, a private foundation, or a professional organization serving *as a broker.* Fourth, a relationship between a university and a firm may be kept "at arm's length" through a related center or foundation created to serve *as a buffer* (or insulator). Fifth, an organization may be established to foster innovations by university and industry entrepreneurs who need special support in the costly developmental stages of reducing new discoveries to practice, thereby serving *as an incubator.* Such agencies are usually referred to as "incubation centers."

These forms of agent ties are not mutually exclusive. Indeed, it is in the layering of several relationships that the most complex issues in academia–industry cooperation arise. Two examples will suffice. First, a faculty scientist may have an individual connection to a firm (as consultant, equity holder, and so on) while also serving as a principal investigator in an institutional agreement between the university and the firm. Actual or perceived conflicts of interest may emerge in such a situation, although that scientist may be the best qualified to serve in both capacities. Another example concerns the combination of the "broker" and "insulator" relationships, where a government agency or private foundation provides targeted funding to promote cooperative research between universities and firms, and does so through an intermediary organization which insulates the principals from the appearance of collusion or conflict of interest.

Figure 1 describes the five forms of agent relationships common to the parties involved in academia–industry interaction.

SCOPE OF PARTICIPANTS

It is also useful to consider relationships in terms of the number of organizations participating on each side—that of academia and that of industry. A cooperative venture may involve: (1) a single firm and a single university; (2) one business concern and several universities; (3) one university and several firms; or (4) multiple universities and multiple corporations, the latter usually organized through a separate educational or research center. In general, conflicts of interest are less likely in situations involving multiple partners than in cases of a primary or exclusive relationship between one party from each sector.

PURPOSES

Relationships will also vary according to purpose. Cooperation between a university and a corporation may involve activities in education, service, and/or research. The university may provide continuing education or special training programs for a firm. The firm may provide opportunities for students to gain practical experiences in their fields of study. Service relationships may involve the sharing of physical plant, equipment, and special expertise as an alternative to capital investments in a specialized or transient area of need. Issues in a relationship involving research purposes may not be pertinent to relationships of an educational or service na-

Figure 1. Agents in Academia–Industry Relationships

1. Individual as Agent

   | University | Faculty Scientist | Firm |

   | University | Industrial Scientist | Firm |

2. University and Firm as Principals

   | University | Firm |

3. Government Agency/Private Foundation as Broker

   | Government/Foundation |
   | University | Firm |

4. Foundation/Center as Buffer

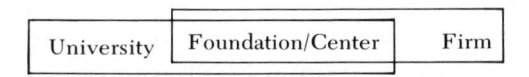

   | University | Foundation/Center | Firm |

5. Budding Entrepreneur Support Agency as an Incubator

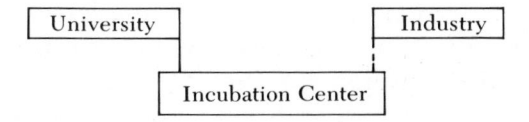

   | University | | Industry |
           | Incubation Center |

ture. Further, it is not uncommon for a university to have a research contract, an educational affiliation agreement, and/or a service provision or procurement pattern with the same firm.

Most of the current interest in industrial–academic collaboration concerns work in research and development. The underlying purposes of research relationships are: (1) to secure adequate resources for research; (2) to provide incentives to discovery and innovation; (3) to expedite technology transfer; (4) to ensure efficacious and safe commercialization in the public interest; and (5) to return and distribute value equitably among the various parties responsible for the chain of innovation and industrial progress.

STRUCTURE OF THE RELATIONSHIP

Classification of research relationships between industry and academia in terms of the commitment established between the parties is perhaps the most useful tool in understanding the structure of a relationship. Six categories are described, progressing from more distant relationships, which carry limited obligations and maximum autonomy, to more intimate ties involving commitments, obligations, restrictions, and possibly shared governance. Each category includes a variety of forms for interaction, some traditional and others quite innovative. They are not mutually exclusive.

1. A Contribution: A Gift or Supply of a Common Good or Service, with or Without Restrictions on Its Use. Private contributions to universities and colleges represented slightly more than 6 percent of total expenditures in public institutions and 12 percent in private institutions during the late 1970s, while federal support represented 50 percent of expenditures. Corporate support to higher education averaged about one-sixth of all voluntary support, thereby representing about 1 percent of the institutional budgets (Haire, 1981). Business increased its contribution to higher education by 15.7 percent in 1980 and by 10.7 percent in 1981, despite a decline of 4 percent in profits. By 1981, the proportion of corporate net income before taxes had increased from 0.35 percent to 0.50 percent (Magarrell, 1983). The corporate contribution for university research and development (R&D) specifically has been estimated at between 6 and 7 percent of the total academic R&D budget, which amounted to about $425 million in 1980–1981 (National Science Board, 1982, p. 27).

While generally not financial in character, universities make valuable contributions to corporations and industry. Such contributions include educational workshops or seminars, reports of research activity and new information, access to faculty and facilities, and placement services to acquaint graduates with career opportunities in the industrial world.

Contributions may be restricted (or designated) to specific purposes, but gifts should not involve the donor in the governance of supported programs. In other words, contributions generally do not have "strings attached."

2. A Procurement: An Acquisition of a Good or Service for a Price, Where the Supplier Is Accountable for Delivery by Specifications of the Purchaser. Firms and universities purchase services from one another for specific needs. Industry procures from universities such services as product testing, consultation, and use of special equipment or facilities. Universities also procure services and facilities from corporations, usually through a subcontract to accomplish a function in which the firm has superior expertise or to use specialized research equipment.

3. A Linkage: A Network Designed to Link Together Two (or More) Parties with Complementary Needs and Interests, Serving as a Communication or Coordinating Mechanism. Sponsored program offices in many universities serve as a linkage mechanism between the university and businesses. Such offices manage activities related to research contracts and other sponsored projects. They identify research endeavors of potential common interest to academia and industry, coordinate negotiations between parties in developing research agreements, monitor ongoing activities in light of policy, and facilitate conflict resolution and communications between the university and the corporation. Likewise, firms are establishing central offices to work out research relationships with universities.

On some campuses, university–industry research development offices serve to link the needs and capabilities of the industrial sector with those of the campus community. They generally provide a staff to facilitate contacts as well as to publish a directory of the research activity and subject expertise of specific faculty. Industrial research staff are assisted in defining problems and seeking out the faculty or library references necessary to solve problems. Staff may visit corporations to inform them of ongoing campus research projects, to coordinate industry visits to campus research laboratories, and to arrange various educational programs for industry. The University of Wisconsin at Madison initiated a University–Industry Research Program (UIR) in 1962 (Murphy, 1980) to encourage Wisconsin's industries to utilize more fully the emerging technologies in space research, solid-state electronics, computer science, and other fields of research stimulated by federal support. It remains a fine example of a "linkage" mechanism.

4. An Exchange: A Reciprocal Trading of Tangible and/or Intangible Values Which Are of Complementary Use to the Parties, Usually Through a Formal Liaison That Defines Each Party's Contribution and Obligations. While linkages are mechanisms to promote communication and problem solving, exchanges are formal relationships involving the trade of tangible and intangible assets. Exchanges between universities and corporations include the exchange of scientists where their expertise has reciprocal value, as well as the exchange of knowledge and money between organizations. The knowledge–value exchange is represented by the technology licensing programs and the industrial liaison (associate and affiliate) programs.

a. *Technology Licensing Programs.* The idea of returning greater value to the university through the exploitation of ideas generated on campus has gained momentum in recent years. Some campuses have established technology transfer programs to facilitate and manage the translation of newly discovered products and processes to industry for commercialization, and to return value to the university in the form of royalties and/or equity. Such programs actively seek patents on discoveries and make efforts to identify potential licensees. New patent legislation allowing universities to retain patent ownership for discoveries made on federally supported projects, the general slump in research funding, and the increasing awareness of the role of technology transfer in building a strong economy are all factors behind this trend to formalize the process. Yet there is controversy as to whether or not universities can or should become competent in technology licensing mechanisms.

Some universities have established in-house technology licensing offices, while others utilize a variety of technology brokerage mechanisms. The latter is usually an independent, nonprofit, campus-based research foundation that licenses patents stemming from the university's research, retains a percentage of royalties for operation, and returns most of the value to the university. The foundation serves as an insulator or buffer between the academy and industry, and as a broker to enhance the value of royalties through investments. An example of each is offered here.

Stanford University has an internal Office of Technology Licensing to manage the identification of potential licensees and the negotiation of licensing agreements. It grants both exclusive and nonexclusive licenses, depending upon the circumstances of the patent and the need for exclusive rights in that product's development. Nonexclusive licensing brings smaller fees and royalties from each licensee, but it is multiplied by many firms seeking the use of the patent. The exclusive license brings a much higher rate of return from a single firm. The office is self-supporting by taking 15 percent "off the top" of income generated in licensing. The remaining 85 percent is allocated based upon the institution's policy: one-third each to the school, the department, and the inventor.

Possibly the best known example of external technology brokerage is the Wisconsin Alumni Research Foundation (WARF). This nonprofit organization was formed in 1925 to help research discoveries support further research within the University of Wisconsin. It serves as a patent-management agent for the university, securing patents and licensing inventions to industry. The inventors receive 15 percent of net royalty income, and the remaining 85 percent is part of WARF's annual research grant to the University of Wisconsin (Fred, 1972). In recent years, WARF has processed more than fifty patent applications each year, and has provided the university with annual research grants of about $5 million. About one-third of this amount comes from current royalty income, while two-thirds is income from the Foundation's investment portfolio.

Other types of external technology brokerage and licensing programs include private research corporations that encourage and sponsor the licensing of university inventions, private consulting firms that act as research or technology brokers between universities and industrial firms (leaving the licensing details to the parties involved), and government sponsored programs organized to facilitate and channel relevant university research into specific fields. New ideas for licensing university discoveries are continually being explored. For example, the concept of a "technology pool" involves an independent foundation to handle the patent and licensing activities for a group of participating universities. The foundation would manage a "pool" of patents, and income from royalties and the investment portfolio would be distributed among the various universities in an equitable manner.

b. *Industrial Liaison/Affiliate Programs.* Industrial affiliate or liaison programs are designed to provide industry with efficient and timely access to the research expertise and new knowledge at the university, and to return financial value to the university for such access. Participating companies belong by paying an annual fee, for which they are provided various forms of contact with university resources. They gain a "window" to research results, methods, students, faculty, and the general direction of basic university research. The dialogue between industrialists and academicians provides insight into researchable problems of interest to faculty and students as well as to industry and society.

The Massachusetts Institute of Technology Industrial Liaison Program (ILP) was founded in 1948, and provides access to the entire institution's resource base. In return for an annual fee based on the size of the firm, the Industrial Liaison Program offers to member firms systematic and efficient access to research results, consultation with leading experts, exposure to students, formal conferences, visitations to the firm by faculty, and advance notice of publications of research activity. In 1981 the program had 280 member companies which gained a "window on science" resulting from MIT's research budget of more than $300 million. An important goal of ILP is to facilitate the transfer of ideas from MIT to industry, particularly technology that can be applied through development and commercialization. Faculty consultancy arrangements and sponsored research projects grow out of ILP connections, but they are not the management responsibility of the Industrial Liaison Office (Bruce, 1981).

MIT also has various "consortia" which function as decentralized industrial liaison programs at the departmental level. An example is the Center for Information Systems Research (CISR), which operates out of the Sloan School of Management. Members pay an annual fee in return for several seminars and conferences, interaction with faculty, and exposure to students for potential recruitment. Research contracts often emerge through CISR and are managed by the program's office. Funds generated are used to support faculty research projects on topics of mutual interest with business.

Stanford University had more than twenty decentralized industrial affiliates programs by 1982. Firms join for annual dues that range from $5,000 to $100,000 per year in exchange for special conferences, formal meetings with department faculty to discuss research methods and results, access to students for recruitment purposes, and one day of faculty consultation each year. Income is used primarily to support research. For example, the program in the biochemistry department supports the work of young research scientists and the purchase of equipment not available on federal grants. Stanford's scientists were reported to view this as allowing "them to keep at arm's length from direct commercial involvement, but still exercise their responsibility to see that research results reach the public domain. The process is seen primarily as a method for keeping companies up-to-date with the university scientists' academic research" (Kalgeris, 1981, p. 66).

5. A Cooperative: A Contractual "Quid Pro Quo" Agreement to Cooperate in a Specific Venture for a Fixed Period of Time, with the Contract Defining the Commitments and Obligations of Each Party, as Well as Conditions for "Ownership" of Future Benefits (and/or Risks) Derived from the Mutual Activity. Cooperative research relationships include a

variety of models that range from straightforward collaboration between industrial and academic scientists to complex and formal arrangements in which two or more organizations agree to cooperate in research activities. Six different forms of a "cooperative" are outlined here:

a. *Peer Collaboration.* It is not uncommon for research scientists to "team up" and collaborate in their work. For example, Bell Laboratories maintains a host of arrangements whereby academic and industrial scientists interact and work on topics of common interest. The research is usually in basic science and engineering and is not proprietary. Such peer collaboration in industrial laboratories depends upon an in-house capability characteristic of only a few corporations (Prager and Omenn, 1980).

b. *Research Agreements.* A research agreement is a contractual arrangement between a university and a firm for the conduct of research in an area of mutual interest. The company provides the funding, usually in return for access to the resulting knowledge and discoveries. The nature of the research can range from development testing to open-ended basic research, but most believe that work done at the university should be fundamental in nature.

The amount of money and the duration of the project are critical features. Fundamental research necessitates long-term commitments. Issues that commonly require negotiation are: (1) influence on the direction of research; (2) licensing and royalty arrangements to any patents which emerge, (3) handling of publications; and (4) access to information on work in progress.

The direction of research usually rests with the academic scientists, although there are instances of shared influence. The university generally retains the patent to any discoveries made, granting firms licenses to use the patent. Agreements vary from a nonexclusive, royalty-free license to an exclusive, royalty-bearing license. In the case of the exclusive alternative, the sponsoring company is given first rights of refusal. If the firm is interested in the patent rights, an exclusive license is granted for a royalty rate that may be negotiated either at the beginning of the contract or after the discovery is made when its value can be assessed more appropriately. If the firm refuses the rights, the patent can be licensed to another firm, on an exclusive or nonexclusive basis. The term of an exclusive license is usually limited to a period that the parties agree is necessary to provide the competitive edge justifying the heavy investments in development. The promise of an exclusive right may not be granted when the contract is formed, thus allowing the university to retain the right to decide at the point of each discovery whether the exclusive or nonexclusive license is appropriate in that case. More often than not, however, firms want as much certainty as possible on a reasonable-term exclusive license as the principal quid pro quo for their funding support. The value of an exclusive license varies from one industry to another. For example, a pattern of cross-licensing in the computer industry makes exclusiveness less important than in the pharmaceutical industry, where proprietary interests are crucial to competitive strength. A nonexclusive license agreement, on the other hand, is usually royalty-free and the university is responsible for licensing any third parties. If it is royalty-bearing, the sponsoring firm may share in any royalty income.

Firms often ask for the right to review publications based on the sponsored research prior to submission. While universities categorically disallow censorship as an infringement on academic freedom and the open exchange of information, many universities allow for a delay of 30–90 days in submission of a manuscript to give sufficient time to develop a patent application. Most firms are content to be early recipients of manuscripts.

Industrial support of university basic research has grown particularly in biotechnology. Examples abound in the recent literature. Mallinckrodt gave the Washington University School of Medicine $3.88 million over a three-year period to conduct research on monoclonal antibodies. Mallinckrodt will be kept informed of all developments and have the right of first refusal for any development that can lead to a commercially valuable method of diagnosis (Lepkowski, 1981).

The DuPont Company and the Harvard Medical School

cooperate in research on molecular genetics concerning a method for the production of large quantities of a form of interferon. DuPont committed $6 million over five years to continue basic studies and to renovate a research laboratory. Any patents resulting from the research will belong to Harvard; DuPont will receive exclusive licenses to develop and market the resulting products. The agreement stipulates that the company cannot control, inhibit, or restrict the conduct of the research or the publication of the results (McDonald, 1981; Kalgeris, 1981).

In May 1981, the Massachusetts General Hospital (MGH) negotiated a large research agreement with the German firm of Hoechst. Hoechst will provide the hospital with more than $50 million over the next decade to finance a major effort in genetic research, including the establishment of the new Department of Molecular Biology at MGH and the construction of a new facility. If research leading to an invention was funded solely by Hoechst, the company will have first rights and exclusive license in the development and commercialization of any resulting discoveries. In the event of collaborative research funded only in part by Hoechst, MGH will grant an exclusive worldwide license for the life of the patent if possible; should this not be feasible, the hospital will grant at least a nonexclusive worldwide license for the life of the patent.

Some research agreements involve a third party as a broker or facilitator. The National Science Foundation (NSF) has provided "seed money" to encourage such relationships. By 1980, the NSF Industry–University Cooperative Program had given grants to seventy-four cooperative research projects, judged on scientific merit and on potential for effective collaboration. The NSF funded all of the university's share and a portion of the firm's share, depending upon the size of the business (Kiefer, 1980).

c. *Research Consortia.* Research consortia are means by which a single university involves a number of companies in its research programs. The member companies pay a fee to support university research activity of mutual interest, and may work closely with certain participants. The university provides ready access to the results, which are shared by member firms. The multifirm approach has been purported to avoid problems associated with exclusive agreements developed with one firm, such as early commitments for an exclusive license to use potential discoveries.

A research consortium may grow out of an industrial liaison or exchange program. The California Institute of Technology's industrial associates program evolved into a major cooperative research consortium involving nine firms which provide research support and some personnel for computer-related work on campus (Murray, 1981).

　　d. *Research Centers (University-based)*. A research consortium may later develop into a major interdisciplinary and long-range research center. One of Stanford University's research consortia contributed for years to semiconductor technology for electronics firms in Silicon Valley. More recently, the university has created the Center for Integrated Systems (CIS), which is supported by funds largely contributed by industry sponsors. The results of research at the Center will be easily accessible to corporate backers and others (Murray, 1981). Stanford will own patents on new discoveries, but the results will become available through licensing arrangements to sponsoring firms. The companies will send their staffs to participate in the research and share new ideas (Lepkowski, 1981). The Center will provide educational experiences for students in all aspects of electronics, telecommunications, and semiconductor technology; and industrial scientists will participate directly in teaching. Member companies will have a "window" and "lead time" on the benefits of the research program, as well as access to graduate students through teaching and thesis activities.

　　e. *Research Laboratory (Industry-based)*. In some ways parallel to the research center at a university, a large industrial laboratory may have sufficient capacity and breadth to establish a similar arrangement whereby many universities participate in research at a single firm. This is the case at Bell Laboratories. However, such arrangements are vastly different because the universities are not formally connected to the laboratory, they do not provide funding support, and the conduct of basic research. Other mechanisms characterize "business partnerships" in which the university either becomes actively and directly involved in the operation of a business or gains access to equity as a means of returning long-term financial growth to the institution from the commercialization of its discoveries.

a. *Research Partnerships.* Perhaps the best example of a recent arrangement in which businesses and universities have beome "partners in research" was the creation of the Center for Biotechnology Research by the University of California and Stanford University, together with the new firm Engenics. Engenics is a new bioengineering concern, interested in the mass production of genetically altered organisms and the development of reliable and cost-effective biotechnical production processes.

The Center for Biotechnology Research will receive a 30 percent equity share in Engenics, and will be provided exclusive licenses to patent rights emerging from university research financed through the Center. In turn, exclusive sublicenses to exploit any patents on discoveries made will be available to the six sponsoring firms and to Engenics at commercial rates. Engenics will conduct developmental work. The sponsoring firms will have the option to exploit any patents and technology which Engenics chooses not to use exclusively, and will have preferential consideration in any contract research which Engenics may subsequently perform for other industries.

The nonprofit Center for Biotechnology Research determines the allocation of research funding, thereby "buffering" the universities from research investments driven by profit aims. It is controlled by a board of trustees which, by charter, is enjoined to act in the best interest of the participating universities. The Center acquires its funding base in three ways: (1) from grant contributions, beginning with $2.4 million; (2) from capital appreciation and dividends on its 30 percent share in Engenics; and (3) from royalty income in sublicensing Engenics and/or any of the other six firms. These funds are funneled back into research projects at universities, among which the two principal participants are now Stanford

University and the University of California. A Scientific Advisory Committee is responsible for judging merit for research funding by peer review. The Center will provide several other benefits to the parties involved such as quarterly reports, annual conferences, communication on industry problems and scientific progress, and research sabbaticals enabling employees of sponsoring corporations to participate in the university research laboratories.

The combined purposes of the for-profit Engenics and the nonprofit Center include: (1) to provide multiyear funding for university research and postgraduate training in biotechnology; (2) to expedite the transfer of results from biotechnology research to commercial development and value; (3) to enable the universities to realize an important share of the economic return from Engenic's commercial activities; and (4) to provide long-term incentives to the corporate financial sponsors that justify their investments. The salient features of this ingenious model were summarized in this way by one of the founders: "the universities which have nurtured basic technologies over the years will participate in an equitable return from their contribution to society that will be used to support new research of benefit to future generations ... [and] each of the groups involved has a common stake in the success of the entire program—from basic research through applied research and development to profitable commercial products and services" (Lindsay, 1981, p. 2). Another advantage of a joint venture is that it allows a contract to be drawn without knowledge of the price of participation given the uncertainties of the market.

b. *Business Partnerships*. There are several modes of industry–academic relationships that might be considered "partnerships in business." The first is the university's approach to investment. Investment mechanisms take many forms, but one that has emerged in recent years is the creation of a venture capital arm of the institution. The University of Rochester became the first American university to create a wholly owned, tax-exempt venture capital arm. University Ventures, Inc. (UVI) was formed as a subsidiary of the private university in order to manage a portion of the university's endowment funds. UVI invests some of its venture money indirectly through other venture capital limited partnerships, but also has a program of direct investments. "The tax-exempt venture arm was created because the university wanted to realize a better return on its investments, become more prominent in the venture capital field, and attract new investment opportunities" (Hillkirk, 1982, p. 6).

A second mode by which universities enter into business relationships is assisting entrepreneurial faculty to start new companies, thereby enhancing the likelihood of keeping the faculty close to the academic community and not losing this valuable resource. The University of Pennsylvania helps to launch new companies through the University City Science Center, which houses sixty-three small companies developing various technologies. The Center provides them access to the university's research resources, low-cost clerical and accounting assistance (Murray, 1981), printing and contract-negotiating services, and access to consultants (Helyar, 1981). The Center has been referred to as a bridge for academicians to enter the business world with the products of their research.

The third model of business partnerships is the ownership (wholly or in part) by the university of a business concern, in partnership with its faculty. This approach was characterized by Harvard University's proposal to establish a genetic engineering firm in which it would have direct ownership of an equity share. The proposal was rejected following intense campus debate (Bok, 1982). Davis (1981) summarized the nature of the "profit sharing plan" as a mechanism that involves patenting a discovery of a professor and setting up a company with outside venture capital. The university would receive a minority share and the company would have the rights to patents held by the university. It has been purported to have these benefits: (1) more effective technology transfer and a greater return to the university than is generally provided by royalties; (2) a response to the criticism that the present system unfairly allows professors to become rich through development of tax-supported research, while distribution of part of the profit to the university would serve the public interest more directly; (3) a means to ensure continual benefits from future discoveries; and (4) the proximity of the industrial laboratory to the university, enabling access to and sharing of resources.

Lepkowski (1981) reported that "Washington University is doing something which Harvard rejected and Stanford has proclaimed it will not do. It is using university funds to establish business enterprises. The Washington University Technology Associates (WUTA) is an off-campus facility which utilizes faculty members to consult with private companies" (p. 31). Its president is the dean of the engineering school, and its board of directors is composed entirely of engineering school faculty. The chairman is the university's treasurer. WUTA employs a small staff, who are not university faculty, and runs the company like a "real business," with stock owned wholly by the university, operating like an R&D firm such as Battelle or A. D. Little. Ownership of a patent or a copyright is shared equally by the faculty inventor and the WUTA, and the products/processes are marketed (Lepkowski, 1981).

A fourth model in the category of business partnerships is the concept of an "investment pool," claimed to serve as an "investment buffer" just as the Center for Biotechnology Research serves as a "research buffer." Such a pool would be comprised of many universities and managed by an independent group that would make investment decisions (like managers of mutual funds) based upon discussion of portfolio choice issues. The universities would set parameters of preference, such as the specification of high technology firms in a particular field or location. The pool would insulate individual universities from decisions about investments in specific firms; therefore, faculty members' firms could be among those investments with lessened conflict of interest.

The Issues and Potential Conflicts

The Fourteenth Annual Report of the National Science Board (1982), entitled "University–Industry Research Relationships," concluded that the future of such relationships will depend upon increased understanding of each other's role. It acknowledged the fundamental question of assessing risks and benefits for the university in particular: "If the university moves nearer to a partnership with industry, more resources can become available, but the university may relinquish some of its unique capabilities for unrestricted exploratory research and freedom of action. There are no absolutes, and the issues become matters of degree and common sense" (1982, p. 32). Another point of view, however, is that federal grant programs place restrictions upon the direction of university research as well. Thus, restriction imposed by industry sponsors is not such a unique phenomenon in the university. But the nature of restrictions imposed by corporations may be quite different from those of a federal agency. The issues are different in nature and degree.

A second subject concerns the assumption that university–corporate relationships may interfere with the university's unique freedoms of action. Whether or not such freedoms are "relinquished" depends upon the clarity of vision about those university freedoms that are nonnegotiable and those that may be restricted to some degree without harm to the integrity of the academic enterprise. One of the fundamental roles of the academy is the promotion of socioeconomic development through advanced training, applied research, and community service. Cooperation among academia, industry, and government is increasingly recognized as essential to the fulfillment of that aim. A parallel goal of the academy is to promote understanding of civilization and the human condition through liberal education, fundamental inquiry, and professional scholarship. It is this role that must be pursued unfettered by the more temporal goals of socioeconomic progress. The future of society depends upon both of these roles in the university's academic mission, and the university is obligated to pursue them in concert and without compromise. Finding effective mechanisms with which to cooperate with industry in the interest of the first role must include careful attention to agreements that preserve the integrity of the second role. This apparent dilemma can become a manageable opportunity for synthesis in higher education and for cooperation among academia, industry, and government. It will require a posture of mutual understanding and respect, clarity on the issues, agreement in negotiated resolutions, and a willingness to experiment.

While the literature of 1980 and 1981 emphasized reports of controversial ventures between universities and firms, more recent reports and articles contribute understanding of the issues and call for informed resolutions. The U.S. General Accounting Office (GAO) initiated a review of the federal role in fostering university–industry cooperation. The resulting report (1983) provided information and guidelines for policymakers in assessing federal initiatives. GAO categorized the issues into those "generic" to any form of university–industry collaboration, and those specific to a particular type of relationship. "Generic issues include the need to reconcile the different objectives, values, attitudes, reward structures, and research agendas of the two sectors; and to locate a source of continuing financial support" (GAO Report, 1983, p. iii). The GAO listed six factors judged as essential to resolving generic issues:

1. the university's commitment to direct some portion of its research and expertise toward industrial needs and opportunities;
2. the firm's commitment to utilize the university's strengths while honoring its objectives;
3. flexibility in university policies and organization, permitting responsiveness to industrial objectives without compromising the academic mission of the university;
4. a strong leader who is respected by both academic and industrial communities;
5. appropriate ways to match the various needs, resources, and interests of each partner, one with the other;
6. sustained funding sources (GAO Report, 1983, pp. iii-iv).

Cautious optimism and challenge is echoed in much of the recent literature along this theme: university–industry cooperation is essential to economic developments and is manageable through conditions of mutual understanding, conflict resolution, and sustained support. Bach and Thornton (1983) emphasize that academic–industrial partnerships are inevitable and desirable, and called for an analytical study of the impact of academia–industry partnerships on issues such as: "inter-scientist communication, direction of research, conflicts in faculty commitments, and transfer of key faculty members and trainees from the academic sector to the industrial sector" (p. 32). Tatel and Guthrie (1983) discuss legal issues and problems in forging new kinds of university–corporate relationships. They emphasize the effect on free exchange of information, effects on academic freedom, conflict of interest for the faculty member who plays the dual role of researcher-teacher and investor-entrepreneur, patent ownerships and licensing, and apportioning of royalty rights. These authors noted that universities have general guiding principles for negotiating research agreements, but advocated "hands on" experience and thoughtful commentary on the legal issues as means to resolving dilemmas.

Perhaps the most important contribution to the recent literature on this subject was the statement of the American Association of University Professors (AAUP) on "Academic Freedom and Tenure: Corporate Funding of Academic Research" (1983a). It discussed several issues such as (1) a possible shift of attention from basic scientific and engineering research to applied research and product development; (2) effects on academic freedom and working conditions of faculty members and students; (3) conflict of interest in faculty consulting and other corporate associations; (4) conflict of interest for the university motivated by corporate temptations; (5) timely dissemination of research results; and (6) choice of research topic. The AAUP document presented a balanced view that acknowledged the benefits and the risks of university–industry cooperation. It also called for the AAUP (in conjunction with organizations representing university administrators) to prepare a statement that would provide suggested guidelines for faculty to minimize potential conflicts of interest, as well as suggested principles governing corporate–university research arrangements. The AAUP advocated more discussion and more information as institutions explore explicit guidelines pertaining to faculty conflict-of-interest and/or corporate–university research relationships.

The remainder of this chapter provides a way of thinking about the prominent issues, intended as a guide for discussing and negotiating relationships. First, the concept of academic integrity is explored in relation to conflicts of interest. Second, the relationship between the flow of funds and the flow of technology transfer is discussed. Both perspectives bear on the principal issues faced in the university when establishing new relationships with industry.

Conflicts of Interest and Academic Integrity

Potential conflicts may emerge simply because conditions that influence industry are different from those that influence academia. An intensely competitive market for high technology development in industry places great value on proprietary information and exclusive rights to reduce a new invention to practice. Yet the preservation of academic values in the university requires free exchange of knowledge and public access to research results. Financial pressures upon universities and faculties encourage efforts to gain access to more resources, such as equity in the future growth derived from the commercialization of discoveries. But an equity interest in a firm may pose potential conflicts of interest for scholars and the academy, conflicts between the interests of professional neutrality and personal or institutional financial interests.

Conflicts of interest for faculty members emerge in situations that interfere with their ability to fulfill their obligations to their university, the academic community, and the public. An essential faculty obligation is to preserve the fundamental principles of academic freedom. A conflict of interest may occur when an individual or an institution assumes substantial authority, responsibility, and/or interest in two or more entities with differing missions. Obligations to principles of academic freedom, on the one hand, and to rendering decisions to advance gains in a business venture, on the other, can generate a conflict of interest when related in a common enterprise. Conflicts of interest may infringe upon the academic freedoms of others in the university community, thereby threatening the integrity of the academy.

Dual loyalties may present: (1) conflicts of *commitment* in time and energy when external activities (consulting practices) draw unduly on effort attributable to university responsibilities; (2) conflicts of *value* when financial interests (employment or stock ownership) in a firm influence decisions related to university work; and (3) conflicts of *judgment* when biased judgments enter into public testimony to protect the interests of a firm (founder or manager). Society relies on academicians for objective and balanced views. The fact that there are at least these three types of conflicts illustrates the complexity of the issue and the need for precision in defining relationships between universities (and faculty members) and corporations.

The basic reason for concern about conflict of interest is the potential impact on academic freedom. Eight dimensions of academic freedom illustrate those rights and obligations that may be affected by agreements between a corporation and a faculty member or university, if such agreements do not provide for their protection.

1. *Exchange of Information:*
   Right: The freedom to have access to information, resources, research property, laboratories, and expertise of the academy.
   Obligation: To share ideas and information freely and openly, and to promote collegial exchange of resources.
2. *Publication:*
   Right: The freedom to communicate, disseminate, and publish freely and openly, without censorship.
   Obligation: To report, publish, and disseminate new knowledge in a timely manner.
3. *Teaching:*
   Right: The freedom to impart knowledge and skills in a

scholarly and objective manner, and to advance candidates for degrees.
Obligation: To educate students on the basis of sound educational principles and to judge them fairly and equitably.
4. *Selection and Promotion of Faculty:*
Right: The freedom to shape the academy by the selection and promotion of its members.
Obligation: To judge other faculty according to criteria that are clear, established by peers, and equitably applied.
5. *Research Direction:*
Right: The freedom to choose one's research topic and direction of inquiry.
Obligation: To promote and conduct research centered upon the pursuit of knowledge.
6. *Governance:*
Right: The freedom to participate in the democratic governance of the scholarly enterprise.
Obligation: To participate in the policies and directions of the academy, and to protect the academy from external pressures.
7. *Collaboration:*
Right: The freedom to collaborate with colleagues in the adventures of science.
Obligation: To invite collaboration among scientists with a shared mission to advance the frontiers of science, independent of immediate interests.
8. *Neutrality:*
Right: The freedom to serve society with objective, unbiased judgment regarding the use, meaning, and implications of science and technology.
Obligation: To remain unbiased in scientific judgments, unfettered by conflicting pressures to advance one's own personal interests.

With this framework on academic freedom, it is possible to examine potential abuses arising from conflicts of interest. Abuses may occur through internal decisions affecting the academy of scholars, or they may emerge in external pressures from industry (or other sector). Table 1 provides illustrations of both internal conflicts and external pressures that have been the subject of concern as related to the potential impact of university–corporate relationships upon academic freedom.

Conflicts of interest may be perceived or real; either presents problems. Commercial interest is only one of many

Table 1. Correlation of Academic Freedom and Potential Abuses

Academic Freedom		Potential Abuses	
Rights	**Obligations**	**Internal Conflicts**	**External Pressures**
Access to Information and Resources	Open Exchange	Secrecy	Expectations to Treat Information as Proprietary
Publication	Disclosure	Sequestering	Prohibitions from Disclosure, Excessive Delays in Publication
Teaching	Sound Educational Principles, Fairness	Servitude	Luring Students to Industry Prematurely
Selection/Promotion of Faculty	Clear, Equitable Peer Review	Favoritism	Inordinate Salary Differentials, and "Brain Drain"
Research Direction	Intellectual Inquiry for Basic Knowledge	Tilting	Constraints/Pressures on Line of Inquiry
Governance	Governance by Democratic Principles	Distortions	Power and Influence
Collaboration	Collegial Participation	Isolation	Exclusiveness
Neutrality	Principal Judgment on Ethical, Social Issues	Bias	"Hooking" Loyalties by Promoting Significant Investments

factors that may pose conflicts of interest for faculty members and the university; this, however, does not diminish the importance of structuring university–corporate relationships to prevent or minimize potential conflicts. Some view the "buffer" mechanism as an effective means for the university to benefit from growth in equity without direct ownership and/or control, while others see it as merely a "smokescreen" to camouflage the conflicts. Innovation in structuring relationships with industry should be encouraged in universities, with the explicit understanding that successful relationships will pass the test of academic integrity.

From the standpoint of the faculty member, consulting practices are gaining greater attention. The benefits of outside professional activity for faculty are recognized. The prevalence and complexity of faculty relationships with firms, however, have elicited widespread concern that these practices, in excess, may threaten the fabric of the academic community and the progress of science. Some believe that fairness is at issue because not all faculty have the same degree of opportunity for consulting, based on differences among disciplines, specialization, and particular skills. The concept of pooling such income for redistribution among colleagues is a laudable goal, but it poses several problems, such as (1) resistance from those able to generate the income; (2) the potential for dual class citizenship in the department (where some are seen as elite in subsidizing others); and (3) inability to use the potential for individual income supplementation as an inducement in recruiting faculty. It is common for clinical faculty in medical schools to use a pooled practice plan to distribute revenue from their patient care service activity. An interesting problem has emerged in that the biologists are no longer the paupers in the system. Many are obtaining substantial individual wealth. Some clinical faculty have suggested that the basic scientists adopt a pooled "practice plan" from external pay opportunities in the practice of their discipline. One of the most significant challenges is to achieve fair practices with innovative proposals that provide some distribution of opportunity and income while retaining reasonable incentive and autonomy for the individual.

The Flow of Funds and Technology Transfer

An arrangement that links commitments for financial support from a firm to commitments for exclusive license agreements from a university poses potential conflicts of interest. Universities, therefore, tend to be skeptical and cautious in negotiating technology transfer agreements. If a university or faculty member holds substantial equity in a firm, there is the possibility that licensing agreements may follow investments as a means to serve one's own financial interests. A university may avoid granting an exclusive license to a firm in which one (or more) of its faculty holds substantial equity.

Universities face several other issues in dealing with technology transfer arrangements. For example, "commingling" involves the rights to inventions made in research funded by two or more sponsors who have provided funds with explicit or implied obligations. The problem is compounded when inventions arise from research sponsored by private as well as public funds. Some argue that the results of research conducted in whole or in part with public dollars should be placed in the public domain for use on a non exclusive basis. Others argue that, when an exclusive license is necessary to justify initial capital costs, the public is best served by allowing a competent corporation to reduce it to practice.

The new patent law allows universities to retain patent rights for inventions made through federal support. Universities can make the judgment to license on an exclusive or nonexclusive basis. But when federal funds are involved the institution must exercise certain restrictions on an exclusive license agreement. A license agreement may provide a shorter term (for example, five years versus the life of the patent), and it may contain diligence-in-use requirements which establish milestones for the licensee to demonstrate to the university its progress in reducing the invention to practice.

When a university negotiates a sponsored project, the firm may ask the university for an exclusive license to any invention that emerges from the sponsored research. Universities try, however, to avoid advanced agreements to exclusive rights because it is often difficult to anticipate: (1) potential commingling of funds in the research; (2) the nature of an invention and the firm most capable of reducing it to practice; (3) the value that should be placed on the license for setting a "price"; and (4) the minimum term necessary to develop a particular invention.

A new twist in technology transfer is the corporate offering of stock or stock options in lieu of royalties as a form of payment in licensing agreements. This is related to the preponderance of entrepreneurial firms with valuable "paper" stock but short cash supply. It is also related to the university's interest in obtaining equity for long-term growth with the exploitation of the invention(s). However, this practice is rejected by many universities as too "intimate" a tie with a firm if that firm provides sponsored research funds to the university and/or if faculty member(s) have interests in that firm.

The potential value of marketing unpatentable know-how, or trade secrets, by universities has been discussed in some university technology transfer or patent offices as another means of generating income from the university's vast resources of new knowledge. But the fact that the value of such know-how could be preserved only through secrecy causes academic administrators and faculties to reject the idea. Any practice, no matter how lucrative, that would require sequestering of knowledge in a university is intolerable.

Some critics suggest that the patent system itself stimulates sequestering of knowledge and distortions in research interests; but most view the patent system as an asset in returning value to the inventor and the institution while allowing free and open publication of the knowledge. The practice of delaying submission for publication of manuscripts for 30–90 days in order to file patent applications is generally regarded as inconsequential in slowing progress in science. However, a faculty member who chooses to delay publication longer in order to protect his or her position in a line of discoveries and/or potential patents may retard the advancement of science. It is not clear whether the desire for a patent adds any more to sequestering behavior than the desire to withhold knowledge of one discovery in the hope that it will lead to successive lines of discovery for which one also wishes the credit, or whether it has any appreciable effect on a scientist's line of inquiry in research. But sequestering based on any motivation is a threat to academic integrity and the advancement of science.

Benefits and Risks

The first step toward the development of informed policies and practices in the negotiation and administration of corporate–university ties is to understand the relative benefits and risks of various approaches. Each party needs to be certain which principles are nonnegotiable. Beyond that, there are important tradeoffs to consider in seeking a tolerable risk–benefit ratio for each party.

For any particular structure the specific benefits sought by corporations and by universities are different, although they should be complementary. Benefits sought by a university are most likely to be financial support for educational research programs and the opportunity to tap some long-term returns from the equity growth arising ultimately from its intellectual property. Benefits sought by a firm usually include acquiring a "window" on new knowledge and technology capacity, and good returns on its investment.

Likewise, the risks are different for each party, and an effort to resolve a risk by one party may pose a risk for the other. For example, a firm supporting university research incurs business costs in agreeing not to treat information from that work as proprietary, whereas it could do so if that work were done in its own laboratory. If the firm attempts to remedy this cost by demanding secrecy, it poses an untenable academic risk to the university in contradiction to its obligation to protect a free and open flow of information. Other risks incurred by corporations include the inability to control the direction of research and the potential inability to secure exclusive rights (or a full term on exclusive rights) to develop a new invention. Universities incur risks to certain academic freedoms and institutional integrity if the flow of research funding and transfer of technology become determinants in the direction of research inquiry.

From a management perspective, the decisions rest on whether or not (and how much) risk can be tolerated in view of the gains sought in a particular cooperative venture. Further, mutual agreements and policies can be instituted to maximize benefits and/or minimize risks.

Of the alternative structures presented here for collaboration between universities and firms, the more distant relationships (for example, linkages) may contribute less direct benefit to research support and/or technology transfer while posing minimal potential for conflicts of interest and threats to academic freedom, institutional integrity, and research priorities. On the other hand, the models that involve more "intimate" ties may maximize potential benefits to each party under conditions that may pose greater risks. Models involving the greatest potential for conflicts of interest in the university are: (1) the *exchange* program in the form of technology transfer agreements if decisions about the flow of funds and the flow of know-how become interconnected; (2) the *cooperative* program in the form of an exclusive agreement between one firm and one university, especially if it involves a faculty principal investigator engaged in consultation or equity ownership with that firm; and (3) the *partnership* program in the form of a direct relationship in which financial decisions and program decisions (research or education) are interrelated and interdependent, without separation of powers or an intermediary "buffer" organization.

The observation that relative benefits and risks move in parallel function may be viewed as a useful generalization in developing university–corporate relationships in all categories discussed except the category of "contributions." Contributions represent the most distant form of relationship in terms of obligations incurred between the parties involved. Contributions from industry to universities may bring the greatest benefits at the lowest risk to universities, while they offer the lowest immediate gains to a firm at the greatest expected cost. However, if firms are willing to provide gifts to universities in support of their research efforts (sometimes restricted to certain types of research), the university has maximum latitude to exercise its collective judgment in educational methodologies and in the direction of inquiry. This implies that industrial donors recognize the unique role of academia in teaching and in fostering fundamental knowledge through a governance system designed to protect the academy from short-range and narrow interests. It further implies that industrial donors believe that such free and protected inquiry has the highest probability of spawning the wholly new industry potential for the future, and that this potential necessitates wise stewardship in balancing basic and applied research activity. This view assumes that industry donors trust universities to recognize the applied value of new inventions, to execute patent applications, and to speed the transfer of new technology to industry for reduction to practice.

Historically, however, universities have been slow to transfer new technology, especially where discoveries emerged from federally sponsored research. The traditional view was that such intellectual property belonged to the government and thus patents were held by federal agencies. Many discoveries (if not most) did not reach industry for development in a manner that allowed the American economy to benefit from its edge on scientific progress and potential innovation. As a result of the Patent and Trademark Amendments of 1980, Public Law 96-517, universities may now secure and manage patents on inventions made from public-supported research. Thus, technology transfer is expected to be more efficient. Major research universities have practiced this for years through waiver of the government's claim on intellectual property. Now, however, the practice of university management of technology transfer is available to all universities. If it is managed well and industry gains faith in the university's ability to make technology transfer decisions in the interest of economic growth, corporations may be persuaded that industrial contributions to universities offer the greatest benefit at the lowest risk. However, the firm desiring at the outset to establish exclusive rights to first refusal on any new knowledge from its investment will still seek more "intimate" ties through other forms of collaboration.

The flow of contributions may be viewed in the opposite direction as well, that is, from universities to industry. It might be argued that universities should give intellectual property to industry for development at no cost or restraint (including exclusive license rights where necessary in development). Underlying this argument is the view that universities can provide industry with the greatest benefit at the lowest cost by contributions of technology transfer. In doing so, universities help industry to get richer; the economy is strengthened; and the universities gain indirectly through increased yield in corporate taxes which are funneled back through public support for education and scientific research.

While this scenario is more complex in reality, it presents a picture of contributions flowing in two directions. If both academia and industry agreed that contributions to each other would provide the greatest benefit to each sector, at the lowest cost/risk, contributions might become a preferred mode of cooperation, leaving each with the greatest degree of autonomy in pursuing its aims. Where the flow of corporate taxes is concerned, the government's role in assuring adequate public support for education and research becomes critical to this argument.

Except for contributions, the progression from procurements to partnerships accelerates the obligation and risks incurred as a consequence of attempts to maximize benefits. Clarity as to desired benefits and the limits on risks to be tolerated and managed is the first order of business in forging academia–industry connections.

Conclusion

Universities and corporations are partners familiar to one another. Consultation by faculty, corporate philanthropy, and many productive associations in teaching and research have a long and productive tradition. The Land Grant Act established a close tie between higher education and American agriculture some 120 years ago. The words of the philosopher José Ortega y Gasset have been used to emphasize the articulation between science and its uses:

> we shall now have to put science in order, to organize it ... for the sake of its healthy perpetuation. To this end we must vitalize science: that is we must provide it with form compatible with the human life by which and for which it was made in the first place. Otherwise, ... science will cease to function; mankind will lose interest in it [quoted in Lepkowski, 1981, p. 32].

Indeed, the industry–academia relationship provides mechanisms to perpetuate science through continued support of its research, as well as an order by which to translate that science to social use.

Within the university, there is a disparity among fields as to their interest in working with industry. The scientists are increasingly ready to cooperate with industry, particularly as their research leads to technological advances. In general, however, the humanists remain reserved with respect to the university's activities with industry. Yet the role of the humanities in today's cooperative endeavors is more important than ever. The rapidly emerging technologies present our institutions and society with moral and ethical dilemmas that must be resolved through the thoughtful rigor and perspective of the humanities. The issues confronting the academy in its venture toward greater cooperation with other sectors of society, while preserving its timeless values, require attention from the entire academic community—the arts and humanities as well as the sciences and technologies. While scientific literacy is purported as a major emphasis in liberal education, the atmosphere of scientific advances demands greater wisdom in the humanities as well. These great domains of academic inquiry must remain in balance or society will not be properly equipped to progress economically, socially, aesthetically, or morally. We must recall that the translation and use of our discoveries will be made by those we educate.

The roles of academia, industry, government, and private

foundations in shaping education and research are profound. Academia is the major source of fundamental research and scientific discovery, and the principal force in educating the public. Science creates the vision and performance capacity for industrial development; education creates the wisdom and intelligence capacity for public policy, as well as the human capital for economic growth. Industry is the primary agent of economic progress and of public access to new technologies through innovation and commercialization. It identifies market needs and potential applications for new discoveries and initiates new business concerns. The government exerts influence through financial support, tax policy, the patent system, and various forms of regulation. The federal government has contributed to cooperative ventures through: (1) support of university research in scientific fields at the frontiers of industrial technology; (2) contract awards to spin-off firms for high technology research and development; and (3) seed funds to stimulate new cooperative research and development centers (GAO Report, 1983, p. v). Foundations remain an important source of financial support, brokerage services, and special initiatives.

The complexity of modern relationships between academia and industry necessitates deliberate and informed planning. The experience of post-World War II endeavors as well as several unique characteristics of high technology industries and contemporary higher education have led to innovation in the university–corporate connections of the 1980s. The creation of a for-profit/not-for-profit pair (exemplified by Engenics and the Center for Biotechnology Research) is a particularly interesting illustration of efforts to shape relationships that allow universities to share in the long-term growth of value from the commercialization of their discoveries without direct interconnections between business decisions (for example, investments and licensing) and academic decisions (such as direction of research), thereby reducing the risk of conflicts of interest.

In its recent report, the General Accounting Office found that the nature and intensity of communication between industry and university parties varies significantly among the different cooperative arrangements and "that the nature of the contributions to innovation most likely to be realized depends on the type of cooperative arrangement" (GAO Report, 1983, p. ii). As an initial step toward comprehending the nature and variety of corporate–university relationships, this chapter offers a framework (or lattice) for recognizing the different forms such relationships may take. The agents of the relationship, its scope, its purpose, and the nature of commitments encountered are the most salient factors in this framework. In general, the more distance maintained in terms of mutual obligations, the fewer the benefits and risks to be expected. The more intimate ties, however, may bring greater benefits and risks. The challenge is to determine the tradeoffs which each party is willing to make, within the limits of explicit principles that are nonnegotiable as a matter of institutional integrity.

Any number of activities can lead to productive and informed relationships between academia and industry, relationships that contribute to social and economic progress in the foreseeable future while preserving the capability of universities to educate students and create new vistas for the scientific, intellectual, artistic, and cultural advancements of future generations. Businesses that embrace this view balance their contributions to universities in an effort to speed developments in science and technology, as well as to enrich the vitality of higher education and research generally. Corporate leaders who serve on university boards can be particularly influential in promoting the dual mission of the academy. Universities are valuable resources in organized efforts to plan socioeconomic developments for a region or state. They can identify their special strengths and potential contributions to industrial progress, seek connections with businesses to further the transfer of technology, and participate in joint ventures where the capacity of the university and that of the firm are complementary. University faculty and administrators can make important contributions as members of corporate boards, or as scientific advisers, but must understand and avoid conflicts of interest.

University administrators carry special responsibilities for leadership in the achievement of these broad aims: (1) to sustain an environment in which academic missions of teaching, research, and service can be carried out; (2) to preserve academic as well as financial integrity; (3) to act in the interest of the public when determining avenues for technology transfer toward effective commercialization and social use; (4) to insure balance and objectivity in the support of programs encompassed in the institution's mission; and (5) to participate in the processes of national policy formulation. In particular, university and industrial administrators are responsible for negotiating specific agreements that foster collaboration in research and technology. Many of the points commonly subject to negotiation are outlined below, but they will depend upon the nature and purpose of the relationship:

I. Purpose of the relationship
II. Funding level
III. Duration of the relationship
IV. Technology transfer
    A. Patentable knowledge:
       1. Patent rights and ownership
       2. Licensing
          a. exclusive vs. nonexclusive
          b. a priori vs. post hoc agreement
          c. duration or term of license
          d. diligence in use requirements
       3. Return of value to the university
          a. direct fees
          b. royalties
          c. stock options
          d. equity ownership
       4. Distribution of revenues within the university
    B. Unpatentable knowledge
       1. Management of the firm's trade secrets
       2. Communication of the university's know-how
    C. Rights and obligations of multiple sponsors, as in commingling of funds
    D. International technology transfer
       1. National security
       2. Economic security

V. Communication of work in progress
VI. Publication rights
VII. Direction of research activities
VIII. Obligations of faculty
IX. Role of students
X. Governance and control
XI. Scientific collaboration

Persistent concern for preserving the values of academic freedom compels institutions of higher education, faculty members, and business leaders to understand potential conflicts of interest and to strike agreements that incorporate appropriate protections. Policy formulation within higher education should progress in the spirit of common law practices, such that codified rules and regulations intended to prevent abuses do not themselves interfere with the freedoms of the academic community to exercise judgment through self-regulation.

Of utmost importance is the university's governance in matters of corporate relationships. The greatest degree of flexibility is desirable, but this is possible only in institutions that have the highest understanding and commitment to fundamental principles of academic freedom. General guidelines are needed, and they should aim primarily to educate for effective self-regulation. Explicit policies may be indicated, such as faculty disclosure of outside consulting practices and interests in any businesses with which the university participates in joint research or other ventures. Open dialogue and refinement of guidelines on campuses will lead to more effective self-regulation in compliance with academic principles, greater peer control in preventing abuses, and richer experimentation with innovative arrangements of consequence to the university and to business. It may be useful to establish an institutional ethics committee that would assist in articulating guidelines, principles, and codes of behavior, and would review cases of alleged abuse. Scientific and humanistic perspectives must play a vital role in this regard.

Such mechanisms of control should not be restrictive but liberating. They should promote experimentation within the limitations of informed, collegial judgment. Just as the patent system offers protection of intellectual property rights while freeing the owner to publish, institutional guidelines should protect academic freedom in the context of university- (and faculty-) industry relationships while providing incentives to those who participate and freeing them to share the benefits with students and colleagues.

Responsible relationships between academia and industry, with enabling support from government and foundations, can and must progress in a way that promotes variety in the models of interaction, furthers the aims and integrity of each organization, and insures accountability to the public. At stake is the design of strong intellectual and economic systems in this country and throughout the world.

References

AAUP, "Academic Freedom and Tenure: Corporate Funding of Academic Research." Report of the American Association of University Professors, Committee A on Academic Freedom and Tenure. In *Academe* (Nov.–Dec. 1983), pp. 18a–23a.(a)

AAUP, "Government Censorship and Academic Freedom." Report of the American Association of University Professors, Committee A on Academic Freedom and Tenure. In *Academe* (Nov.–Dec., 1983), pp. 15a–17a. (b)

ASSOCIATION COUNCIL FOR POLICY ANALYSIS AND RESEARCH. *America Has a New Urgency.* (Washington, D.C.: American Council on Education, 1984), p. 11.

BACH, MARILYN AND THORNTON, RAY. "Academic-Industrial Partnerships in Biomedical Research: Inevitability and Desirability." *Educational Record* (Spring, 1983), pp. 26–32.

BOK, DEREK C. "Academic Science and the Quest for Technological Innovation." In *Beyond the Ivory Tower: Social Responsibilities of the Modern University* (Cambridge, Mass.: Harvard University Press, 1982), pp. 136–168.

BRODSKY, NEAL, KAUFMAN, HAROLD, AND TOOKER, JOHN. *University/Industry Cooperation: A Preliminary Analysis of Existing Mechanisms and Their Relationship to the Innovation Process* (Center for Science and Technology Policy, New York University, June 1980), pp. 1–97.

BRUCE, JAMES D. "University/Industry Interactions: The MIT Experience." Keynote Address, International Association of Consultants, Danbury Park, United Kingdom, Sept. 13–15, 1981.

DAVIS, BERNARD. "Profit Sharing Between Professor and the University." *The New England Journal of Medicine*, 304 (May 14, 1981), pp. 1232–1235.

FRED, E. B. *The Role of the Wisconsin Alumni Research Foundation in the Support of Research at the University of Wisconsin* (A document on WARF History and Activities), 1972.

GENERAL ACCOUTING OFFICE, "The Federal Role in Fostering University-Industry Cooperation" (Washington, D.C., May 25, 1983, GAO/PAD-83-22).

HAIRE, JOHN R. "Voluntary Support in the 1980's." In *Competition and Cooperation in American Higher Education;* ed. Thomas Stauffer. (Washington, D.C.: American Council on Education, 1981), pp. 139–145.

HELYAR, JOHN. "Center Gives Campus Research Bridge to Enter Business World." *Wall Street Journal* (Feb. 2, 1981).

HILLKIRK, JOHN. "University of Rochester, First School to Set Up Venture Fund." *Venture* (March, 1982), p. 6.

"Improving Research Links between Higher Education and Industry." *Report of the Advisory Council for Applied Research and Development and the Advisory Board for the Research Councils* (London: Her Majesty's Stationery Office, June, 1983).

KALGERIS, DAVID. "The Role of the University in the Commercialization of Biotechnology." Unpublished Research Document, Dec. 21, 1981, pp. 1–168.

KIEFER, DAVID. "Forging New and Stronger Links Between University and Industrial Scientists." *Chemical and Engineering News* (Washington, D.C., Dec. 8, 1980), pp. 38–51.

LEPKOWSKI, W. "Research Universities Face New Fiscal Realities." *Chemical and Engineering News* (Washington, D.C., Nov. 23, 1981), pp. 23–32.

LINDSAY, FRANKLIN. "A Cooperative University/Industry Program in Biotechnology." Unpublished Paper (Dec., 1981).

MAGARRELL, JACK. "RPI Netting $3 Million on High Technology Industrial Park." *The Chronicle of Higher Education*, vol. 22, April 20, 1981, p. 21.

MAGARRELL, JACK. "RPI Betting $3 Million on High Technology Industrial Park." *The Chronicle of Higher Education*, Vol. 22, April 20, 1981, 1983), p. 14.

MCDONALD, KIM. "DuPont Gives $6 Million to Harvard for Research in Molecular Genetics." *The Chronicle of Higher Education* (1981).

MURPHY, TOM. "UIR: In Business for Your Business." *Wisconsin Alumnus Magazine* (July/Aug., 1980), pp. 5–7.

MURRAY, THOMAS. "Industry's New College Connection." *Dun's Review* (May 1981), pp. 52–59.

NATIONAL SCIENCE BOARD, *University–Industry Research Relationships: Myths, Realities, and Potentials*. Fourteenth Annual Report of the National Science Board, National Science Foundation (Washington, D.C.: U.S. Government Printing Office, 1982).

OMENN, GILBERT. "University/Industry Research Linkages: Arrangements between Faculty Members and their Universities." Paper presented at AAAS's Symposium on Impacts of Commercial Genetic Engineering on Universities and Non-Profit Institutions (Washington, D.C., Jan. 6, 1982), pp. 1–16.

PRAGER, DENNIS J. AND OMENN, GILBERT S. "Research, Innovation, and University–Industry Linkages." *Science* (Vol. 207, Jan. 25, 1980), pp. 379–384.

TATEL, DAVID AND GUTHRIE, CLAIRE. "The Legal Ins and Outs of University–Industry Collaboration." *Educational Record* (Spring, 1983), pp. 19–25.

TEICH, JUDITH. *Inventory of University–Industry Research Support Agreements in Biomedical Science and Technology* (Bethesda, Md.: National Institute of Health, Jan., 1982), pp. 1–28.

Self-Regulation of the Use of Human and Animal Subjects in Academic Inquiry

KARL J. HITTELMAN
ERICA J. HEATH

Self-Regulation: How Did We Get Where We Are?

Regulation means control, and control is a sensitive issue for academic institutions. Under the rubric of academic freedom, they tend to guard very jealously the things they do and their prerogatives to do them as they best see fit. For a long time, while the public's level of confidence in them was high and federal funding to them was low, academic institutions were left relatively alone, if not encouraged, to pursue the truth and better the lot of both man and beast. After all, traditional (that is, self-regulated) ways of doing things had helped this nation build one of the most productive systems of higher education in the world. From this system there continues to emanate a seemingly endless stream of truly outstanding intellectual achievements. Not the least of these are major advances in the biomedical sciences, which rely on the use of humans and animals as experimental subjects.

But things are no longer done as simply or as traditionally as they once were. Beginning just after World War II and continuing through the 1970s, the convergence of a number of factors has affected how academic institutions are regarded in our society and the way they do business. Many of these factors are related to broad social and political events. In the late 1940s and early 1950s, McCarthyism drove a wedge between the public and some academic institutions, and between some institutions and their faculties. Although a fair recovery followed, vulnerability to external forces was readily apparent. Then the rise of student activism in the 1960s, which developed into intense, campus-based opposition to the Vietnam War in the 1960s and 1970s, seriously compromised the general trust and confidence which the public had customarily accorded academic institutions. In some quarters, strong public outcry demanded that academic institutions cease tolerating rebellious students and get about the business of education. More "accountability" was demanded by critics who questioned the wisdom of opening the public treasury to the education establishment. It did not help that a growing number of college graduates, many from minorities and probably the first in their families to receive a college education, could not find employment. Some social commentators have also asserted that these historic events were being played out against a background of persistent anti-intellectualism.

But it is widely acknowledged that the most important single factor in bringing regulation to the realm of academic inquiry was the increasing amount of financial support which the education system accepted from government. Of particular interest, for purposes of this discussion, is that the post war period bore witness to explosive growth in biomedical research, due in large part to the development and maturation of the National Institutes of Health (NIH) and their extramural programs. This expansion was undoubtedly a major factor in the steadily increasing amount of research done on both human and animal subjects during this period, and it led inevitably to increased scrutiny and control of research activities, including the involvement of human and animal subjects.

There were also painful lessons to be learned from the

way in which humans could be mistreated in the name of research. In the mid-1940s, the world became aware that unimaginable acts of cruelty had been committed in German concentration camps during World War II, some ostensibly in the name of a grotesquely misguided "science." Man's inhumanity to his fellow man became a real, contemporary horror which virtually co-opted the meaning of the word "holocaust." Out of the Nuremberg Military Tribunal which followed the war evolved the Nuremberg Code, the first widely accepted code of practice for the use of human subjects in research.[1]

Then, in the 1960s and early 1970s, there was a series of revelations about research practices on human subjects in the United States, the cumulative effect of which was virtually to ensure that regulations would be imposed upon the academic community.[2] It became known that in experiments designed to test cellular rejection responses, a number of elderly patients at the Jewish Chronic Disease Hospital in Brooklyn had been injected, without their knowledge or consent, with live human cancer cells. At Milledgeville State Hospital in Georgia, psychiatric patients were used as subjects in experimental drug studies without benefit of consultation with the psychiatrist responsible for their care and without their consent or that of a surrogate. In the course of a study on viral hepatitis, retarded children at Willowbrook State Hospital in New York were deliberately infected with the disease with parental consent, though that consent was obtained under arguably coercive circumstances. And finally, it was revealed that black American men who were enrolled in the 1930s in the United States Public Health Service's now infamous "Tuskegee study" were allowed to suffer and die of syphilis, even though effective treatment had become available.[3] This last incident is all the more disturbing because it came to light *after* federal regulations for the protection of human research subjects were well developed.

With the clarity of hindsight, it is now apparent that the imposition of some form of control over the use of human subjects in biomedical and behavioral research was inevitable. The driving forces were obvious: the axiom that federal financial support will surely have strings attached, the haunting mistakes of the recent past, and the prudent view that as the intensity of activity accelerated, so, too, grew the need for reliable controls to avert future tragedies.

It is also clear that the biomedical community was neither standing idly by nor reacting rigidly as events unfolded. A review procedure with the purpose of protecting human subjects was required of some NIH research programs as early as 1953. By 1967, such review was required of all intra- and extramural Public Health Service research and training programs in which human subjects were to be used. In 1971, the Department of Health, Education, and Welfare published an *Institutional Guide to DHEW Policy on Protection of Human Subjects*, followed by formal regulations which became effective in 1974.[4] These regulations, developed with the active participation of the academic community and based largely on the procedures shaped at NIH, rely heavily on *self-regulation* for their implementation.

Academic institutions are fortunate indeed that the present mandates regarding protection of human subjects allow the flexibility of implementation by self-regulation. Ironically, there is a chance they may not do quite as well in the future for the use of laboratory animals. A very important battle is now being waged over this emotional issue between the animal rights movement and the academic community, in particular its biomedical sector.

The animal rights movement, also referred to as the antivivisection or animal welfare movement, dates back well into the nineteenth century. Particularly strong in England, its strength is attested to there by long-standing laws which, by United States standards, markedly restrict the use of animals in instruction and research. Once characterized in this country as a fringe element of neo-Luddites dominated by stereotypical "little old ladies" bent on bringing scientific progress to a halt, this movement has now attracted the interest and attention of some serious philosophers, scientists, and legislators, and is very well funded.

The movement is not a monolithic one. One segment of it, which acknowledges the benefits to both humans and animals of using animals for research, presses for reform in the form of better treatment and husbandry conditions, prohibition of painful or minimally useful tests and techniques, and assurances that no more animals will be sacrificed in experiments that merely replicate many that have already been done before. Another segment of the movement regards the use of animals in research (or for food and fiber, for that matter) as "species-ism," a practice deemed as morally repugnant as genocide, and it presses for outright abolition of the use of animals in instruction and research.

As was the case for human research, animal research has also fallen under governmental scrutiny and control as a quid pro quo for the funding for that research. In 1963, the NIH published the first *Guide for the Care and Use of Laboratory Animals*.[5] This was truly just a guide which codified laboratory animal practices then prevalent at NIH. Regarded as a fluid document intended to be responsive to changing conditions and new information, it has undergone several revisions.

With the enactment in 1966 of the Animal Welfare Act, a legislative link was forged between research funding and the welfare of laboratory animals. The act contains provisions to ensure that laboratory animals receive humane care and treatment. Now, in the climate of intense animal welfare activity, the animal rights movement is lobbying heavily to have the Animal Welfare Act (and other legislation as well) extensively amended so as to make its requirements and prohibitions much more stringent.

The most influential public policy document relating to the use of laboratory animals is probably the *Public Health Service Grants Administration Manual.* First, it promulgates a set of principles regarding the use of laboratory animals; these will be discussed below. Second, it requires institutions receiving NIH funding to provide assurance in writing that they are committed to following the *Guide.* Third, it requires that institutions either be accredited by the American Association for Accreditation of Laboratory Animal Care (AAALAC) or have an institutional committee (that is, a *self-regulation* committee) that reviews laboratory animal facilities and practices for compliance with the *Guide*. And fourth, the *Manual* requires NIH staff and reviewers to consider animal welfare policies and principles in their reviews of grant applications. The Public Health Service is currently proposing to amend the *Manual* with a new "Policy on Humane Care and Use of Animals by Awardee Institutions." It bears many similarities to the regulations for the protection of human research subjects.

The battle over animal research is being fought in the courts, in legislative chambers, in the media, and within the walls of academic institutions themselves. Its outcome will obviously be of great significance for the conduct of academic inquiry. In a very real way, this is a test of the academic community's prerogatives to teach and do research as it best sees fit. To win the battle, it will have to convince the public that it can do things its way and still live within acceptable societal norms. Failure will mean that control will be imposed from without.

With regard to the use of human and animal subjects in instruction and research, then, self-regulation is in fact a *privilege* granted to academic institutions that allows them rather broad discretion in choosing the mechanisms they use to ensure their adherence to prevailing ethical standards and to implement regulatory mandates. It is, quite simply, self-policing. Often, as long as the spirit of a regulatory requirement is observed, its letter may be implemented differently from institution to institution.

In practice, self-regulation means that a person or group from within the institution, usually a "third" or "disinterested" party not directly involved in the particular activity being regulated, reviews and monitors compliance with specific standards of performance. These standards may be specified by regulations, they may be developed internally, or both.

The most common model for accomplishing self-regulation of human and animal research is for a review of a proposed activity to be conducted prior to its being initiated. For human research, prior review is required in federally funded studies. It is explicitly forbidden that an activity commence before it is approved by a review committee, or that it commence at all if it has been disapproved.

In the prior-review process, proposed activities are openly assessed against the standards of performances an institution has adopted. For instance, does the design of a faculty member's proposed study of child abuse meet the institution's standard for protecting the privacy of the subjects and the confidentiality of the research records? Does the post-surgical care proposed for a series of animal experiments fulfill institutional criteria? Questions such as these are at the heart of self-regulation activities as they play themselves out on a day-to-day basis.

There are numerous ways of implementing self-regulation. In higher education, it has historically been done on an individual basis through teaching or mentorship, such as when a faculty member oversees a student. There are also several types of group control. In most institutions, group control will be exerted by a committee, such as a "Committee on Human Research" or a "Committee on Animal Research." Yet another possibility, one which has not been fully explored, is regional committees comprised of representatives from cooperating institutions. While regional committees offer many advantages, particularly to smaller institutions with limited resources, there are obstacles to their acceptance. The route an institution takes toward implementation, like the standards it adopts, will depend upon the overall goals of the self-regulation program and the resources available for its implementation.

The Goals of Self-Regulation

At the outset, an institution must make an important philosophical choice: will its self-regulation process be cast to meet a minimum standard, such as might be required solely for compliance with regulatory mandates, or will the institution go further, using the process to achieve something more than the minimum, such as a consultation service, educational opportunities, or an enhanced public image? Such a decision will obviously require many choices, and in this discussion we will explore some factors to be considered.

ADHERENCE TO ETHICAL PRINCIPLES

Decisions affecting experimental subjects are made on the basis of a contemporary body of ethical principles which derive from the Nuremberg Code. The basic principles of the Code were subsequently adopted by the World Medical Association, first in 1964 as the Declaration of Helsinki, and then as revised in 1975 at its World Assembly in Tokyo.[7] These codes were developed in the biomedical community without reference to behavioral or social research.

The principles embodied in the Nuremberg Code and its revisions have been further elaborated through the work of the National Commission on Protection of Human Subjects of Biomedical and Behavioral Research, which extended the principles to behavioral and social research. In one of the Commission's reports, entitled *The Belmont Report*, three paramount ethical principles were identified: beneficence, justice, and respect for persons.[8] While not universally accepted, these have been incorporated into almost all existing United States regulations.

By citing beneficence, the Commission incorporated the Nuremberg Code's principle of requiring that studies on human subjects be designed so as to yield fruitful results. That is, when subjects are to be placed at risk, there must be reasonable justification in terms of benefit to the subject and or society. Hand in hand with this goes the obligation to do no harm.

Of the many formulations of justice, the commission adopted as its model a traditional system of distributive justice.[9] They stated that "there should be a distribution of the burdens and the benefits of participation...." One direction in which this might lead would be a national lottery to determine who would be a subject in any research requiring human subjects. In practice, this is unworkable for a number of reasons, but the requirement remains that one group not be used as subjects for the benefit of another group.

Finally, the concept of respect for persons requires that each subject be viewed as an individual, rather than as a member of a group. The obligations that derive from this are considered to be truth-telling, promise-keeping, and informed consent. This concept translates directly into the need for review committees to understand that subject populations consist of individuals, each with personal fears, needs, and priorities, whose willingness (or not) to participate must always be respected.

While the Nuremberg Code, its successors, and the *Belmont Report* provide essential codification of the ethical principles underlying the protection of human research subjects, these documents are not of sufficient authority in practice. Thus, federal funding agencies have incorporated the principles into comprehensive regulations which govern the use of human subjects in that research which they support. The most important of these are the regulations of the Department of Health and Human Services and the Food and Drug Administration.[10] In addition, some branches of the military and several individual states have special requirements.

Although there is presently no direct analogue of the Nuremberg Code or the *Belmont Report* pertaining to the use of laboratory animals in research, an emerging body of literature addresses philosophical principles embedded in the relationships of humans to other animals and the use of animals for research purposes.[11] Even in the absence of generally accepted ethical principles, however, a widely observed statement of principles for research using animal subjects can be found in the *Public Health Service Grants Administration Manual*. In addition, scientific societies whose members use animals for research have codes of ethics for the use of experimental animals.

The majority of the principles in the *Manual* seem to echo the Nuremberg Code. They require that research be such as to yield fruitful results for the good of society and not be random or unnecessary in nature. Experiments should be based on sufficient knowledge and be designed so that the anticipated results will justify the study. There is an admonishment to avoid unnecessary suffering and to minimize discomfort. In the same way that a review of a study using human subjects would ask if animal models might not be substituted for the humans, the principles for use of animals suggest that an investigator consider whether alternatives to the use of animals are available. Of course, the principles for use of human and of animal subjects do differ. The crucial ethical difference is with respect to informed consent, which, of course, is inapplicable to animal research.

Beyond the primary goal of adherence to ethical principles, a number of other goals can be achieved by an institution's self-regulation program, and the decision to pursue these additional goals will also affect the structure of the program. For example, an institution might elect to use its program to provide educational opportunities for students, faculty, and staff, to define its ethical standards, to increase its protection from civil or criminal liability, or to enhance community relations. If these are the carrots, the stick is the minimum standard required simply to meet the letter of any applicable regulations.

EXPLOITATION FOR EDUCATIONAL VALUE

The actual process of self-regulation can provide an opportunity to involve individuals from all segments of an institution in the application of ethical principles to actual circumstances. Faculty involvement in the process can increase their awareness of ethical issues, expand their understanding of research paradigms different from their own, and confront them with others' perceptions of their work and their institution. For students, whether participants in or consumers of the self-regulation process, there can be "hands on" experience with real ethical issues, which can only enrich the educational experience. And for staff, there are not only learning opportunities but also the increased morale and sense of pride and commitment that can come from active participation in institutional governance.

DEFINING OR CLARIFYING INSTITUTIONAL STANDARDS

At any institution there is likely to be a wide spectrum of views on the level at which standards imposed by self-regulation should be set. For some, it would be sufficient simply to meet the minimum standard described by compliance with the letter of the relevant regulations. For others, this would not be enough. For example, an institution might decide that its animal care facility should meet the standards of accreditation of the AAALAC even though the institution receives no extramural funding from a source requiring that such a standard be met.

In those institutions that elect to pursue a standard higher than the minimum, the participants in the self-regulation process will play a featured role in defining standards. Through ongoing interplay between the review committee and those being regulated, consensus will be achieved and the institution's standards defined. Note that under such give-and-take conditions, the standards may change from time to time within the boundaries established by the regulations.

PRUDENCE AND PREVENTION

Institutions of higher education must protect themselves from the potential liability that comes with using humans or animals in research and instruction. Simple prudence would seem to dictate at the very least that an institution have in place procedures to ensure within reason that no harm come to any human subject of sanctioned instructional or research activity. But while it may not seem at all apparent that a student's simple questionnaire about health, say, might embarrass or otherwise injure a subject, the subject might subsequently take vigorous exception, and force litigation. An institution's exposure is lessened, however, if it can demonstrate that it has made a good-faith effort to develop a well-documented and well-executed program of self-regulation to ferret out potential liability problems in its use of human and animal subjects.

FORGING A POSITIVE IMAGE

If an institution of higher education is to thrive, it is important for it to be perceived positively by both its internal constituencies and the external forces that affect it. Thus, it borders on an act of self-destruction for an institution to tolerate cavalier treatment of human or animal subjects. What citizenry, legislature, philanthropic foundation, or alumnus would support an institution that courted such a notorious reputation? And what effect might this have within the institution's own walls? On the other hand, much may be gained from being seen as an institution that is both protective and compassionate toward human and animal subjects, and at which high ethical standards in practice are part of the commitment to quality.

The collective image of institutions of higher education should not be neglected. Everyone is aware that the careless, negligent or malevolent actions of a few can reflect on the many. The high level of current activity among radical animal rights activists illustrates how this phenomenon can be exploited as an emotional propaganda weapon, and the use of animals for instruction and research becomes generally threatened by the exposure and widespread publicity of a very few serious cases of maltreatment. In no small way, then, we are each responsible for our collective as well as our individual images.

Conceptualizing a Self-Regulation Program

In this section we will describe a general framework within which institutions can examine their needs for self-regulation programs.

WHAT ARE THE PRIORITIES OF THE SELF-REGULATION PROGRAM?

Once the program's goals have been decided upon, they must be translated into the process of self-regulation. But some goals will be of higher priority than others, and this will shape the development and implementation of the program. In regulating animal research, for example, an institution that receives NIH funding might be expected to place its highest priority upon implementation of minimum NIH regulatory requirements so as not to jeopardize that funding.

Other goals will have different priorities. Responding constructively to community criticism of vivisection is becoming a common secondary goal, for this clearly will reflect on an institution's image. In addressing this issue, some institutions now go beyond the minimum requirements of NIH by opening the review process to public participation, for instance, by appointing lay members from the community to their animal research review committees. Note that this may have the additional effect of modifying the institution's self-regulation standards.

At the far end of the spectrum of goals will probably lie adherence to ethical principles, not because of any cynical disregard or devaluation of these, but simply because as a goal this is intangible and diffuse. Nevertheless, the powerful, underlying force of such principles will confer upon them a central role in the discussions that establish the more concrete goals, and especially in the implementation of the self-regulation process itself, when institutional standards are actually applied in practice.

HOW EXTENSIVE NEED THE SELF-REGULATION PROGRAM BE?

It is now necessary to define as precisely as possible what specific activities under the rubric of human or animal research are to be regulated. In practical terms, this means establishing the boundaries of the self-regulation program. The first question asked should be, "Are we engaged in any activity which compels us to have a self-regulation program?" If the answer is "no," the issue could be dropped. However, even without compulsion the decision might be made to develop a program in order to meet goals other than compliance with external requirements. But self-regulation can be complex, controversial, and costly. The decision to undertake it voluntarily should not be taken lightly.

If it is deemed necessary to establish a self-regulation program, more questions arise. With respect to human research, for example, the next one to be answered is, "What categories or kinds of human research should we self-regulate?" Any and all of it? Only that which is extramurally funded? Only the biomedical? Only the behavioral? Only that which is physically invasive? Simultaneously, an institution might ask, "What kinds of human research should we prohibit?" Any which is not under the direction of full-time faculty? That which uses prisoners? Minors?

Three major factors will shape the self-regulation program. One, of course, is the nature of ongoing or planned instructional and research activities. A second is the thoughtful selection of goals for the program from among those described above. A third is the resources available for implementation of the program. The broader the scope of the program, the greater will be its demands for review committee activity, staff, space, and other items necessary for the program's support.

WHERE DOES AUTHORITY LIE?

Here it is necessary to distinguish between two types of relevant "authority." One is institutional knowledge, expertise, the capacity to mount a well-informed program. The other is institutional authority, corporate control, the power to make the process work.

The first kind of authority which must be considered in developing and implementing a self-regulation program is institutional knowledge. Are there enough people with the background, knowledge, and skills to be able to develop a program? Are there enough people who have the respect of the institutional community and the personal interest and commitment to be able to implement a program? These are very important questions, for unless an institution proposes simply to install a program by administrative fiat, it is necessary to have skilled leadership, broad participation, and a knowledgeable focus if a consensus on institutional standards is to be achieved and a program embodying them is to be implemented successfully.

The other kind of authority, institutional authority, is absolutely essential to the success of a self-regulation program. The reference here is to "real" authority, not merely that portrayed on an organizational chart. At some institutions, that may indeed mean the administration. At others, it may mean the faculty senate. At yet others, it may mean a functional coalition of faculty and administration. But regardless of where this authority resides, it must be perceived as being clearly and unequivocally committed to upholding the standards adopted for self-regulation. This is not always easy, as when an influential faculty member demands of the administration that it overrule a review commitee's negative decision and allow conduct of experiments that violate the standards adopted by the institution. Moreover, a self-regulation program is merely a fiction if research subject to regulation proceeds without explicit approval. Clearly, a program that is defenseless against the end run eventually will collapse in chaos.

Under certain circumstances, strong protection is available for the standards adopted for an institution's self-regulation program. This occurs, for instance, in the case of institutions that file what is known as an "Assurance of Compliance" with the federal regulations for protection of human subjects. Such an assurance is submitted to the Office for Protection from Research Risks (OPRR) at NIH, and commits the institution to meeting all the requirements of the regulations. One of these is a stipulation that the disapproval by a review committee of a proposed study cannot be overturned at any other level in the institution, but only upon reconsideration (presumably of a modified proposal) by the review committee itself.

A test of the level of commitment of an institution to its

self-regulation program is to assess the degree to which implementing authority is delegated. To ask the question another way, "How much autonomy has been granted to those charged with implementing the self-regulation program?" In the foregoing example of an institution with an approved "Assurance of Compliance" on file with OPRR, implementing authority has been delegated to the institution's review committee and its staff, and the standards adopted by the institutional community should prevail without interference from dissenters or administrators.

For other models, implementing authority may be less fully delegated, or perhaps more diffusely delegated. While this does not necessarily mean that the program's standards will be abused, it does suggest that there will have to be a very strong internal commitment to them. This is especially true insofar as standards must be upheld without the benefit of external authority, such as that which stands behind an approved "Assurance of Compliance."

There is, of course, another way to assess the level of commitment of an institution to its self-regulation program: look at the budget. Even the most exquisitely designed program will not be worth much if the resources committed to it are inadequate. Staff support, space, and time demands placed upon reviewers are some of the more important resource factors, and must be carefully tuned to institutional needs. Excess is as much a problem as inadequacy.

WHO ARE THE PLAYERS IN THE SELF-REGULATION PROCESS?

There are obviously two central roles to be played in the self-regulation process, that of the regulator and that of the regulated. Among the former, there may in turn be two distinct roles, that of the reviewer or member of a review committee, and that of staff to the reviewer or committee. It is useful to make this distinction among the regulators because some institutions will choose to establish a staff separate from the reviewer or review committee, and because in some cases staff play a special, highly differentiated function in the process.

The regulators, or members of a review committee, evaluate proposed research in light of ethical principles, current knowledge in the field, generally accepted techniques and practices, and accepted institutional standards, and by these criteria approve or disapprove projects. In practice, most committees seldom disapprove projects outright, choosing instead to be a consultative resource to investigators, and negotiate modifications that bring otherwise unacceptable proposals up to required standards. In doing this, institutional precedents are established and standards are refined, analogous to the way in which our judicial system functions. Moreover, as individual regulators change, as new knowledge and techniques are developed, as experience accumulates, and as community mores evolve, so will an institution's standards for self-regulation undergo change.

There is a very broad range of activities in which staff may be involved. At one extreme, they may have strictly clerical functions, serving simply as a typing and filing service and a largely passive conduit between the regulators and those regulated. For example, in a small undergraduate college with a little research activity limited to behavioral studies, staff support for a self-regulation program for human research (which might exist primarily for exposing students to the principles, methods, and responsibilities of protecting subjects) could simply consist of a secretary devoting an occasional hour or two to record-keeping chores on behalf of the institution's regulator, who might be the chair of the psychology department.

At the other end of the spectrum are the major research universities, particularly those involved in large amounts of basic and clinical biomedical research. These institutions invariably rely on NIH for a large part of their research funding, and do not have the option of adopting self-regulation standards below those mandated by federal regulations. These regulations stipulate a healthy number of documentation and reporting requirements. Thus, there is literally no way that these research activities could proceed without staff dedicated solely to the task of supporting the self-regulation process.

There are, of course, a variety of options between these two extremes. An institution could elect to restrict its staff's support to the required clerical activities. This would mean that the burden of other essential activities, such as consulting and negotiating with investigators and writing correspondence, would fall largely upon the members of the institution's review committee. Moreover, ad hoc institutional studies and the maintenance of any data bases might have to be undertaken by others who were relatively unattuned to the intricacies of the institution's self-regulation procedures for human and animal research.

Perhaps the most advanced staff model is that used at institutions heavily involved in biomedical research. There, staff are highly trained professionals who handle the bulk of the institution's self-regulation activities. They interpret the various regulations, provide guidance and consultation to investigators, participate in instructional programs as appropriate, analyze the potential impact of legislation or proposed changes in regulations, and conduct institutional studies on self-regulation activities. Such staff also provide continuity for the program as review committee membership changes over the years.

Obviously, this type of staffing requires substantial resources, but in institutions with major human and animal research commitments it also provides a very high level of technical and educational support for investigators and students. At the same time, it frees the members of the review committee to concentrate their efforts on evaluating research proposals. The seasoned observer will also realize that there is a far better chance of recruiting faculty to serve on review committees that are expertly staffed than on those that will demand a very heavy—perhaps disruptive—burden of responsibility.

Finally, the role of those who are regulated needs to be considered. It is not likely to be a merely passive one. For one thing, as we have already discussed, these players can be expected to take an active, ongoing interest in the discussions by which the institution's standards are developed and evolve, for it is by these standards that their proposed work will be judged. Their acceptance of the program in principle, their participation (as both advocates and adversaries) in the process, and their commitment to upholding the standards adopted by the institution are all essential if the program is to succeed.

In thinking about the roles of both the regulators and those who are regulated, the traditional concept of distributive justice again comes to mind. This is because of the potential interchangeability of the regulators and the regulated. It is likely, especially where a review committee is used in the self-regulation process, that some of the regulators will eventually become the regulated, and vice versa, as membership on the review committee turns over. Indeed, this interchangeability may be a key feature of successful self-regulation, for it requires participants to act in a manner consistent with being either. That is, regulators and regulated alike may share the burdens and benefits of participation in both roles.

Of course, it should not be overlooked that those in government agencies charged with administering regulations are also interested in institutional programs for self-regulation of both human and animal research. While the reflex assumption may be to see them as obfuscatory bureaucrats, many of these people, when approached with discretion, are genuine assets who can be very helpful both in instructing newcomers in the intricacies of implementation of self-regulation programs and in problem-solving with the veterans. Indeed, it can be very useful to have these friends in the wings.

Some Brief Comments on Implementation

Although it is possible under some circumstances for an individual to carry out an institution's self-regulation functions, the most widely used mechanism for this is review committees. An institution may use any name it wishes for its committees, but the generic term for those constituted according to federal regulations governing the use of humans is Institutional Review Board (IRB); for the use of animals it is Animal Research Committee (ARC). In this section, we will describe briefly some of the types of committees that can be used for self-regulation and comment on some issues related to operating procedures.

TYPES OF COMMITTEES

The Pure Regulatory Committee. If an institution were simply to operationalize regulations governing the use of human or animal subjects in research, the result would be a single-function committee which could be called a pure regulatory committee. In practice, institutions adopting this model use the regulations as a minimum standard and embellish them to reflect better their own goals and standards. This model may be found at institutions of all sizes, though it might be expected to be most common at large research universities with high levels of human and/or animal research activities, and where it is necessary to restrict committee activities to a manageable level that does not interfere with the productivity of members or applicants.

There are variants of the pure regulatory committee. Some institutions have found it useful to divide responsibilities for reviewing human research between two committees, one to review biomedical research, another to review behavioral and social research. Similarly, institutions have divided the responsibilities for review of animal research between two committees, one to review research proposals per se, the other to monitor the animal care facility's physical plant, procedures, recharge rates, and so forth.

The Mixed Function Committee. Many institutions have found the self-regulation functions are best met by what can be called "mixed function" review committees. As the name implies, such committees undertake several distinct activities, usually in order to avoid proliferation of committees, to spare resources, or both. In so doing, they provide convenient, "one-stop shopping."

The three most important activities usually undertaken by mixed function committees include peer review for scientific merit, regulatory review for adherence to self-regulation standards, and policy and procedure review for development and refinement of standards and procedures. Other responsibilities may be assigned as well.

While there are some obvious benefits to this labor- and resource-sparing model, there are also substantial drawbacks. The most difficult of these problems arises when the committee finds itself in a conflict of interest with itself. This will not necessarily be an infrequent dilemma, since the charge of a committee with such broad responsibilities will include protecting the interests of the institution, the faculty, the individual investigator, and the human or animal subjects. The best interests of each of these do not always coincide.

The Regional Review Committee. Since self-regulation activities inevitably consume resources, an institution may find that an optimal program may be beyond its means. Thus, it may be useful to explore alternatives to going it alone. One potential solution is uniting with other resource-limited institutions in the region to share the burdens of implementation of a joint self-regulation program. This approach need not be limited to academic institutions. Indeed, doing so would fail to take advantage of the variety of talent, the cross-fertilization of ideas, and the sharing of expertise that is possible through joint ventures. For example, small colleges in a community could collaborate with a local hospital and social service agency to establish a broadly based IRB which could serve the needs of all the participants.

The major obstacle to the establishment of regional review committees is the perceived threat to institutional autonomy. Closer examination reveals that there are really two distinct problems embedded in this. One is the issue of standards and the other is operating procedures. Standards will obviously vary—indeed, they may well conflict—among the many institutions in the academic community. The differences may be multiplied when nonacademic institutions are entered into the equation. Procedural problems may be equally difficult, for their resolution requires reaching agreement about such issues as representation, frequency of meetings, sharing of costs, quality assurance, and site of ultimate authority. In spite of these many difficulties, the advantages could well outweigh the disadvantages.

OPERATING PROCEDURES

There are probably as many variations in operating procedures as there are self-regulation committees. It may be useful, however, to mention several relevant key issues, and comment briefly on them.

Responsibilities. It is of paramount importance that the responsibilities of self-regulation bodies be very clearly understood by all involved. In the most general terms these will include the protection of research subjects through objective prior review of research proposals. It is crucial that a clearly written charge to a self-regulation committee be published, and that it include definition of its primary goals and its jurisdiction.

Membership. Institutions that establish review committees in response to regulatory requirements will find that to a degree, membership will be stipulated by the regulations. Underlying this are three important factors of general applicability to membership, and they are interrelated. First, there must be sufficient expertise among the members to provide rigorous, thorough reviews of the kinds of research conducted in the institution. But obviously, a committee cannot always have the comprehensive capability it might like, so it should be understood by all—committee members and investigators alike—that occasionally outside consultation must be sought. Second, a committee must have sufficient diversity so that the court is not packed, as it were, exclusively with clinical investigators or animal users, and so that the major constituencies in the institution's community are represented. For example, IRBs at Veterans Administration hospitals have at least one member who is a veteran, in addition to the physicians, nurses, scientists, and others who serve. This should not be interpreted to mean that every constituency need be represented, lest the size of the committee burgeon to the point of being unmanageable. And third, the membership must have the respect of the institutional community, which can be earned and maintained only through the high quality, consistency, and fairness of its actions. This point cannot be overemphasized. Without this respect, an institution will have a troubled self-regulation program.

Staffing. Some of the possible staffing arrangements for review committees were discussed above. The key issue here is whether staff will serve only a clerical function; will provide a broad range of consultative, support, and research functions in addition to clerical functions; or will be some place in between. In any case, the quality of the individuals who comprise the committee staff will be a very important determinant of the quality of the self-regulation program.

Procedures. Here, a number of factors need to be considered, a few of which are: How many members will the committee have and by whom will it be appointed? To whom in the administration will it report? How shall it structure its interactions with investigators? With the administration? With its staff? With regulatory agencies? How will a chairperson be selected? How will the committee and the institution handle reports of injury or other unanticipated "incidents" involving subjects? What principles will be used to assign applications for review among committee members? How will the committee deal with reviews that might not require action by the whole committee, that is, those that can permissibly be expedited or exempted? How will appeals be handled? What mechanisms will the institution use to ensure that the committee remains current as regulatory requirements change? As new ethical issues arise, how will these be resolved within the committee and the broader institutional community?

Record-Keeping. This is a very important function of the self-regulation program; must be done well if only for the legal protection it might provide. Besides recording committee correspondence and the minutes of meetings, good documentation can provide a variety of benefits ranging from educational examples of informed consent forms to the accumulation of data for institutional studies of self-regulation activities. With modern computer technology for office automation, only a very modest investment is required to achieve integrated data-base management, report-generating and word-processing capabilities that greatly simplify record-keeping and other clerical responsibilities, while simultaneously providing powerful, additional possibilities for institutional studies.

Legal Issues. Any self-regulation committee or office ought to have immediate access to institutional legal counsel. Although many committees, especially human research committees, may have an attorney member, there is no requirement that that person act as legal counsel for the institution. In fact, a person with such a dual role runs the risk of a conflict of interest between the responsibility to represent the institution and that to protect subjects.

Compliance. As mentioned earlier, a program is merely a fiction if research subject to regulation proceeds without explicit approval. Although self-regulation programs are based on a foundation of integrity, experience has already taught us that an institution must have the means to know that the self-imposed rules of the game are being observed. Some institutions choose to do this by conducting straightforward, on-site observations of regulated activities. At other institutions, more informal mechanisms predominate, such as peer pressure and "the grapevine." And at all institutions, there is the possibility that a whistleblower will appear, and that a formal inquiry will have to be conducted into an alleged violation of regulations or institutional standards.

Although it may seem that the obvious choice for monitoring the program is the review committee itself, this is probably the poorest choice. The stature and effectiveness of a review committee are almost certain to be undermined if it must serve in both the review and the surveillance capacities. Moreover, review committees are often ill-equipped to perform the surveillance function. But most important, it is ultimately the responsibility of the highest levels of administration at an institution to ensure that its self-regulation program is honored.

A Glimpse into the Future

Current events suggest that some changes may be coming to self-regulation of animal and human research. At present, for example, *in vitro* fertilization, artificial-heart implantation, and manipulation of the human genome are prominent scientific issues in the attention of the news media and the interest of the public. So are the issues of the care and use of laboratory animals in research. It is probable that continued interest and inevitable pressure from segments of both the general public and the academic community will lead to increased regulation of activities such as these, if not also legislation that directly affects them. Such changes are already afoot with respect to animal research.

Another change, one which ought to be welcomed insofar as it could simplify life for self-regulation committees, would be development of uniform sets of regulations for the use of human subjects and of animal subjects in research. The use of humans in research, for example, is subject to the requirements of such various agencies as NIH, FDA, the Veterans Administration, the Department of Agriculture. There are enough different regulatory requirements for human research—none of them offering any more substantial protection for subjects than do the NIH regulations alone—to make the process of self-regulation sometimes confusing or unnecessarily complex. Regulation of animal research is in an equally diffuse state. Uniform regulatory codes would better serve the interests of both the subjects they are intended to protect and the self-regulators.

Notes

1. *Trials of War Criminals before the Nuremberg Military Tribunals under Control Council Law No. 10.* Vol. 2. U.S. Government Printing Office, Washington, D.C., 1949. See Robert J. Levine, *Ethics and Reg-*

ulation of Clinical Research (Baltimore-Munich: Urban & Schwarzenberg, 1981), pp. 285–286.
2. Hershey, Nathan and Miller, Robert D. *Human Experimentation and the Law* (Germantown, Md.: Aspen Systems Corporation, 1976). Brady, Joseph V. and Jonsen, Albert R.. "The Evolution of Regulatory Influences on Research with Human Subjects." In *Human Subjects Research,* ed. Robert A. Greenwald, Mary Kay Ryan, and James E. Mulvihill (New York: Plenum Press, 1982). Jonsen, Albert R. "Public Policy and Human Research." In *Biomedical Ethics Reviews,* Vol. 2, ed. James F. Humber and Robert F. Almeda (Clifton, N.J.: Humana Press, 1984).
3. Jones, James H. *Bad Blood: The Tuskegee Syphilis Experiment* (New York: Free Press, 1981).
4. *Institutional Guide to DHEW Policy on Protection of Human Subjects.* DHEW Publication No. (NIH) 72-102 (Washington, D.C.: U.S. Government Printing Office, 1971).
5. *Guide for the Care and Use of Laboratory Animals.* DHEW Publication No. (NIH) 78-23 (Washington, D.C.: U.S. Government Printing Office, 1978).
6. "Animal Welfare." Chapter 1-43, PHS Supplements, *Public Health Service Grants Administration Manual,* 1978.
7. *Declaration of Helsinki: Recommendations Guiding Medical Doctors in Biomedical Research Involving Human Subjects,* World Medical Association. See Robert J. Levine, *Ethics and Regulation of Clinical Research* (Baltimore-Munich: Urban & Schwarzenberg, 1981), pp. 287–289.
8. *Belmont Report: Ethical Principles and Guidelines for the Protection of Human Subjects of Research.* DHEW Publication No. (OS) 78-0012, (Washington, D.C.: U.S. Government Printing Office, 1976).
9. Rawls, John. *A Theory of Justice.* (Cambridge, Mass.: Harvard University Press, 1971).
10. Title 45, *Code of Federal Regulations,* Part 46; Title 21, *Code of Federal Regulations,* Parts 50 and 56.
11. Singer, Peter. *Animal Liberation: A New Ethics for Our Treatment of Animals.* New York: Avon Books, 1975. Rowan, Andrew. *Of Mice, Models, and Men: A Critical Evaluation of Animal Research.* (Albany, N.Y.: State University of New York Press, 1984).

Resources

Human Research

1. Title 45, *Code of Federal Regulations,* Part 46.
   Title 21, *Code of Federal Regulations,* Parts 50 and 56.

These are the regulations from the Department of Health and Human Services (Title 45) and the Food and Drug Administration (Title 21) pertaining to protection of human subjects of research. There are many other pertinent sections in Title 21.

2. Office of Protection from Research Risks
   Office of the Director, National Institutes of Health, 9000 Rockville Pike, Bethesda, MD 20205, (301) 496-7005

   This is the Office at NIH responsible for overseeing implementation of the DHHS regulations.

3. Office of Health Affairs
   HSY-20, Food and Drug Administration, 5600 Fishers Lane, Rockville, MD 20857, (301) 443-1382

   This office handles inquiries relating specifically to the FDA regulations.

4. *IRB: A Review of Human Subjects Research.*
   360 Broadway, Hastings-on-Hudson, N.Y. 10706

   This journal is dedicated to discussions of Institutional Review Board issues and activities. Published 6 times per year.

5. *The Hastings Center Report.*
   360 Broadway, Hastings-on-Hudson, N.Y. 10706

   Bimonthly journal dedicated to discussion of ethical problems in the biomedical, behavioral, and social sciences and issues in professional and applied ethics.

6. Levine, Robert J. *Ethics and Regulation of Clinical Research* (Baltimore-Munich, Urban & Schwarzenberg, 1981).

   This is currently the definitive monograph on ethics and regulation of biomedical research. Much of it is also useful for behavioral and social science research. It has a very good bibliography.

7. Hershey, Nathan and Miller, Robert D. *Human Experimentation and the Law* (Germantown, Md.: Aspen Systems Corporation, 1976).

8. Robertson, John A. "The Law of Institutional Review Boards." *UCLA Law Review*, Vol. 26 (Feb. 1979).

9. Greenwald, Robert A., Ryan, Mary Kay, and Mulvihill, James E., eds. *Human Subjects Research: A Handbook for Institutional Review Boards.* (New York: Plenum Press, 1982).

10. *FDA Information Sheets*
    Associate Commissioner for Health Affairs, Food and Drug Administration, Rockville, Maryland 20857, (301) 443-1382

FDA publishes a series of information sheets covering commonly raised questions. Institutions forming a new program would be particularly interested in "A Suggested Self-Evaluation Guide: Human Subject Protection Institutional Review Boards."

11. Public Responsibility in Medicine and Research (PRIM&R)
    132 Boylston Street, 4th Floor, Boston, MA 02116

    This is a regional organization which offers worthwhile semi-annual, national meetings of use to both beginning and advanced IRB members, chairs, and staffpersons.

12. Office of Small Manufacturer's Assistance
    HFK-60, Bureau of Medical Devices, Food and Drug Administration, 8757 Georgia Avenue, Silver Spring, MD 20910

    This office is extremely helpful with questions related to research on medical devices, and is an excellent source of information about the regulations linking research to manufacturing and marketing.

13. *The Gray Sheet* and *The Blue Sheet*
    Drug Research Reports, Inc., One National Press Building, Washington, D.C. 20045

    These are weekly publications. The Blue Sheet carries news from FDA about drugs; the Gray Sheet provides medical device information.

14. *The Official IRB Guidebook.* Prepared by the President's Commission for the Study of Ethical Problems in Medicine and Biomedical and Behavioral Research.

    Potentially useful, but incomplete and currently out of print. NIH encourages making copies of existing volumes. Expressions of interest may help revive it. Call (301) 496-7005 (NIH) or (301) 443-6143 (FDA) for information.

15. *Reports of the National Commission on Protection of Human Subjects of Biomedical and Behavioral Research.* Available from the U.S. Government Printing Office, Washington, D.C.

    The Commission has published a variety of reports, with appendices, on a number of human research issues. The topics range from the ethical issues in research, to the use of special subject populations, to exploring the boundary between research and innovative practice.

16. *Reports of the President's Commission for the Study of Ethical Problems in Medicine and Biomedical and Behavioral Research.* Available from the U.S. Government Printing Office, Washington, D.C.

    This Commission also published a series of reports, with appendices,

Self-Regulation of the Use of Human and Animal Subjects 243

on a broad spectrum of health-related topics such as access to health care, the definition of death, and whistleblowing.

Animal Research

1. *Guide for the Care and Use of Laboratory Animals.* DHEW Publication No. (NIH) 78-23 (Washington, D.C.: U.S. Government Printing Office, 1978).

   Details many technical specifications recommended by the NIH for the proper care and use of animal subjects.

2. "Animal Welfare." Chapter 1-43, PHS Supplements, *Public Health Service Grants Administration Manual*, 1978.

   A proposal, dated April 5, 1984, for revision of the policy section of this chapter is currently under review.

3. Office of Protection from Research Risks (OPRR) Office of the Director, National Institutes of Health, 9000 Rockville Pike, Bethesda, MD 20205, (301) 496-7005

   This is the Office at NIH responsible for overseeing implementation of the DHHS extramural policies regarding animal welfare.

4. Office of Science Coordination
   HF-8, Food and Drug Administration, 5600 Fishers Lane, Rockville, MD 20857, (301) 443-1587

   This Office at FDA is becoming increasingly involved with animal welfare issues.

5. American Association for Accreditation of Laboratory Animal Care (AAALAC) 208A North Cedar, New Lenox, IL 60461, (815) 485-7101

   This organization has assumed a leadership role in the accreditation of laboratory animal care facilities.

6. Singer, Peter. *Animal Liberation: A New Ethics for Our Treatment of Animals.* New York: Avon Books, 1975.

7. Rowan, Andrew. *Of Mice, Models, and Men: A Critical Evaluation of Animal Research.* Albany, N.Y.: State University of New York Press, 1984).

PART FOUR
The Future

The Role of the Academy in a Nuclear Age

THEODORE M. HESBURGH, C.S.C.

I WOULD LIKE TO DISCUSS THE FUNCTION of our academic institutions as shaping the future, and I would presume to speak particularly of the moral dimensions of higher education and some of the impending ethical questions that attend such a consideration. Although I speak directly to my fellow educators, the message is for everyone, everywhere. We have all been schooled in the proposition that the life of the university is the life of the mind, the free search for truth and its dissemination to the upcoming generation. This is at first glance an intellectual, not a moral task. Why then, the ethical or moral concern?

I think it is fair to say that education, lower or higher, involves more than the mind. We are educating the human person, that most marvelous of all visible realities. Jacques Maritain, the late French philospher, said of the person:

> What do we mean precisely when we speak of the human person? When we say that a man is a person, we do not mean merely that he is an individual, in the sense that an atom, a blade of grass, a fly or an elephant is an individual. Man is an individual who holds himself in hand by intelligence and will. He does not exist only in a physical manner. He has a spiritual superexistence through knowledge and love; he is, in a way, a universe in himself, a microcosm, in which the great universe in its entirety

can be encompassed through knowledge; and through love, he can give himself completely to beings who are to him, as it were, other selves, a relation for which no equivalent can be found in the physical world. The human person possesses these characteristics because in the last analysis man, this flesh and these perishable bones which are animated and activated by a divine fire, exists "from the womb to the grave" by virtue of the very existence of his soul, which dominates time and death. Spirit is the root of personality.

The notion of personality thus involves that of totality and independence; no matter how poor and crushed he may be, a person, as such, is a whole and subsists in an independent manner. To say that man is a person is to say that in the depths of his being he is more a whole than a part, and more independent than servile. It is to say that he is a minute fragment of matter that is at the same time a universe, a beggar who communicates with absolute being, mortal flesh whose value is eternal, a bit of straw into which heaven enters. It is this metaphysical mystery that religious thought points to when it says that the person is the image of God. The value of the person, his dignity and his rights belong to the order of things naturally sacred which bear the imprint of the Father of being, and which have in Him the end of their movement.[1]

I have cited at some length Maritain's eloquent description of the person for two reasons. First, it is persons, not minds, not hearts, that we educate, individuals, worlds unto themselves, the most sacred of all visible realities, the repository of all rights and obligations, the only free and intelligent agents in all the visible universe. If you view persons as unfree or totally dependent on society for all they have, you are speaking of a completely different world than that we educators visualize in a free democracy. My second reason for quoting Maritain at length is that I have been unable to find a more eloquent portrayal of what it really is to be a human person, the exalted subject of all education, the hope of a better world.

In educating those persons who will form the leadership of all the other great institutions in our present and future, the family, church and state, the great business organizations and labor unions, the military, the many voluntary organizations that so enrich our lives and our professions, we must face the reality that our universities and colleges are perhaps the most important element in shaping the future. How we educate these student-persons will have an all-important influence on what our future will be.

How we educate, this is perhaps the greatest moral dilemma of all, because there is all too little agreement among us as to what is right or wrong in what we are purporting to do. We have many hints from the past.

Plato speaks of knowledge as a completion and a concomitant to virtue. Concomitant perhaps, but I think all of us would agree that while knowledge is power, it is power for good or evil, not necessarily virtue. Knowledge acquired at our best universities was the entrée for the young leaders in President Nixon's White House. After the Watergate debacle, they admitted that they learned how to use methods that were effective, but not to ask whether what they were doing was right or wrong. Augustine, a well-educated man who sowed his share of wild oats before becoming Bishop of Hippo and a saint, described education as working toward *ordo amoris,* putting order into what we love. I suspect that this insight, like others in his *Confessions,* came somewhat later than during his formal education as a rhetorician. Thomas Aquinas is in the same line, saying that the truly educated person is the one who knows the right things to have faith in, to hope for, and to love.

Matthew Arnold speaks of studies that will quicken, elevate, and fortify the mind and the sensibility. I like that and I would hope that our future leaders would lead better if their minds and sensibilities are quickened, elevated, and fortified. However, as I look at universities today, my own included, I would say as an honest moral judgment, "Easier said than done." Martin Buber and Ghandi, too, to cite two more modern observers of the educational scene, speak of the education of character as the only worthy outcome. Another modern, Robert Hutchins, described education: "the prime object of education is to know ... the goods in their order." Again, I must repeat, easier said than done. What agreement is there, in most faculties, on the "order of goods"?

William Bennett, secretary of education and former chairman of the National Endowment for the Humanities, noted some of these goods in a recent speech to the Association of Catholic Colleges and Universities. Culminating his list was a quote from Robertson Davies, who said, "The purpose of learning is to save the soul and enlarge the mind." If I might speak for the Church, I would frankly admit that it has its hands full in the effort to save souls and probably envies the universities in their easier task of enlarging the mind.

What do we do when students are not particularly excited about enlarging their minds, but would prefer to learn how to operate effectively as chemical engineers in a worldwide oil company, lawyers with a lucrative practice, accountants in one of the big eight firms, or physicists in a national weapons laboratory? It may be our moral dilemma, but it is theirs, too. The rub is, we are the educators, we establish the curriculum, we teach the courses, we demonstrate what we think is all-important in a total education, giving wholeness of knowledge, not bits and pieces.

Again, I trust that I am not overstating the ultimate moral dilemma that we face, how we educate, but there it is, notwithstanding Plato, Augustine, Aquinas, Arnold, Buber, Ghandi, or even Robertson Davies. Their vision is, I fear, far from our present reality.

Modern youth, in their jargon, would say we ought to "get our act together," but I doubt we will do whatever that means unless we can at least agree on something not too popular in modern universities and colleges: defining what we most fundamentally believe higher education to be, what we deeply believe future leaders should learn from us.

Doing this will require something even more unpopular: spending time to consider transcendentals like the true, the good, the beautiful, and the moral imperatives that flow from them. We need to discern their relevance to what we are educating young persons to be. We need to decide what it is we can teach the young that will enable them to lead us out of the present wilderness into a better future. This will require more than simply useful knowledge, in the most pragmatic sense of "useful." I need not insist here that if we, the faculty, do not see the road ahead fairly clearly, it is unlikely that we will surmount this moral dilemma in time to help our present students become effective leaders in a world of considerable moral confusion.

Let me begin with something that we will all agree with, I hope, whatever we think about Plato and Aristotle or whatever we print in our catalogues. In simplest terms, I assume that we all agree that we are mainly, but not exclusively, concerned with the first of those transcendentals, truth. We all want to grow in knowing the truth, which is a road to wisdom as well as knowledge and which indeed does make us free. We cannot be like Pilate who asked the Lord, "What is truth?," and then walked away before getting a response.

Whatever else we do, we spend most of our lives seeking truth—about our world, about ourselves, about God, about how we go about knowing truth on a wide variety of levels: scientific and technological (really the easiest because mathematics is a precise language), and humanistic truth through literature and history, and the social sciences, again with mathematics as a helpful aid in these latter approaches to truth. Then we learn, too, through art and music and, perhaps most of all, through poetic intuition. At the core of all, there is philosophy, which puts it all together, we hope, in some meaningful rational synthesis. If we want to go still further in seeking truth, and here I speak of my own profession, we study theology, which I did for six years after college. We call it all truth, and indeed it is, although we come to it by many paths of learning. The more, the better if we are looking for wholeness of knowledge, not just tidbits of this or that truth, quarks at the heart of matter or black holes amid the galaxies.

The pursuit of truth lends excitement to our profession and coherence to our institutions. James Billington, director of the Woodrow Wilson International Center for Scholars, recently said at Catholic University in Washington:

> The pursuit of truth is the highest form of the pursuit of happiness—and the surest way to keep us from the pursuit of one another. Truth is noncompetitive; the discovery of one can

benefit all. Truth is bigger than all of us, and can be pursued by each of us wherever we are with whatever we have at hand.

The open, unlimited search for truth is a major source of hope for a free society—not because it offers easy answers, but because it offers a shared enthusiasm that threatens no one and can involve everyone. Only in the life of the mind and spirit can the horizons of freedom still be infinite in an era of growing physical limitations.[2]

It would seem to me that the pursuit of truth is a good shared goal with which to begin to reorient and revivify our institutions as we attempt to shape the future through our students. At least, it has been the inspiration of all of our lives, and we should be able to inspire our students to see it as the best and continuing result of their higher education. The pursuit of truth and the full transmission of truth is at heart what makes educators and education interesting, even exciting, and at its best, fulfulling and inspirational. *Universitas,* which gave the name to our institutions, means pursuing truth in its fullness.

Let me add another thought or two to the general theme, with the help of two good friends. We may think that our moral concern for shaping the future through our students is a modern concept. Hanna Gray of the University of Chicago puts the same idea in historical perspective:

> People tend to think of the Renaissance as a period of self-conscious new beginnings. The humanists thought it possible that they might produce great reform in the world.... Their educational thinking was the vehicle by which they criticized the society of their own time: its ethical values, its culture. The humanists believed that the kinds of knowledge and of scholarship and of advanced education, which characterized the university system of their own day, were too academic, too narrow, too pedantic, too specialized.... From their critique of what was wrong with contemporary thought and scholarship in the university, the humanists concluded that by contrast an education in the liberal arts was that form of learning most relevant to the development of people who would become masters of their own world and leaders toward an improved future. They thought it was not enough to know what ethics was; they believed it important to know how to apply ethics, how to

become more moral, how to shape the will—and not only the intellect—of morally aware and active human beings.[3]

I read the Henry Lecture after practically completing this article and all I could think was: *Plus ça change, plus c'est la même chose.* The Renaissance educational problem is our own today, only the stakes are higher in our modern world, as I will demonstrate later on.

Hanna Gray's thought is put into modern context by Ambassador Charles Malik when he delivered the Pascal Lectures at the University of Waterloo, Ontario, in March of 1981.

> The fundamental spirit of the whole university is determined by the humanities. Philosophically and spiritually, where the humanities stand, the entire university stands, administrators, professors, and students, individually and, what is more dominant, in their meetings, in groups, their view of the nature and destiny of man, the general outlook on life and being, the interpretation of history, the fundamental orientation of the mind, the formation of personal character and the fixing of basic attitudes and habits, the nature of good and bad and right and wrong, the meaning and purpose of human existence, the whole spirit which stamps the individual human person—all of these radiate in the first instance, not from the sciences, but from what is taught and presupposed in the humanities.... The scientist himself, both when he takes courses in general education as an undergraduate student, and from the general climate of opinon of the university, is stamped in his mind and character by the pervasive spirit of the university.[4]

Hanna Gray writes as a historian, Charles Malik as a philosopher, a student of Alfred North Whitehead at Harvard and Martin Heidegger at Freiburg. They are saying the same thing, I believe. All truth is important, but some truths are all-important. Education is the key to the future, but it had better include education in what is most important in life.

I found Gray and Malik, not just in these few words but in their total lectures, quite helpful in the quest with which I began: trying to find some intellectually and morally coherent philosophy of education that can help us shape the future through the students we educate in our institutions. Our best goal is not just to educate in a thousand different ways—although we will do that too—but to give a vision of truth, a zest for the pursuit of truth, along all the avenues to truth, that might well lead these young persons to nobility of spirit and a commitment to do what each can do to create a world of greater justice and beauty, in a word, to educate persons really capable of shaping the future, not dull and drab practitioners of what is and has been and still needs changing.

Perhaps I am being too idealistic, but I do believe after living since age seventeen in a university, that students do react positively to a great vision of what they and their world might become. If we really want to shape the future, the operative question is: do we want to shape it in truth, justice, beauty, the good, and, yes, in love, too? If we are unclear or less than enthusiastic about this, who will follow the uncertain trumpet? Certainly not our students. We all know we are decent people, totally engaged in a noble quest. But let it not be forgotten that how we think, what we do is so much more important than what we say. Every act of ours is teaching. Our words are buttressed by our deeds, and our deeds are inspired by our convictions. If we are not deeply concerned about truth, justice, beauty, and the good as we know it, how will the students be?

Perhaps I can cap this discussion of our greatest moral challenge as educators by making it concrete in seeing how we might face the greatest moral problem confronting humanity today or ever. Weak tea will not do here. I speak of the nuclear threat to humanity.

I could speak of a whole series of other ethical challenges that confront us: how to preserve excellence in a time of retrenchment (the Carnegie Commission has the ultimate word on this one); how to preserve our freedom while seeking new and massive funding from business enterprises (we have at times had this same problem with government support); how to respond to the legitimate desires of women and minorities when there are so few openings on our faculties; how to reach out effectively to poor and minority students when student aid is shrinking; how to balance vocationalism and the humanistic concerns in higher education; how to relate to

Third World yearnings for development and human rights; how to sustain support for the fine arts in our institutions when all the emphasis is on computers which are basically uncreative—I know that computers have composed symphonies, but spare me from listening to them—; how to inspire our business and engineering students to be not just consultants but creative managers of greater productivity without which we will not make it in the world markets; how to inspire our lawyers to work for justice, whatever the cost, not just for profit whatever the manipulation of the law involved; how to graduate physicians who care about people, whose deep personal concerns transcend cat-scans and electromagnetic machines; how ultimately to reproduce ourselves, not practicing celibacy as regards the most important cohort to come and the one with the least attraction today, great teachers. All of these are fundamental moral concerns for our educational endeavors. I could say something about all of them, but just let me address the most important, the nuclear dilemma. If we do not learn and teach our students how to cope with this primordial nuclear problem, we need not worry about all the others. After total nuclear conflagration, all human problems are moot.

problems. Then and there it seemed important to disengage myself from these other concerns, except education, and to do whatever I might about this quintessential threat of nuclear annihilation.

I am often asked, "Why the sudden concern? The nuclear threat has been with us since the obliteration of Hiroshima and Nagasaki. Somehow we have survived."

I believe the sudden concern stems from the accelerating trend of utter disaster of the past three or four years. In 1945 Albert Einstein prophesied: "The unleashed power of the atom has changed everything except our mode of thinking —and we thus drift towards unparalleled disaster." We now have available a million times the destructive power of those primitive yet devastating bombs that ushered in the Atomic Age in Japan in 1945. There are now four tons of TNT equivalent available in the form of nuclear bombs for every man, woman, and child on earth. That awesome destructive power is not just theoretically there, it is processed into warheads, targeted, poised on delivery systems, hair-triggered to very fallible computers. There is a decision time of ten or fifteen minutes on whether or not to fire them, even less time on the field of battle, and there will be practically no time for decision once these systems are placed in space, as is now being planned by both the U.S.S.R. and the United States.

To give some small sense of the rate of escalation, we have been told in recent years that the Russians are escalating wildly—which they have been doing: one new SS-20 a week aimed at Europe—while we have presumably been sitting on our hands. Well, while we have been sitting on our hands, we have developed the MX with ten warheads; the Triton submarine with new super-accurate, more powerful missiles; the Pershing II; the cruise missile to be launched at sea, in the air, and from the ground; the B-1 bomber; the upcoming Stealth bomber; and now Star Wars. What would we have done if we had not been sitting on our hands? One Triton submarine alone represents three times the total fire power exploded by both sides during World War II and we are building more than thirty of them. So are the Soviets.

All the movement, on both sides, has destabilized an already very touchy political situation between us. All of this is happening in a very volatile climate, where arms control talks go nowhere, and the leaders of the superpowers have not met since President Carter signed the SALT II Treaty with Brezhnev in Vienna, a treaty still unratified. As the little girl, Samantha, who visited Russia at Andropov's invitation in the summer of 1983, asked: "If both sides say they will not start a nuclear war, why do they both continue to build more weapons?"

Never before has humankind—mostly mankind—had in their hands the power to destroy the total work of creation, fourteen times over, in a few moments, even accidentally. The newer weapons are greatly destabilizing, because they are either nonverifiable, like mobile SS-20s or cruise missiles that evade radar and defense systems, or they are offensive, first-strike, like MX and its Soviet counterparts, rather than defensive and deterrent. The military on both sides are jittery and for good reason. Once the nuclear barrier is breached, for whatever reason, nonreason, or mistake, it is bound to escalate. Limited or winnable nuclear war is a most foolish illusion. As a Russian scientist recently put it: "These are not weapons because weapons are to defend yourself and if you defend yourself with this weapon, you are dead." "Neither," he added, "is nuclear war, war in any rational Clausewitzian sense of a continuation of politics by other means. Wars are won, but in nuclear war, there is nothing left to win, all is death, destruction, and devastation, your country and ours and probably most others." If you still have any illusions about this, read the recent novel *Warday*, which portrays America and Russia after a modest exchange of some fifty missiles each. (We each have thousands.) Or read Carl Sagan on the nuclear winter that would follow a modest exchange of nuclear weapons.

It has to be the worst sin, the worst blasphemy, to destroy utterly God's beautiful creation, Planet Earth, the gem of our solar system, and all we have created here, so painstakingly, in a few thousand years: all our institutions that we have labored to perfect, all learning, all science and technology, all art, all books, all music, all architecture, every human treasure, everything, but especially millions of men, women, and children, all their future and all futures, utter obliteration at worst, a return to the Stone Age at best. It has to be utter insanity for rational creatures to have painted themselves into such a corner, to have created such a monster. But in freedom, what we have created, we can uncreate, dismantle, and we must.

It will require, most of all, hope that it can be done, the beginnings of serious, high-level conversations, with creative options on the part of the superpower leaders. All movement must be reversed—downward for a change—done mutually and done in a totally verifiable manner. This is not a Russian or American problem. It is a threat that profoundly affects every human being on earth.

Hope that we can turn the tide is central to the task ahead. Otherwise, we are lost. The need for hope is implicit in a recent Leslie Gelb article:

> In nuclear doctrine, it is necessary to have choices between massive retaliation and surrender. But it is risky to assume, as current doctrine would have it, that once a war begins, it can be controlled. And it is downright dangerous to believe there can be meaningful winners and losers, as some strategists in this administration believe. These recent trends in strategic thinking are highly questionable.
>
> But what has to be understood now is that the future could be different, that the nuclear peace of the last 40 years could be transformed into nuclear nightmare. What is in the offing is not simply another weapons system or two, not just another phase of the old arms race, but a package of technological breakthroughs that could revolutionize strategic capabilities and thinking.
>
> To be sure, there is time before all of these technologies mature into reliable weapons systems. But not much time.
>
> Meanwhile, arms-control talks between the United States and the Soviet Union are getting nowhere. The two sides have not even been negotiating with each other for months. And when the negotiations resume this year or next, it must be remembered that they deal only with reducing and limiting numbers of nuclear weapons, not with the broader technological problems described here.

Most lamentable, there seems to be habit of mind developing among Soviet and American officials that the problems cannot be solved, that technology cannot be checked, a kind of combination of resignation and complacency. They have gotten used to both the competition and the nuclear peace. Mankind may not survive on that alone.[5]

Barely a week before, Freeman Dyson, a physicist at the Institute for Advanced Studies at Princeton, had addressed the same problem in the fourth article of a series in *The New Yorker* (February 21, 1984). Dyson had begun his series, now a book, *Weapons and Hope*, with the concept that this discussion is always torn between the warriors (the hawks) whose battle cry is "Don't rock the boat" and the victims (us) who seem too easily to say "Ban the bomb." This is indeed, as he remarks, a dialogue of the deaf. Each side is speaking to itself and nothing really happens. After an exhaustive analysis and a choice of a position "Live and let live" (read the book), Dyson concludes his analysis on a call for hope.

> The moral conviction must come first, the political negotiations second, and the technical means third in moving mankind towards a hopeful future. The first, and most difficult, step is to convince people that movement is possible—that we are not irredeemably doomed, that our lives have a meaning and a purpose, that we can still choose to be makers of our fate.
>
> This lesson, not to give up hope, is the essential lesson for people to learn who are trying to save the world from nuclear destruction. There are no compelling technical or political reasons that we and the Russians and the French and the Chinese, too, should not, in time, succeed in negotiating nuclear weapons down to zero. The obstacles are primarily institutional and psychological. Too few people believe that negotiating down to zero is possible. What is needed to achieve this goal is a worldwide awakening of moral indignation, pushing the governments and their military establishments to get rid of these weapons which in the long run endanger everyone and protect nobody....
>
> [t]he basic issue before us is simple: are we, or are we not, ready to face the uncertainties of a world in which nuclear weapons have been negotiated all the way down to zero? If the

answer to this question is yes, then there is hope for us and for our grandchildren.[6]

Dyson's final answer is to quote Clara Park, "Hope is not the lucky gift or circumstance or disposition, but a virtue like faith and love, to be practiced whether or not we find it easy or even natural, because it is necessary to our survival as human beings."

Curiously, hope, like faith and love, is not a moral but a theological virtue. It becomes even more necessary to transmit hope to our students, who so often feel hopeless in the face of such cataclysmic issues, when we consider how the purely intellectual approach to this nuclear problem has brought us even closer to the abyss. Fred Kaplan, in a recent book, *The Wizards of Armageddon,* portrays the efforts of the intellectuals who have elaborated American nuclear policy while rotating between the Department of Defense and State and the national think tanks. After almost 400 pages of record, he concludes:

> They performed their calculations and spoke their strange and esoteric tongues because to do otherwise would be to recognize all too clearly and constantly, the ghastliness of other contemplations. They contrived their options because without them, the bomb would appear too starkly as the thing that they had tried to prevent it from being, but that ultimately it would become if it ever were used—a device of sheer mayhem, a weapon whose cataclysmic powers no one had the faintest idea of how to control. The nuclear strategists had to come to impose order—but in the end, only chaos still prevailed.[7]

Is it conceivable that universities and colleges who traditionally have been rational and objective critics of our society, local and global, can be silent in the face of the nuclear threat? Is it possible that our students can prepare to be future leaders and still not learn from us the dimensions of this nuclear threat, the moral problems involved, and possible solutions, if only they have hope that a solution is truly possible? It is mainly of their futures that we speak. Our lives are on the downside.

I have spoken of the pursuit of truth as our greatest moral

imperative. There is no truth about the world and humankind today that does not become darkened in the shadow of the thermonuclear mushroom and nuclear winter.

What to do? Many things. Although the problem is fundamentally geopolitical, politicians are mostly concerned with what their constituents are saying, especially if it is loud and clear and universal. I fully realize that our opportunities for political action far transcend that of those in controlled societies, especially behind the Iron Curtain. But even there, one finds great and, I think, sincere concern. One would have to be crazy not to be concerned. Again, as a top Russian scientist told me: "I'm really worried about your computers, and ours are worse."

Each of us and each of our institutions must do what we can do best, and there are some things we can do together. The nuclear problem involves the expertise of all our faculties and departments.

There is no dearth of intellectual materials. I have already quoted several authors. In the short time that I have become involved, dozens of books and hundreds of articles have come my way.

The book (earlier a *New Yorker* series) that I read first and found better at description than prescription was Jonathan Schell's *Fate of the Earth* (Alfred A. Knopf, New York, 1982). He has just published another, *The Abolition* (Alfred A. Knopf, New York, 1984). Dyson's four articles, now *Weapons and Hope* in book form, are, I think, better at prescription and right on target in sensing that hope is the most important factor of all, especially for young people.

Then came the Catholic Bishops' Pastoral, "The Challenge of Peace: God's Promise and Our Response," followed by two commentaries by Philip Murnion ("Catholics and Nuclear War"), and James Castelli, ("The Bishops and the Bomb") for both of which I wrote introductions. The great virtue of the Bishops' Pastoral is that, for the first time, the problem is put into a rational and faith framework. It is modestly reticent in making final judgments, but it does assert unequivocally that there is no possible moral justification for killing hundreds of millions of innocent people. If so, we have a compelling moral problem with offensive weapons and also with deterrence as long as there is not a serious effort right now to reduce and eventually eliminate nuclear weapons.

On the difficulty of nuclear negotiations, there are two fine studies: *Kennedy, Khrushchev and the Test Ban* by Glenn Seaborg (University of California Press, Berkeley, 1981) and Gerard Smith's *Doubletalk: The Story of Salt I* (Doubleday & Company, Inc., Garden City, New York, 1980).

I have mentioned a recent novel, Whitley Streiber and James Kunethka's *Warday* (Holt, Rinehart, & Winston, 1984). Another is Larry Collins and Dominique LaPierre's *The Fifth Horseman* (Avon Books, New York, 1981). Somehow novels and films (of which there are many) can grip us and our students in ways that serious factual books cannot. Perhaps they strike our emotions in ways that intellectual arguments do not.

In addition to these recent books, articles, and films, it would be useful to inform our students that professionals—which many of them will soon enough be—are organizing on this subject of the nuclear threat, almost by spontaneous combustion. The physicians are best organized at the moment. After their second international meeting in 1982 at Cambridge University, the three American leaders, two of them Notre Dame graduates, joined three Russian medical colleagues to discuss the medical effects of nuclear war on Soviet national television. The videotape is available.

At the third international meeting in Amsterdam in 1983, Dr. Bernard Lown, the Harvard co-founder of International Physicians for the Prevention of Nuclear War (IPPNW), said in his presidential message:

> We can and must instill a sense of moral revulsion to nuclear weaponry and the Orwellian term, "deterrence" which is but a sanitized word for indiscriminate and colossal mass murder. Our goal should be the widest conditioning of an anti-nuclear instinct as potent as hunger. Moral arousal, I believe, will help tilt the perilously balanced scale in world affairs towards survival.

President Eisenhower predicted that there will come a day when the people will generate such a mighty popular groundswell for peace that governments will be forced to get out of their way. Such a day is no longer remote for it is beckoned by the unleashing of the deepest forces embedded in humankind when threatened by extinction.[8]

Lawyers have begun to organize. We have a chapter at Notre Dame. Business leaders are essential in this crusade because they are presumed to be on the other side. Some assume that profits are all that concern them, and again, as President Eisenhower pointed out in his farewell address, there is a military-industrial complex. However, there are many deeply responsible business leaders who share the common concern. Many of them are grandfathers, too. Anyone in doubt should read Henry Willens, *The Trimtab Factor* (William Morrow, New York, 1984). A group of young businessmen, many from Silicon Valley, have retired prematurely from business to promote "A World Without War."

To mention an unusual group, I am currently attempting to bring worldwide scientific and religious leaders together —making common cause for the first time since Galileo —against the nuclear threat.

The scientific statement, written and signed by representatives of thirty-six national academies of science at the Vatican in September 1982, is very explicit, calling for moral judgment from religious leaders and indicating some possible first steps toward the ultimate elimination of all nuclear weapons. The statement was reproduced in full in the most popular technological review in the Soviet Union, with a circulation of 3,000,000. We were able to reproduce it in *Science*, which reaches 100,000 American scientists.

May I quote just one paragraph from the preamble of this five-page statement, which has been translated into the principal world languages and was also discussed by representatives of world religions in Vienna, with plans for discussions in Tokyo (on the fortieth anniversary of Hiroshima and Nagasaki), New Delhi, and Cairo.

The existing arsenals, if employed in a major war, could result in the immediate deaths of many hundreds of millions of people, and of untold millions more later through a variety of after-effects. For the first time, it is possible to cause damage on such a catastrophic scale as to wipe out a large part of civilization and to endanger its very survival. The large-scale use of such weapons could trigger major and irreversible ecological and genetic changes, whose limits cannot be predicted.[9]

The first religious reaction to this statement studied by an influential group of religious leaders in the company of American, Russian, and other scientists who wrote it, is completely supportive. I quote only their concluding paragraph:

> What faith impels us to say here in Vienna must be fortified by the hope that it is possible to build a world which will reflect the love of the Creator and respect for the life given us, a life certainly not destined to destroy itself. Because of the deterioration of the international political atmosphere and the great danger posed by the rapid developments in military technology, humanity today is in a critical period of its history. We join the scientists in their call for urgent action to achieve verifiable disarmament agreements leading to the elimination of nuclear weapons. Nothing less is at stake than the future of humanity, with its rich and variegated cultures and religious tradition.[10]

Among the signatories of this statement were the principal Protestant and Roman Catholic religious leaders of the United States, as well as religious leaders from as far away as Delhi, Cairo, Sanaa, North Yemen (the Grand Mufti), and, of course, Franz Cardinal König, Archbishop of Vienna, who was central to this whole endeavor. These statements in their entirety are available on request.

We are education persons, teaching students the wisdom of the past and pointing them toward the future. Their future, all of it, is threatened as never before in the history of humankind. There may be no future if the nuclear threat is not immobilized. As I asked before, is it conceivable that students spend four years or more with us without being confronted with this unprecedented threat, at least to understand it in all of its dimensions, all the moral problems it implies, and what possible actions on their part might neutralize the threat lest it increase and eventually bring their world to utter devastation? At Notre Dame, we have begun a course on the nuclear threat, involving many of our departments, and using many of the books mentioned above. We have also launched an Inter-Faith Academy of Peace at our Ecumenical Institute for Advanced Theological Studies in Jerusalem, under the presidency of Landrum Bolling, a distinguished Quaker, and Dean William Klassen, a Canadian Mennonite with much concern for this effort.

These efforts will touch a few hundred students each year; through the videotape of the course, we hope to reach many others. But a way must be found for all of our institutions to become involved as widely as possible. I have no magic answers, but if the nuclear threat is all that I have described it to be, there is no moral concern more threatening in our times and we, as educators, simply cannot fail to find a way to use our enormous influence to find a strategic breakthrough. If we could influence our counterparts in the Soviet Union to meet and discuss informally and unofficially our common interests in preserving the future for our students, it might be a beginning. I close by appealing to the most creative company I know, academe, to make a move in the hope that it might reverse the present headlong dash to the ultimate catastrophe—an end to all we hold dear, all good, all true, all beautiful, all persons.

Notes

1. Maritain, Jacques. *Principes d'une politique humaniste* (Paris: Paul Hartmann, 1945), pp. 15–16.
2. Billington, James. Commencement Address, The Catholic University of America, Washington, D.C., May 21, 1983.
3. Gray, Hanna. "The Liberal Arts Revisited." Henry Lecture, University of Illinois, 1982, pp. 14–15.
4. Malik, Charles. *A Christian Critique of the University* (Downers Grove, Ill.: Inter-Varsity Press, 1981), p. 70.
5. Gelb, Leslie. "Is the Nuclear Threat Manageable?" *New York Times*, March 4, 1984.

6. Dyson, Freeman. *Weapons and Hope* (New York: Harper & Row, 1984).
7. Kaplan, Fred. *The Wizards of Armageddon* (New York: Simon & Schuster, 1983), p. 390–391.
8. International Physicians for the Prevention of Nuclear War. *IPPNW Report*, Vol. I, No. 2 (1983), p. 15.
9. Statement by Scientists, Pontifical Academy of Sciences, Vatican City, September 24, 1982.
10. Statement by Religious Leaders, Vienna, January 15, 1983.

DISCHARGED

DEC 19 1989

NOV 24 1998